D1642873

EYEWITNESS TRAVEL GUIDES

NAPLES
& THE AMALFI COAST

EYEWITNESS TRAVEL GUIDES

NAPLES
& THE AMALFI COAST

LONDON, NEW YORK,
MELBOURNE, MUNICH AND DELHI
www.dk.com

Produced by Fabio Ratti Editoria Libraria
e Multimediale Milano, Italy

PROJECT EDITOR Giovanni Francesio
EDITORS Barbara Cacciani, Giorgia Conversi, Elena
Marzorati, Michele Di Muro
DESIGNERS Paolo Gonzato, Carlotta Maderna, Stefania Testa
MAPS Paul Stafford

Dorling Kindersley Ltd
PROJECT EDITOR Fiona Wild
EDITORS Francesca Machiavelli, Naomi Peck, Rosalyn Thiro

CONTRIBUTORS Patrizia Antignani, Mariella Barone, Ciro
Cacciola, Angela Catello, Daniela Lepore, Emilia Marchi,
Kirsi Viglione, Beatrice Vitelli
ILLUSTRATORS Giorgia Boli, Paola Spampinato, Nadia Viganò

ENGLISH TRANSLATION Richard Pierce

Reproduced by Lineatre Service, Milano
Printed and bound by L. Rex Printing Company Limited, China

Published for the first time in Italy in 1997, under the title *Guida
Mondadori: Napoli e Dintorni*.
© Fabio Ratti Editoria, Milan 1997
© Dorling Kindersley Ltd, London 1997

First published in Great Britain by Dorling Kindersley Ltd,
80 Strand, London WC2R ORL

Reprinted with revisions 2000, 2001, 2003

Copyright © 1998, 2003 Dorling Kindersley Ltd, London
A Penguin Company

ALL RIGHTS RESERVED. NO PART OF THIS PUBLICATION MAY
BE REPRODUCED, STORED IN A RETRIEVAL SYSTEM, OR TRANSMITTED
IN ANY FORM OR BY ANY MEANS, ELECTRONIC, MECHANICAL,
PHOTOCOPYING, RECORDING OR OTHERWISE, WITHOUT THE PRIOR
WRITTEN PERMISSION OF THE COPYRIGHT OWNER.

A CIP CATALOGUE RECORD IS AVAILABLE FROM THE BRITISH LIBRARY.

ISBN 0 7513 4813 9

FLOORS ARE REFERRED TO THROUGHOUT IN ACCORDANCE WITH EUROPEAN
USAGE; IE THE "FIRST FLOOR" IS THE FLOOR ABOVE GROUND LEVEL.

**The information in this
Dorling Kindersley Travel Guide is checked regularly.**
Every effort has been made to ensure that this book is as up-to-date
as possible at the time of going to press. Some details, however,
such as telephone numbers, opening hours, prices, gallery hanging
arrangements and travel information are liable to change. The
publishers cannot accept responsibility for any consequences arising
from the use of this book, nor for any material on third party
websites, and cannot guarantee that any website address in this
book will be a suitable source of travel information. We value the
views and suggestions of our readers very highly. Please write to:
Publisher, DK Eyewitness Travel Guides,
Dorling Kindersley, 80 Strand, London WC2R 0RL, Great Britain.

CONTENTS

HOW TO USE THIS GUIDE 6

The Farnese Hercules

INTRODUCING NAPLES

PUTTING NAPLES ON THE MAP 10

THE HISTORY OF NAPLES 14

NAPLES AT A GLANCE 28

The Spaccanapoli district

◁ **Overview of the city with the distinctive dome of San Francesco di Paola in Piazza del Plebiscito**

Panoramic view of the Forum at Pompeii, with Vesuvius in the background

Outdoor eating, Bay of Naples

Pizza Napoletana

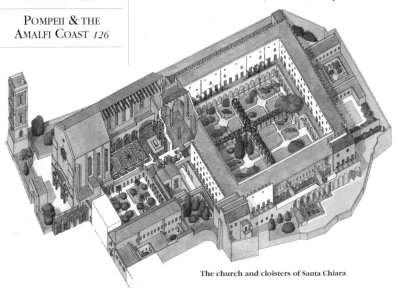
The church and cloisters of Santa Chiara

HOW TO USE THIS GUIDE

THIS GUIDE helps you to get the most out of your visit to Naples. It provides both expert recommendations and advice as well as useful practical information. The first chapter, *Introducing Naples*, sets the city in its rich and varied geographical and historical context. *Naples at a Glance* gives you a brief overview of the main sights in the city, as well as cultural background. *Naples Through the Year* describes events and festivals season by season. *Naples Area by Area* describes the main sightseeing areas in detail, with maps, illustrations and photographs. *Pompeii and the Amalfi Coast* covers this region's splendid archaeological sites and also features an itinerary for a coastal boat trip. Information on hotels, shops, restaurants and bars is covered in *Travellers' Needs*, while the *Survival Guide* contains practical advice – for example, how to use the local transport networks.

FINDING YOUR WAY AROUND THE SIGHTSEEING SECTION

The city has been divided into six colour-coded areas, each with its own chapter. A description of the history and features of each area is followed by a Street-by-Street map focusing on the main attractions. The sights are numbered for easy reference. The most important sights in each area are described in detail in two or more pages.

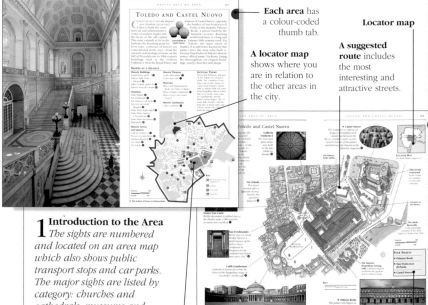

Each area has a colour-coded thumb tab.

Locator map

A locator map shows where you are in relation to the other areas in the city.

A suggested route includes the most interesting and attractive streets.

1 Introduction to the Area
The sights are numbered and located on an area map which also shows public transport stops and car parks. The major sights are listed by category: churches and cathedrals, museums and galleries, streets and squares, marketplaces, historic buildings, parks and gardens.

The area shaded pink is shown in greater detail on the Street-by-Street Map on the following pages.

2 Street-by-Street Map
This gives a bird's-eye view of the heart of the sightseeing area. The numbers refer to the fuller descriptions provided on the following pages.

The list of star sights indicates places no visitor should miss.

NAPLES AREA MAP
The coloured areas on this map (see inside front cover) correspond to the six main sightseeing areas. Each area is covered in full in the Naples Area by Area (see pp44–125) section. The map showing the centre of Naples (pp12–13) also locates all of the major sights and monuments in the city.

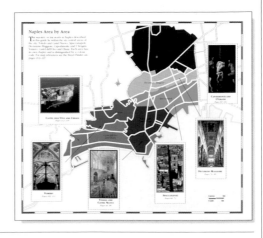

Numbers refer to each sight's position on the area map and its place in the chapter.

Practical Information provides all the information you need to visit the sights, including map references to the Street Finder (see pp212–27).

The Visitors' Checklist provides all the practical information needed to plan your visit.

3 Detailed Information on Each Sight
All the most important sights in Naples are described individually. They are listed in order, following the numbering on the area map, which appears at the beginning of each chapter. The key to the symbols used is shown on the back flap for easy reference.

Stars indicate the features you should not miss.

The timeline lists the most important events in the history of the building.

4 Naples' Top Sights
Historic buildings are dissected to reveal their interiors. Museums and galleries have colour-coded floorplans to help you locate the major works exhibited.

INTRODUCING NAPLES

Putting Naples on the Map

NAPLES IS THE
third largest city
in Italy after Milan and
Rome, and the largest city
in Southern Italy. The
population of the city proper
(see pp12–13) is 1,250,000, rising
to almost three million when the
suburbs are taken into account.
The city faces the great sweep of
the splendid Bay of Naples, extends
into the fertile Campania plain, and
occupies high ground and hollows
formed by ancient volcanic craters.

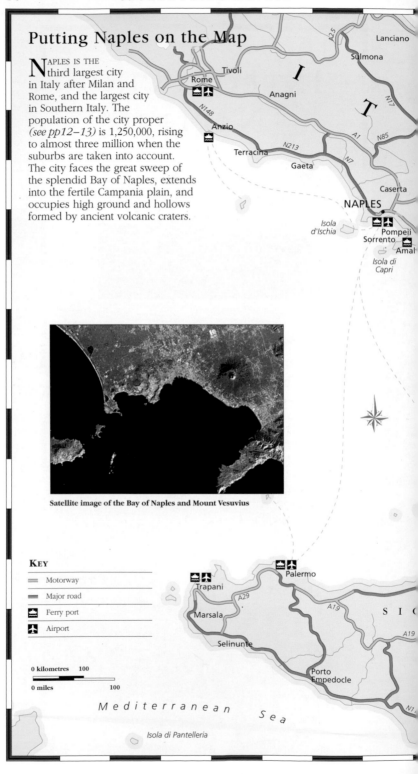

Satellite image of the Bay of Naples and Mount Vesuvius

KEY

═══	Motorway
──	Major road
⛴	Ferry port
✈	Airport

0 kilometres 100

0 miles 100

Mediterranean Sea

Isola di Pantelleria

Aerial view of Naples

Greece →

Lucera
Foggia
Trani
Bari
ento
Melfi
erno
Matera
Paestum
Agri
Maratea
Rossano
Cosenza
Catanzaro

Brindisi
Taranto
Lecce
Galatina

_A14_
_N89_
_A16_
_N96_
_N16_
_N407_
_N7t._
_N18_
_N106_
_A3_
_N18_
_N16_

Tyrrhenian

Sea

Ionian

Sea

Isole Eolie
or Lipari

Milazzo

Reggio di
Calabria

Catania

Siracusa

_A3_
_N106_
_A18_

Malta →

EUROPE

NORWAY
SWEDEN
FINLAND
ESTONIA
RESSIAN
FED
LATVIA
LITHUANIA
DENMARK
REPUBLIC
OF
IRELAND
GREAT
BRITAIN
NETHERLANDS
BELORUSSIA
POLAND
BELGIUM
GERMANY
LUXEMBOURG
CZECH
REPUBLIC
SLOVAKIA
UKRAINE
FRANCE
SWITZERLAND
AUSTRIA
HUNGARY
ITALY
ROMANIA
BULGARIA
ALBANIA
GREECE
PORTUGAL
SPAIN
Naples
ALGERIA
TUNISIA

Central Naples

THE OLD TOWN is divided into six distinct areas. From the 16th century on, the administrative and commercial centre of Naples developed around Toledo and Castel Nuovo. The old city centre is described in the chapters on Spaccanapoli and Decumano Maggiore. The Vergini district, immediately north of the Foria gorge, leads to the park of Capodimonte with its Royal Palace. The Certosa di San Martino and Castel Sant'Elmo dominate the Vomero hill. In the Chiaia area, a few steps from the most elegant shops in Naples, places such as Castel dell'Ovo and Mergellina are surrounded by greenery and the sea. To the west are the lovely inlets and villas of Posillipo.

The Certosa di San Martino, on the Vomero

The Cappella Caracciolo di Vico in San Giovanni a Carbonara

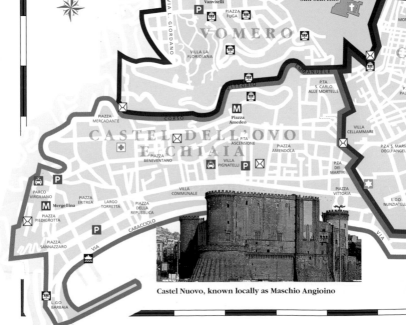

Castel Nuovo, known locally as Maschio Angioino

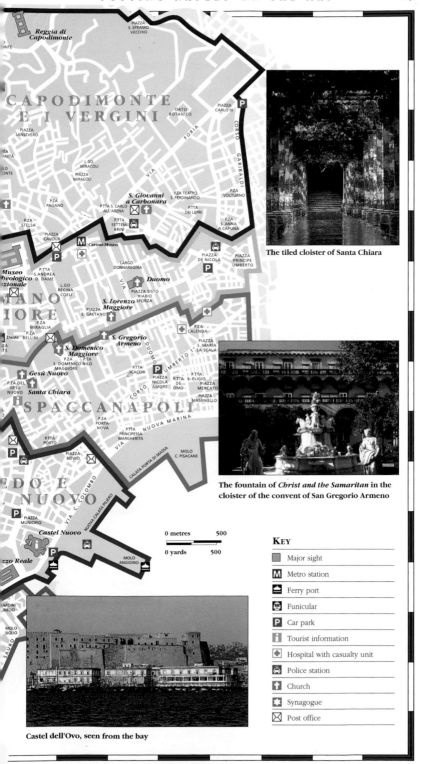

Reggia di Capodimonte

PIAZZA S. EFRAMO VECCHIO

CAPODIMONTE E I VERGINI

ORTO BOTANICO

PIAZZA CARLO III

PIAZZA SANSEVERO

FORIA

L.GO MIRACOLI

PIAZZA MIRACOLI

VIA

CORSO GARIBALDI

P.ZA PAGANO

S. Giovanni a Carbonara

P.TTA S. CARLO ALL'ARENA

P.ZA TEATRO S. FERDINANDO

P.ZA VOLTURNO

P.ZA STELLA

P.TTA SETTEM-BRINI

PITTA DEI LEPRI

P.ZA S. ANNA A CAPUNA

PIAZZA CAVOUR

M Cavour-Museo

LARGO DONNAREGINA

PIAZZA DE NICOLA

PIAZZA PRINCIPE UMBERTO

Museo Archeologico Nazionale

P.TTA S. ANDREA D. DAME

L.GO REGINA COELI

VIA

Duomo

PIAZZA SISTO RIARIO SFORZA

ROMANO MAGGIORE

S. Lorenzo Maggiore

PIAZZA S. GAETANO

P.ZA MIRAGLIA

P.ZA BELLINI

P.ZA Dante

S. Gregorio Armeno

PITTA LA SCALA

P.ZA S. MARIA

PITTA CALENDA

S. Domenico Maggiore

P.ZA S. DOMENICO MAGGIORE

NILO

P.TTA SCACCHI

DUOMO

Gesù Nuovo

P.ZA DEL GESÙ NUOVO

Santa Chiara

CORSO UMBERTO 1°

PIAZZA NICOLA AMORE

P.TTA DE. OMO

PITTA S. ELIGIO

PIAZZA MERCATO

PIAZZA MASANIELLO

SPACCANAPOLI

P.ZA PORTA-NOVA

VIA NUOVA MARINA

P.TTA PRINCIPESSA MARGHERITA

P.TTA PORTO

PIAZZA BOVIO

MOLO C. PISACANE

CALATA PORTA DI MASSA

LEDO E NUOVO

PIAZZA MUNICIPIO

VIA C. COLOMBO

NUOVA CALATA PILIERO

Castel Nuovo

MOLO ANGIOINO

zzo Reale

GARDINI PUBBLICI

MOLO SIGLIO

SAURO

0 metres   500
0 yards   500

The tiled cloister of Santa Chiara

The fountain of *Christ and the Samaritan* in the cloister of the convent of San Gregorio Armeno

Castel dell'Ovo, seen from the bay

KEY

	Major sight
M	Metro station
	Ferry port
	Funicular
P	Car park
	Tourist information
	Hospital with casualty unit
	Police station
	Church
	Synagogue
⊠	Post office

THE HISTORY OF NAPLES

IN GREEK MYTHOLOGY, Naples was built where the Siren Parthenope was washed ashore after she had been rejected by Odysseus. Greek colonists, perhaps from Rhodes, may have founded a colony at this point as early as the 10th century BC, but this too may be the stuff of legend. What is certain is that Greeks from Cumae built a new city nearby, calling it *Neapolis* (new city), while the original town was renamed *Palaeopolis*, or old city. Neapolis was a leading commercial centre and the Greek language and customs survived even during the Roman period, when it was a favourite area of the elite.

Gorgon, 6th-century BC Cumaean antefix

After the fall of the Roman Empire and a wave of invasions, the city, though it retained some independence, came under Byzantine influence and went through a period of rebirth. In the 10th century the invading Normans succeeded in conquering the whole of Southern Italy, a kingdom initially ruled from Palermo, under Roger II. Norman rule finally came to an end in 1189. With the Angevin (French) and Aragonese (Spanish) dynasties, Naples itself became a capital, and the court began to attract famous artists. The 1400s were a golden era for Naples, but there followed two centuries of direct rule by Spain. The Spanish viceroys were oppressive rulers and the era is remembered for unjust taxation, the Inquisition, plague, overpopulation and the rebellion of Masaniello. Creativity flowered however, despite the widespread poverty.

In 1734 Charles III began the period of Bourbon hegemony. With the exception of the short-lived republican government in 1799 and the subsequent decade of French dominion, the Bourbons ruled Naples until 1860.

Since the unification of Italy the city's problems have become national issues – for example the markedly different level of development between Northern and Southern Italy.

Map of Naples in 1790

◁ *Paquius Proculus and His Wife*, 1st-century AD wall painting from Pompeii

Greco-Roman Naples

Pompeian cameo

B Y THE 8th century BC, Greeks had founded a settlement at Cumae, one of the earliest Greek colonies in Italy. From there they established a new town on Pizzofalcone hill, known as Parthenope, and trade prospered. Population growth led to the founding of Neapolis, or new city, nearby, and victory over the Etruscans in 474 BC brought further expansion. Neapolis came into contact with the growing power of Rome during the latter's protracted wars with the Samnites, and in the 4th century BC the citizens agreed to become an "allied city" of Rome.

In AD 79 an erupting Vesuvius buried a number of ancient Roman cities, including Pompeii.

EXTENT OF THE CITY

☐ 8 BC ☐ Today

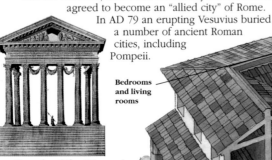

Bedrooms and living rooms

Temple of the Dioscuri
This 16th-century print shows the Roman temple which once stood on the site of San Paolo Maggiore (see p79). The temple façade collapsed in the 1688 earthquake.

Atrium

Via Anticaglia
The "street of ruins" acquired its name from the brick arches connecting the Ancient Roman bath house and the theatre (see p84).

Ornamental basin (impluvium)

TIMELINE

1000–900 BC According to Greek myth, city of Parthenope founded		**328 BC** War with Rome; Naples is defeated but a treaty sanctions the city's freedom	**90–89 BC** People of Campania become Roman citizens
900 BC	**600 BC**	**300 BC**	**100 B**
600 BC Greeks from Cumae found *Neapolis* or "new city"	*Red-figure vase (5th century BC)*		**100 BC** Tunnel built in Posillipo hill connecting city with Phlegraean Fields area and its trade and military ports

THE HOUSES OF POMPEII

The Roman houses in Pompeii *(see pp146–7)* are among the best-preserved examples of Roman civilization in Campania. This illustration shows a typical patrician house in Pompeii, displaying characteristic features of Roman and Greek domestic architecture. The houses were generally rectangular. To ensure privacy, they faced inwards, as can be seen by the few windows on the outer walls, and the rooms were built around an atrium or courtyard, which was the focal point of domestic life. Wealthier houses were richly decorated.

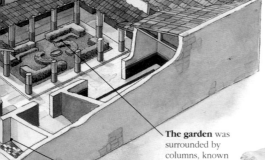

The garden was surrounded by columns, known as a "peristyle".

The kitchen and dining room (triclinium) were in this part of the house.

The Greek Walls
Made of large tufa blocks, the city walls date from the 5th century BC. Remnants can be seen in present-day Piazza Bellini (see p78).

WHERE TO SEE GRECO-ROMAN NAPLES

Beneath the cloister *of San Lorenzo (see p80) layers of the ancient city are still visible.*

Although not much is left of Greco-Roman *Neapolis*, some traces are visible in Piazza Bellini *(see p78)*, around Santa Chiara *(see pp66–7)* and under the Duomo *(see pp82–3)*. Outside the city, Pompeii and Herculaneum are vivid records of ancient Roman life. The Museo Archeologico Nazionale *(see pp86–9)* in Naples houses rich finds. Amphitheatres survive at Pozzuoli *(see p132)* and Santa Maria Capua Vetere *(see p159)*, and Greek ruins at Cumae *(see p134)* and Paestum *(see pp156–7)*.

The Diadumeno Torso from Castel Capuano

Statue of Aphrodite, Museo Archeologico

350–400 Christianity gaining in acceptance

500 Bishop Severus builds the first parish church, now San Giorgio Maggiore *(see p70)*

AD 1	AD 300	400	500

79 Vesuvius erupts; Pompeii and Herculaneum destroyed

The Siren Parthenope on a Roman coin

476 Romulus Augustulus, last Roman emperor of the West, imprisoned in the *Castrum Lucullanum (see p116)*

536 Byzantine General Belisarius wins Naples, entering city via the aqueduct

From Byzantine Rule to the Aragonese Dynasty

Angevin lily

IN THE 6TH CENTURY AD, Naples became part of the Byzantine (Eastern Roman) empire. Despite incursions into Southern Italy by Goths, Lombards and Saracens, it remained a semi-independent duchy, nominally under Byzantine rule, until it became part of the Norman kingdom of Sicily in the 12th century. By the 13th century the French House of Anjou had taken over and Naples became the capital of the Angevin kingdom. Ambitious schemes were begun: land reclamation and building of new castles, churches and monasteries. In 1421 the last Angevin queen, Joan II, named Alfonso V of Aragon as her successor.

GROWTH OF THE CITY
■ 500   □ Today

Tombs in Santa Chiara
The Angevin rulers were buried in Santa Chiara, which contains superbly crafted tombs such as this one by an unknown artist (first half of the 14th century).

Louis of Anjou took vows after refusing the crown of Naples and was canonized in 1317.

Tomb of Ladislas of Durazzo
This tomb is in San Giovanni a Carbonara (see p96), chosen by Ladislas to house the tombs of the Angevin kings.

The Pietrasanta Bell Tower
This is among the few remaining examples of medieval architecture in Naples (see p78).

TIMELINE

553 Naples again under Byzantine rule

7th-century Byzantine fibula

902 After many attempts to conquer Naples, the Saracens are defeated at Garigliano

600	700	800	900

600 Naples resists Lombard siege and remains an independent duchy

763 The duchy becomes hereditary and independent

Statue of Frederick II, Holy Roman Emperor

Frescoes of the Giotto School
Giotto lived in Naples from 1328–33. His influence can be seen in the frescoes in Santa Maria di Donnaregina Vecchia (1332–5).

The crown Louis is placing on the head of his brother Robert legitimized the Angevin dynasty.

ST LOUIS OF TOULOUSE

This Gothic portrait was probably painted in 1317, after Louis of Anjou was canonized. Louis is shown as a Franciscan saint crowning his younger brother Robert King of Naples. Simone Martini's masterpiece is now in the Museo Nazionale di Capodimonte *(see pp98–101)*.

Robert of Anjou

WHERE TO SEE ANGEVIN AND ARAGONESE NAPLES

Evidence of this period is everywhere in Naples, although successive reconstructions have often obscured the original architectural styles. Rather than civic buildings such as Castel Capuano *(see p81)*, it was the churches that changed the face of the city: Santa Chiara *(see pp66–7)*, San Lorenzo *(see p80)*, San Domenico Maggiore *(see p68)*, and Santa Maria di Donnaregina Vecchia *(see p84)* with its wonderful cycle of frescoes painted by the school of Giotto.

Castel Nuovo, *originally Angevin, also has Aragonese elements (see pp54–5).*

King Roger II
The first great king of Naples is depicted in one of the eight statues placed in the niches of the Palazzo Reale façade in 1888 (see pp50–51).

1100	1200	1300	1400
1139 Neapolitans consign city to Roger II, Norman king of Sicily	**1194** The city ruled by Henry VI Hohenstaufen, Roger II's son-in-law **1224** Frederick II founds the University	**1343** Petrarch stays at San Lorenzo	**1443** Alfonso of Aragon enters Naples **1496** Threatened by France and Spain, the king cedes Naples to the French
1165 Castel Capuano built in strategic position to control communications with interior	**1266** Charles I of Anjou enters Naples and makes it the capital of the new Angevin kingdom	**1279** Construction of Castel Nuovo begins	**1421** Joan II, last Angevin sovereign, names Alfonso V of Aragon her heir **1485** The Barons' Conspiracy fails

Bust of Alfonso V

The Spanish Viceroyalty

Masaniello

IN 1503 NAPLES ceased to be an independent kingdom, and became a colony of Spain, ruled by a viceroy. The city began to expand unchecked in the suburbs and beyond the walls. Palazzo Reale was built near Castel Nuovo, and courts assembled at Castel Capuano. With the construction of Via Toledo and the restructuring of Via Chiaia in the mid-1500s, the focus of city development shifted: aristocratic palaces were built along the Riviera and Toledo and the need to accommodate the troops led to the building of the Quartieri Spagnoli district. New churches and monasteries were built. By now Naples was by far the largest city in Italy, with consequent problems of overcrowding and poverty. A famous figure in this period is Masaniello, the revolutionary who was first considered a hero, and then killed by the people who had supported him. Spanish rule came to an end in 1707 when, with the Treaty of Utrecht, the kingdom of Naples was ceded to Austria.

GROWTH OF THE CITY
☐ 1500　☐ Today

Santa Maria del Carmine *(see p73)*, which gave the square its name.

Don Pedro de Toledo
A controversial figure, Don Pedro was viceroy from 1532 to 1553. He promoted new town planning, but also wanted to bring the Inquisition to Naples, triggering a popular revolt.

Masaniello, born Tommaso Aniello in 1620, was an illiterate fisherman.

TIMELINE

1503 Gonzalo Fernández de Cordóba, sent by the King of Spain, enters the city

1510 Failure of the viceroy's attempts to bring the Inquisition to Naples

1532–52 The first modern town plan of Naples put into effect

1536 Via Toledo opened

Palazzo Reale

1600 Construction of Palazzo Reale, by Domenico Fontana

1606–7 Caravaggio in Naples

The Eruption of Vesuvius by *Philipp Hackert*

1631 Eruption of Vesuvius

1637–60 Construction of Guglia di San Gennaro to thank the patron saint for saving the city from the eruption of Vesuvius

1500　1600

Statue of San Gennaro
The Neapolitans gave their venerated patron saint credit for having stopped the eruption of Vesuvius in 1631.

This memorial stone was to record all the concessions obtained from the viceroy by Masaniello.

MASANIELLO'S UPRISING

This painting by Micco Spadaro depicts Piazza Mercato *(see p73)* during the 1647 riot. A tax levied on fruit sparked the riot which rapidly grew into a fully-fledged uprising against the aristocracy. However, the attempt was soon crushed, as the city's moderates managed to persuade people to rebel against their revolutionary leader. He was killed the same year on 16 July.

WHERE TO SEE VICEROYAL NAPLES

The original 17th-century façade of the Palazzo Reale *(see pp50–51)* has changed little over the centuries. The Cappella del Tesoro di San Gennaro *(see pp82–3)* is one of the richest Baroque monuments in Naples. A short distance from the Duomo is a small area with a wealth of 17th-century treasures: the Guglia di San Gennaro *(see p81)* and Pio Monte della Misericordia *(see p77)*, which houses the canvas that marked a turning point in 17th-century Neapolitan painting – *The Seven Acts of Mercy* by Caravaggio, who stayed in Naples in 1607.

The Certosa di San Martino (see pp108–11) *was extended and decorated in the late 1500s.*

At San Gregorio Armeno (see p80), *the cloister is decorated with this striking fountain.*

Giambattista Vico
The famous philosopher and historian, author of La Scienza Nuova (The New Science), *was born in Naples in 1668, the son of a bookseller.*

1647 Masaniello's uprising

The plague in a painting by Micco Spadaro (detail)

1707 Beginning of Austrian viceroyalty

1723 Pietro Giannone flees to Vienna after publishing his *Civic History of the Kingdom of Naples*, which is banned by the Church

1650

1700

1656 Devastating plague epidemic; Naples loses one-third of population

1688 Earthquake damages most of old city

1701 Failure of the Prince of Macchia's conspiracy in favour of the Austrians

1697 Giambattista Vico becomes professor of rhetoric at Naples university

Bourbon Naples

Portrait of Charles III

I**N** 1734 THE MUCH-ABUSED kingdom of Naples changed hands once more, with the arrival of the Bourbon king Charles III, who set out to make Naples into a metropolis. He suspended church building in favour of large-scale public works and new industries. He also built a Royal Palace in Caserta modelled on Versailles, which was to be the focal point of an entire city. At the same time, art, antiquities, music and even the *lazzari* (street urchins) attracted travellers making the Grand Tour. The royal schemes lacked a coherent plan, however, and fundamental problems failed to be addressed. Bourbon rule ended in 1860, when Garibaldi arrived in Naples, having won over Sicily and Calabria. In the same year Naples became part of the new kingdom of Italy.

GROWTH OF THE CITY

| ■ 1700 | □ Today |

The Palace of Capodimonte

III

Charles III's Porcelain
The king was so proud of his porcelain factory that when he returned to Spain he closed it down and took his best craftsmen with him.

The Beheading of Ettore Carafa
This relief in the Museo di San Martino depicts the execution of one of the martyrs of the Parthenopean Republic on 17 August 1799.

Antonio Genovesi (1713–69)
A leading figure in the Neapolitan Enlightenment movement, he became the first professor of political economics in Italy in 1754.

TIMELINE

Statuette found in Herculaneum

1738 Beginning of excavations at Herculaneum

Ancient finds at Herculaneum transferred to Palazzo degli Studi

1734 Under Charles of Bourbon Naples becomes an independent kingdom again

1740 Church building suspended

1759 Charles III returns to Spain, his son Ferdinand becomes king

1777 The university moves to the Jesuit College, now a banished society. Ferdinando Fuga turns Palazzo degli Studi into a museum

Cappella di San Gennaro

19th-century Neapolitan painting often featured landscapes and picturesque settings – as seen in this work by Gigante (1806–76), showing the chapel of San Gennaro – as well as the rural scenes of Palizzi (1818–99) and the realism of Morelli (1826–1901).

THE DUKE OF NOJA'S MAP

This was the first modern relief map, the work of Duke Giovanni Carafa di Noja in 1775. The map shows the full extent of the city of Naples and the monumental buildings in the newly developed districts. In this detail the impressive Royal Palace of Capodimonte dominates the city skyline.

Naples appears as a chaotic muddle of buildings here.

WHERE TO SEE BOURBON NAPLES

The most important architectural achievements of the Bourbons are the Teatro San Carlo *(see p53)*, the Palace of Capodimonte *(see pp98–101)* and the Albergo dei Poveri *(see p97)*. Urban projects such as the Foro Carolino and the Villa Reale at Chiaia also date from the Bourbon period. The passion for antiquity inspired collecting and the setting up of the Museo Archeologico *(see pp86–9)*. But Bourbon influence is mainly to be seen outside the city, where kings built hunting lodges as well as royal palaces, such as Caserta *(see pp160–61)*.

***The Bourbon court** on a shoot in a painting by Jakob Philipp Hackert (1783)*

The Naples-Portici Railway

The first Italian railway was inaugurated in 1839, when the Bayard locomotive took 9 minutes 30 seconds to travel about 7.5 km (4.5 miles). This painting of the Vesuvio by Fergola is in the Museo di San Martino.

1806 Napoleon gives the role of king of Naples to his brother Joseph Bonaparte

1808 Bonaparte goes to Spain and is replaced by Joachim Murat. The French promote great public works and administrative reforms

1848 Popular revolt restores constitution but it is annulled by Parliament in 1849

Giuseppe Garibaldi

1799 Birth of Neapolitan Republic, overthrown six months later by the counter-revolution. Its leaders are executed in Piazza Mercato

1820 Constitution granted but is repealed the following year

1815 Murat executed at Pizzo Calabro. Ferdinand returns to throne as King of the Two Sicilies

1839 First railway in Italy, Naples–Portici, inaugurated

1860 Garibaldi enters city on 21 October; after plebiscite Naples becomes part of newly united Kingdom of Italy

Naples after Unification

The philosopher Benedetto Croce

I N A CROWDED, DENSELY POPULATED CITY, the 1884 cholera epidemic brought ancient problems to a head. An attempt to face them was made with the Urban Renewal Plan. Slum clearance was carried out around the port and new districts were created in the centre and towards the hills. However, the Plan failed to solve many basic problems, work took much longer than expected, and triggered a wave of corruption. The Fascist regime contented itself with a new series of public works and the creation of more built-up areas. A leading local figure of the time was the philosopher Benedetto Croce, one of the few Italian intellectuals who openly opposed Fascism.

GROWTH OF THE CITY

☐ *1850*   ☐ *Today*

Santa Chiara
Restoration of Santa Chiara was carried out after the 1943 fire, re-creating its presumed original appearance.

THE ILVA STEELWORKS IN BAGNOLI

This plant, later known as Italsider, was built near the beach and the ancient hot springs in 1907 *(see p132)*. Renovated for the last time in 1987 and now closed, it has become a symbol of modern development carried out with total disregard for the natural context and scenic beauty of the area.

Matilde Serao (1856–1927)
"Naples must be gutted" declared the prominent author on the eve of the Renewal Plan. A few years later, disappointed by the results, she described Corso Umberto I as a "screen" concealing old and new misery.

TIMELINE

The Mount Vesuvius funicular

1880 Inauguration of Vesuvius funicular, which inspires the famous song *Funiculi Funicula*

1891 First city funicular connecting Vomero with centre becomes operative

1850	1880	1890

1868 Via Duomo begun with first city demolition and finished in late 1800s as part of Urban Renewal Plan

1885 Special law for Urban Renewal Plan: demolition of slum areas begins

1884 Cholera epidemic

The Rettifilo
This eclectic and stately avenue, officially called Corso Umberto I and built after the Urban Renewal projects ended, is a good example of late 19th-century bourgeois Naples.

WHERE TO SEE POST-UNIFICATION NAPLES

The Caffè Gambrinus *(see p52)* was the haunt of Italian avant-garde artists, like the Futurists, as well as such illustrious visitors as Oscar Wilde. During the Urban Renewal period that changed the face of civic Naples, the Art Nouveau style prevailed in the new residential districts and the small villas in Chiaia *(see pp112–19)* and Vomero *(see pp102–11)*. Monumental Fascist architecture is represented by the Palazzo delle Poste e Telegrafi *(see p57)* and the Stazione Marittima (the port). Via Toledo *(see p53)* boasts an important Novecento-style building constructed in 1939 to house the main offices of the Banco di Napoli.

The Caffè Gambrinus *was popular in the early 1900s.*

The Mostra delle Terre d'Oltremare
This huge exhibition and recreational complex was one of the Fascist regime's most notable architectural achievements. Work on the site began in 1937 after the demolition of the Fuorigrotta quarter.

1901 Saredo judicial inquiry reveals government–Camorra rapport

1925–7 Naples incorporates surrounding towns, formerly independent

1940 Mostra delle Terre d'Oltremare, a huge exhibition, recreational and sports complex built by the Fascist regime

Entrance to Mostra d'Oltremare

1900 | **1920** | **1945**

Benito Mussolini

1899 First stretch of Cumana railway built

1922 On October 24, Fascists meet in Naples on eve of "March on Rome"

1928–41 Rione Carità district replaces old San Giuseppe quarter

1944 Last eruption of Vesuvius

1943 *"Quattro giornate"* uprising: Germans driven out of Naples

Present-day Naples

Eduardo De Filippo

AT THE END of World War II the city had to cope with the appalling damage inflicted by all the bombardments. The 1950s and 1960s were marked by the large-scale, indiscriminate building activity promoted by politicians who looked only for short-term gain. The closing down of some large factories in the 1980s aggravated the acute unemployment problem. However, Naples has always distinguished itself by its irrepressible vitality and creativity, especially in the fields of music and theatre. Today the city is rediscovering its past, and there is a new commitment to city regeneration, as well as a resurgence of cultural programmes.

GROWTH OF THE CITY

■ *1945*　　□ *Today*

Vesuvius
This work by Andy Warhol was produced in 1985 for an exhibition held at the Museo di Capodimonte, where the canvas is now on display. It is the American artist's tribute to the most recurrent artistic motif relating to Naples – an erupting Vesuvius.

San Paolo Stadium
Built in the 1960s, this football stadium has a seating capacity of 80,000. Famous players for Naples include Dino Zoff and Diego Maradona.

TIMELINE

1945 Eduardo De Filippo writes *Napoli milionaria*. Town council approves reconstruction project

1949 Curzio Malaparte's novel *La Pelle*, set in Naples, causes a scandal with its raw descriptions

1952 Shipowner Achille Lauro, leader of the monarchist party, becomes mayor. Period of building speculation begins

Achille Lauro

1962 Centre-left coalition governs city

1963 Francesco Rosi directs film *Hands over the City (see p36)*

1972 Town-planning regulations (still partly in force) protect historic old town, considered a cultural heritage

1950　　1960　　1970

Posillipo Today
Among the many examples of building malpractice in Naples, Posillipo is one of the most tragic. The hill, known the world over for its ancient history and lovely scenery, has been defaced by unchecked and unscrupulous development.

Pedestrian avenue

Skyscrapers are a novelty in Neapolitan architecture.

CENTRO DIREZIONALE
This district of futuristic administrative office buildings in the heart of the city, near the central railway station, is an example of "rational" modernization. The original plan dates from the 1960s, but in 1982 the famous Japanese architect Kenzo Tange began a new design. The layout of the area is such that traffic, which runs along underground streets, is separated from pedestrians.

The underground roads are an attempt to solve serious traffic problems.

Montagna di Sale
Mimmo Paladino's Salt Mountain was installed in Piazza del Plebiscito for New Year's Day 1996. The square, restored for the G7 summit and now a pedestrian zone, has become a symbol of the new Naples.

NAPLES AT A GLANCE

NAPLES IS FILLED with evidence of many centuries of occupation blended into the fabric of the present-day city. This complex heritage, from ancient Greeks and Romans to the dukes, kings and queens of the Middle Ages and beyond, has contributed to a rich store of galleries and museums, ancient amphitheatres and ruins, as well as churches, monasteries, royal palaces and monuments. While the *Area by Area* section *(pp45–125)* describes the various places of interest in detail, the following ten pages will provide some background and cultural context. Each corner of Naples has something different to offer, but below is a selection of attractions that no visitor to the city should miss.

NAPLES' TOP TOURIST ATTRACTIONS

Castel Nuovo *See pp54–5*

Santa Chiara *See pp66–7*

Museo di Capodimonte
See pp98–101

Certosa di San Martino *See pp108–11*

Mergellina *See p119*

Castel dell'Ovo *See p116*

Museo Archeologico Nazionale
See pp86–9

Posillipo
See pp120–25

◁ The seafront with its historic hotels, Castel dell'Ovo and the Borgo Marinaro

Naples and the Bay

The Faraglioni of Capri

FORMED BY AN IMMENSE CRATER, the Bay of Naples is both sheltered and exposed; sheltered by the curve of hills to the east which create a natural semi-circular amphitheatre, but open to the sea. The zone is volcanic, shaped by cones and craters of all ages, some submerged, some still bubbling with thermal springs and jets of steam. Now that Vesuvius is quiet (the last smoke trail was seen in 1944), the most active crater in the region is the Solfatara at Pozzuoli *(see p133)*. The living, breathing quality of the land led Homer to choose the coastline as the setting for parts of the *Odyssey*. Chaotic development along the coast has not deterred visitors from seeking out and appreciating the beauty of the bay.

Ischia has small sandy beaches that are a great tourist attraction.

Gaiola is the largest of the three islands facing the Gaiola quarter. The coastline is rocky and precipitous with natural caves.

Posillipo

Castel dell'Ovo

THE BAY OF NAPLES

Mount Vesuvius stands guard over a bay which owes its beauty and characteristic curves to the violent and often deadly explosions of a series of volcanoes. The conical shape of Monte Epomeo on Ischia still shows its volcanic origin; one submerged crater now does service as the port of Ischia and hot springs abound. Capri, once joined to the mainland, is geologically an extension of the Sorrento peninsula; time has carved beautiful caves along the island's precipitous coastline. Just beyond Punta Campanella are islands known to Homer as the home of the Sirens.

THE BAY FROM MERGELLINA

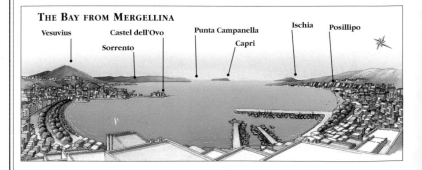

Vesuvius · Castel dell'Ovo · Sorrento · Punta Campanella · Capri · Ischia · Posillipo

The port of Naples, once a disembarkation point for transatlantic ships, is now the centre of intense ship, ferry and hydrofoil traffic for tourists along the coast and to the islands of Capri, Ischia and Procida. The Angioino wharf is also important commercially.

The fertility of the soil in Naples was proverbial in ancient times. To this day you can still find unexpected pockets of terrace cultivation in built-up areas.

Riviera di Chiaia

San Francesco di Paola

Palazzo Reale

The pebble beaches under Castel dell'Ovo and Palazzo Reale serve as small marinas for all kinds of boats, especially leisure craft.

The natural grottoes of Sorrento, with their original shapes produced by water erosion, are a characteristic feature of the southern stretch of the bay.

The Architecture of Naples

O NE FEATURE of the architecture of Naples is the way in which traces of various epochs and styles can be seen in one short section of street, from Roman foundations and remains to the turn-of-the-century galleria made of iron and glass. Little remains within Naples of its Greek heritage, yet in the heart of the city you can still discern the regular grid layout adopted in 5th-century BC Neapolis: the three main streets going east–west – present-day Via Anticaglia *(see p84)*, Via Tribunali *(see pp76–7)* and Via San Biagio dei Librai – and the north–south roads that intersect them at right angles. Along the waterfront (Lungomare) and the Riviera di Chiaia, more modern buildings can be found, elegant palazzi alternating with villas and splendid luxury hotels.

The ancient grid layout of Neapolis (red lines) over a plan of the modern city

VIA FORIA

Caserma Garibaldi

VIA DUOMO

1956–7

RIVIERA DI CHIAIA

The wide, elegant Riviera di Chiaia, flanked by fine buildings, mostly dating from the 18th and 19th centuries

1940–41

LUNGOMARE

1955–6

Faculty of Business Administration, 1934

Hotel Royal, 1956

A MULTI-LAYERED CITY

San Lorenzo Maggiore *(see p80)* is one example of a layered building. Remains of the ancient city are visible under the monastery. The church itself is also the result of a series of reconstructions; the Angevin basilica, built over the ruins of a 6th-century church, was completely rebuilt in the 1700s, and then restored to its original medieval state in the last century. The 18th-century façade still has the original 14th-century wooden doorway.

Greco-Roman remains

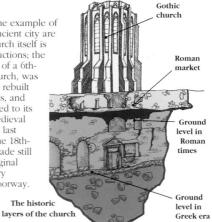
Gothic church
Roman market
Ground level in Roman times
Ground level in Greek era
The historic layers of the church

The Galleria Principe di Napoli, built in 1883, the oldest galleria in Naples

San Giuseppe a Chiaia, dating from 1666–73

The Neo-Classical Villa Pignatelli, 1826, designed by Pietro Valente, now a museum *(see p118)*

Hotel Continental

Hotel Vesuvio (reconstruction), 1948

Santa Lucia, 1902

Writers and Artists in Naples

Portrait of Virgil

THE BEAUTY OF THE BAY OF NAPLES and the fascination of Vesuvius have inspired writers and painters for hundreds of years. The Greeks wove stories around the landscape, seeing in it a variety of mythological creatures; volcanic activity was regarded as the work of the gods. The poet Virgil so loved Naples that he spent his last years there while writing the *Georgics* and the *Aeneid*. The city's rich classical inheritance again attracted travellers with the advent of the Grand Tour, over 17 centuries later, when no young man could be considered well educated without a visit to Italy.

"Virgil's tomb" *(see p119)*

FROM CLASSICAL WRITERS TO THE RENAISSANCE

BEFORE THE eruption of Vesuvius in AD 79, the volcano had been quiet for 1,200 years, but the inhabitants were nonetheless aware of the living nature of the land. In Greek myth, the Olympian gods had buried defeated giants in the Phlegraean Fields; the ground was said to stir if they moved. Pliny the Elder, author of the *Naturalis Historia*, lost his life at Pompeii in AD 79; his insatiable curiosity tempted him to go closer to the volcano and he was suffocated by the fumes. His nephew Pliny the Younger was an eyewitness.

The Renaissance brought a revival of interest in Greek and Latin culture. In the 14th century the great lyric poet and scholar Petrarch was one of many writers, artists and architects attracted to the court of Robert of Anjou. Boccaccio and Giotto were also at the court at this time. Torquato Tasso, a native of Sorrento, worked on his epic poetry at the monastery of Monteolivetoat the end of the 1500s.

Petrarch

TRAVELLERS AND THE GRAND TOUR

THE GRAND TOUR first became a custom in the 16th century and had become an English fashion by the 18th century. Young aristocrats were expected to study Europe's classical past to complete their education. The route took in the main classical sites and focussed on Rome and Naples as the highlights of the trip. Sir William Hamilton, envoy to Naples from 1764, entertained Grand Tour travellers at the embassy. An archaeologist and collector as well as a diplomat, his collections now form part of the classical antiquities section at the British Museum in London. (Sir William's wife Emma was another source of attraction at the embassy, and became notorious as the mistress of Nelson.)

In 1775 Goethe visited the city with the painter Tischbein and was overwhelmed. He later wrote: "One may write or paint as much as one likes, but this place, the shore, the bay, Vesuvius, the citadels, the villas, everything, defies description".

Tischbein, *Goethe in the Country* (Museo di San Martino)

Goethe was not the only visitor to produce a book from his travels *(Italian Journey)*. Classical Italy inspired numerous diaries and descriptions, and guidebook writing began to flourish. When excavations began at Herculaneum in 1711 and at Pompeii in 1733, this only added to the enormous appeal of this part of Southern Italy.

Catel, *Death of Tasso* (San Martino Museum)

ROMANTIC NAPLES

THE 1800s brought writers and artists from all over Europe to Naples. The French writer Stendhal, who regarded Italy as his adopted country, left Naples in 1817 swearing he would never be able to forget Toledo and the Teatro San Carlo, the glories of the "most beautiful city in the universe". In 1812, another French writer, Alphonse de Lamartine, recalled his experiences of Naples in *Graziella*, which featured a girl from Procida, and the *Gulf of Baia*.

In the field of classical music, Rossini's *Othello* was performed at the Teatro San Carlo, the composer being forced to work at break-neck speed by his opera impresario friend Barbaja. Two of Rossini's operas had their world premieres in Naples. *Mosè in Egitto* (1818) was written for the opera singer Isabella Colbran, later to be Rossini's wife. *La Donna del Lago* (1819) was based on Sir Walter Scott's romantic poem *The Lady of the Lake*; the role of Ellen was written for Colbran. Scott's work was also the inspiration for Donizetti's *Lucia di Lammermoor*, first performed at the Teatro San Carlo in 1835.

Under Bourbon rule Naples became a grand and even sophisticated place for those who could afford luxury. In 1828 the American author James Fenimore Cooper was so taken by the city that he managed to find good qualities even in its negative aspects. In his description of the area around Castel Nuovo, he declares: "This was the area of the *lazzaroni*; and it is no easy task to find lovelier or happier vagabonds than the ones here".

The San Carlo theatre *(see p53)*, which began its great tradition in the romantic period with world premieres of Rossini and Donizetti

Gioacchino Rossini

Foreign artists were drawn to the city by its beauty. In 1816 the Dutch landscape painter Anton Pitloo set up a private art academy, influencing a group of young local artists who later founded the Posillipo school of landscape painting. In 1825 Sylvester Scedrin, another landscape painter, came from St Petersburg to work here. Charles Dickens paid a long visit to Italy in 1844, which resulted in a book, *Pictures from Italy*. He also distilled his experiences into lively despatches for the benefit of the readers of the *Daily News*. The end of Bourbon rule and the cholera epidemic of 1884 brought about a decline in the appeal of Naples. Visitors could not fail to be enchanted by Naples and the bay, but by degrees the city became a stopping point for visitors heading for Pompeii or the temples of Paestum.

TO THE TWENTIETH CENTURY

THE ROMANTIC POET Leopardi (1798–1837) spent the last years of his life in Naples. In his poem *La Ginestra*, he makes the "destroyer Vesuvius" the

symbol of the destructive power of nature. He had a love/hate relationship with Naples, liking some aspects but mistrustful of the Neapolitans: "Scoundrels and buffoons, both noblemen and plebeians, all of them thieves and wretched barons most worthy of the Spanish and the gallows".

More recently, the Neapolitan writer Matilde Serao depicted the hectic life of Naples in *Il Paese di Cuccagna* (1891), a vividly written account of the hopes and passions inspired by the lottery. Fellow Neapolitan author Curzio Malaparte looks at the city in *La Pelle* (1948): "Naples is the most mysterious city in Europe. It is the only city of the ancient world that has not perished. ...It is not a city: it is a world – the ancient pre-Christian world – which has survived intact on the surface of the modern world".

Portrait of Giacomo Leopardi

Naples and the Arts

Silent film stars of 1914

NAPLES WAS FAMOUS in the 19th century for its spectacular operas and the emotional power of its popular songs, and in more recent times, Neapolitan performers such as Eduardo De Filippo, Totò and Sophia Loren, have all gained worldwide acclaim. But the city is not content to dwell on past glories. The arts scene is very much alive, with creative experiments ranging from modern variations on the melodramatic *sceneggiata* to the new cinema of Mario Martone, and from the traditional melodies of Roberto Murolo to rock and rap.

Eduardo De Filippo and Totò

A scene from *The Gold of Naples*

CINEMA

ONE OF THE FIRST cinema companies in Italy, Lombardo Film, was founded in the early 1900s in the Vomero district of Naples. However, the first major film to be produced in Naples was probably *Assunta Spina* (1915), based on a novel by Salvatore di Giacomo. In its most memorable scene, the heroine, played by Francesca Bertini, has her face slashed in the Mergellina quarter. Many of the silent films made in this period were realistic works based on stories of everyday life, often acted by locals taken off the streets.

More familiar are the films made in the 1950s, many featuring famous songs or plots based on the traditional melodrama of the *sceneggiata*. Most of these were fairly lightweight and commercial, but they did include the occasional masterpiece, such

as Eduardo De Filippo's *Napoli Milionaria* (1950). Two other notable exceptions were *Un Turco Napoletano* (1953) starring the great comic actor Totò, and Vittorio De Sica's *The Gold of Naples* (1954) with Sophia Loren. Ten years later, the director De Sica and Sophia Loren collaborated once again in *Marriage Italian Style*, an adaptation of one of Eduardo De Filippo's best-loved stage plays, *Filumena Marturano*. For her services to Italian cinema over five decades, Sophia Loren was dubbed Knight of the Italian Republic in March 1997.

Many of Italy's greatest film directors have been inspired to communicate their personal impressions of Naples. The portrait of the city in Roberto Rossellini's *Viaggio in Italia* (1953) is unsentimental. In Francesco Rosi's *Mani sulla Città*, the Neapolitan

director attacks the corrupt links between the city's politicians and developers. This marked an awareness of social reality in the 1960s. The film won first prize at the 1963 Venice Film Festival. Opposing views of Naples can be seen in Nanni Loy's mysterious *Mi manda Picone* (1983) and Ettore Scola's sunny, life-enhancing *Maccheroni* (1985).

Loren and Mastroianni in *Marriage Italian Style* (1964)

Then there are the touching films of the late actor/director Massimo Troisi. The young man he plays in *Ricomincio da Tre* finds it impossible to live a normal life away from Naples; he is always made to feel an "emigrant". Notable recent films include Mario Martone's *L'Amore Molesto*, in which the city, for all its faults, still exerts a powerful pull on those who want to leave, and Antonio Capuano's *Pianese Nunzio, 14 Anni a Maggio*, shown at the 1996 Venice Film Festival.

Massimo Troisi on the set of *Ricomincio da Tre* (1980)

OPERA AND THEATRE

ENTERTAINMENT in Naples has always catered for a broad range of tastes. The opera season at the San Carlo Theatre *(see p35, p53)* is well subscribed, but the theatre has a wider appeal, thanks to the great tradition of plays in Neapolitan dialect and the comic talents of native actors such as Eduardo Scarpetta (1853–1924), Totò (1898–1967) and Eduardo De Filippo (1900–84). De Filippo combined the roles of actor, manager and play-wright. His brilliant comedies, which usually revolve around

THE SCENEGGIATA

The *sceneggiata*, or popular Neapolitan melodrama, dates from the turn of the century. With the simplest of plots and characters crudely drawn in black and white, it was a grotesque mixture of tragedy and farce; audiences cheered the hero and booed the villain. Music played an important part in the show and there was always a rousing title song, the *pezzo forte*. The genre was revived

Mario Merola

in the 1970s. The modern version is more sophisticated, but has perhaps lost a little of the original flavour. The leading exponent of the *sceneggiata* today is Mario Merola.

Eduardo De Filippo on stage

the apparently petty concerns of family life, were performed by his famous family troupe.

The works of the actor and playwright Raffaele Viviani (1888–1950) also portray daily Neapolitan life with irony as well as affection, often with the use of local dialect.

Experimental theatre has been active in Naples since the establishment of the "Falso Movimento" in 1979. Its founders are now involved in the Teatri Uniti, staging avant-garde plays at the Teatro Nuovo and the Galleria Toledo, where the leading actors are Enzo Moscato and Tonino Taiuti.

NEAPOLITAN SONGS

FOR MANY, the spirit of Naples is embodied by the sound of Neapolitan songs, overflowing with powerful expressions of love, longing and melancholy, and filled with images of the sun and the sea. The songs' romantic melodies have always had a profound influence on the development of Italian music and are familiar the world over through the recordings made by Enrico Caruso and other great tenors.

Naturally, the best-known songs are the classics, first and foremost *O Sole Mio*, composed in 1898 and still as popular as ever.

Present-day masters of the tradition include Sergio Bruni, famous for his song *Carmela*, and Roberto Murolo, who is known respectfully as the "singers' singer". Their work is true to the spirit of Neapolitan songs, but is fresh and original rather than mere pastiche.

Other less well-known traditional forms include the *macchietta* (a comic song routine) and *tammorriate* (dances accompanied by songs). These both enjoyed a revival in the 1970s. There is also an extensive repertoire of so-called "modern-traditional" songs. These are virtually unknown outside Naples but are extremely popular with the locals and sometimes

Roberto Murolo

sung by famous performers such as Nino D'Angelo.

Some composers graft Neapolitan songs onto other musical forms such as jazz, blues, rock and even rap. Among the more successful experiments of this kind are Eugenio Bennato's "pop" songs, the delicate melodies of Eduardo De Crescenzo and the poetic accounts of everyday life by Pino Daniele, who has achieved fame outside Naples as well. The Almamegretta group *(see p197)* set their songs in Neapolitan dialect to typical British electronic music.

Pino Daniele

Symbols of the City

NAPLES IS A CITY that defies rational explanation, yet visitors have always found a wealth of sights and sounds that sum up aspects of its character. Some are positive: the beauty of the bay, the romantic melodies of Neapolitan songs, the craftsmanship of the cribs in the churches. Others are quite the opposite. Northern Europeans (and Northern Italians) are often shocked by the contrast between the city's general air of *dolce far niente* and its widespread poverty and superstition. All these things have become clichés, making it even harder to distinguish the true nature of Naples.

The pazzariello and his band

Street life: colourful stalls in a city market

FIRST IMPRESSIONS

NAPLES HAS ALWAYS been famous for the vivacity of its alleyways, streets and squares. The zest for life in the Toledo district amazed foreign visitors such as Goethe and Stendhal *(see pp34–5)*. The *lazzaroni* (ruffians) lounging around on street corners made such a strong impression on foreign visitors to Naples in the 18th and 19th centuries, that they became more or less synonymous with the city. Ferdinand I, King of the Two Sicilies from 1759 to 1825, was even nicknamed the *Re Lazzarone*.

Today, many people are struck by the ubiquitous street pedlars. There have been many attempts to regulate their activities, but most have come to nothing.

Old water-seller's marble stand

THE WATER-SELLER

THE NEAPOLITAN water-seller (*l'acquaiolo*) was once a very common sight on the streets of the city, offering refreshing drinks to passers-by on torrid summer afternoons. The water often came from the sulphurous springs of Chiatamone, which used to rise near the church of Santa Lucia *(see p116)*. It was kept cool in clay jugs, known as *mummere*. If you paid extra, you could have lemon or orange juice added to make a *spremuta*. In some parts of the old city you can still spot a *banco dell'acqua* or water stand with its solid marble counter and decorative citrus fruit. Most, however, have been modernized by the addition of stainless steel and sell cans of Coca-Cola as well as traditional drinks.

THE PAZZARIELLO

A curious and unique figure, sadly now defunct, the *pazzariello* could be seen dressed in an old-fashioned military uniform, wielding a long ceremonial baton with a gold pommel at one end and leading a small marching band. The amusing and immensely popular character, he was originally a town crier, but his duties were later extended to include leading parades on local feast days and advertising goods for sale in a new shop. The *pazzariello* was immortalized by Totò in Vittorio De Sica's film *The Gold of Naples (see p36)*.

THE SCUGNIZZO

THE STEREOTYPE of the cheeky, but basically good, street urchin, plays a major part in the folklore of the city. Living by his wits, ready to run errands for anybody who would give him money or food, he made an indelible impression on the American troops based in Naples during World War II. The true *scugnizzo* no longer really exists. Yet one can perhaps sense his streetwise spirit in the many small boys who now whizz about the city on mopeds.

A scugnizzo

PULCINELLA

THE CHARACTER of Pulcinella, stupid, yet at the same time cunning, dogged by chronic bad luck and always hungry, is the stock comic figure of a Neapolitan. One can never be quite sure, as the philosopher Benedetto Croce remarked, whether he represents a faithful portrait, a caricature or an ideal to which Neapolitans aspire. Either as a puppet (he was the model for the English Mr Punch) or in the theatre, Pulcinella has always made people laugh. With his crazy schemes, wild grimaces and the comic effects of his permanently empty stomach, he personifies the city's age-old scourge of famine.

The character of Pulcinella, as we know him today, seems to have first appeared in about 1600, but he may well have had a Classical ancestor in the equally hungry Macchus, a character from the ancient farces of Atella, a town northeast of Naples.

The greatest interpreters of the role within living memory were naturally the two actors who most fully represented the spirit of Naples – Eduardo De Filippo and Totò (see pp36–7). Their performances were especially poignant in the period of famine during and after World War II.

Pulcinella

THE CHRISTMAS CRIB

NOBODY KNOWS when the custom of representing the nativity of Christ in a sculpted tableau began. One of the earliest examples is the 13th-century sculpture by Arnolfo di Cambio at the Basilica of Santa Maria Maggiore in Rome, but the tradition may well be much older. In Naples it became such an important feature of the Christmas celebrations that people came to think

Detail of historic crib scene at the Museo di San Martino (see p111)

of the crib (il presepe) as a Neapolitan institution. The traditional local craftsmen, who, in many cases, have produced magnificent works of art (see p111), do not limit themselves to the central figures of the nativity grouped around the baby Jesus in the manger. The scene expands to become a miniature representation of the whole of Naples, with all its characteristic sights and personalities. Look closely at the figures in a modern crib scene and you may spot Pulcinella, Totò or even the current mayor of Naples, Antonio Bassolino.

THE LOTTERY

THE DRAWING of the lottery, in which a blindfolded child extracts the winning numbers, has remained unchanged, but the lottery is not quite the force it once was. Founded by Ferdinand I

in 1774, il lotto can be said, without exaggeration, to have ruled the lives of many 19th-century Neapolitans. It is still very popular and La Smorfia, a book that claims to interpret dreams and events to help you choose the winning numbers, has been reprinted many times (see p71).

PIZZA AND PASTA

Ingredients for the topping of a pizza Margherita

THE GASTRONOMIC symbols of Naples, pizza and pasta, were not always the city's staple foods. Before the population explosion of the 1600s, the poor lived mainly on cabbage and other vegetables. These were then replaced as the staple food by wheat flour, which was less perishable, and the Neapolitans acquired the nickname "macaroni eaters".

Pizza, in its present form, dates from the end of the 18th century. It may not have been a Neapolitan invention, but it was Naples that gave the world the napoletana and the Margherita (see p180), its two most enduring varieties.

Period print showing the traditional lottery drawing ceremony

NAPLES THROUGH THE YEAR

THERE IS NO SINGLE ideal season for visiting Naples; the temperate climate means a pleasant stay at any time of year. However, every season has its particular attractions. In May, an increased number of churches and monuments are open to the public; while July and August are perfect for the beach. The miracle of the city's patron saint San Gennaro is celebrated in May and September. In December, local craftsmen create traditional Christmas crib scenes. In the outlying areas, old traditions, with processions at sea and feasts celebrated in historical costume, are still vital to local life.

SPRING

THE MILD SPRING climate is perfect for enjoying drinks at an outdoor café, walking around the town centre, or visiting the surrounding countryside, which is relatively uncrowded during this season compared with summertime. At Easter it may be warm enough to swim in the sea, although traditionally 1 May marks the beginning of the bathing season. The months of March and April can be unsettled, however, and a brief spell of fine weather may be interrupted by a cold snap or even hailstorms. According to a local proverb, the weather experienced in Naples on 4 April will continue for the following 40 days.

San Giuseppe's day *zeppole*

MARCH

Feast of San Giuseppe (19 March). A bird festival is held in Via Medina, with *zeppole* (doughnuts) in every bar, bakery and home. At one time the festival marked the change from winter clothes to the new spring wardrobe.

EASTER

In many outlying districts and in some quarters of Naples there are **Good Friday** processions. One of the most

Madonna dell'Arco, Easter Monday

interesting takes place on the island of Procida. The cortege of priests and parishioners leaves at dawn from the top of Terra Murata and ends up at Marina Grande.

Easter Monday, or "Pasquetta" is the day for outings, when the whole family goes for a meal in a trattoria out of town. For the more traditional, a ceremony is held at the sanctuary of Madonna dell'Arco, near Sant'Anastasia, 15 km (9 miles) east of the city. Barefooted men, known as *fuijenti*, ask for alms, and a statue of the Madonna is carried on flower-laden carts into the countryside. Here the occasion turns into a lively "pagan" feast.

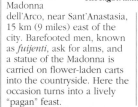

The *Inghirlandata* ceremony

Trotting races at the Agnano racetrack

APRIL

The Agnano racetrack hosts trotting races for the **Gran Premio della Lotteria di Agnano** in April. Dog races are held all year round at the Cinodromo.

MAY

One of the two annual celebrations of the miracle of **San Gennaro** *(see p83)* takes place on the first Sunday in May. The procession starts off at the cathedral (*duomo*), with the statue of San Gennaro, the patron saint of Naples, being carried from the church. The procession is known locally as the *Inghirlandata* (garlanding) because it was traditionally accompanied by flowered decorations, and the faithful would throw rose petals over the statue of the saint.

During May visitors can make the most of the **Maggio dei Monumenti**, when buildings and churches which are normally closed are open to the public. The scheme, also known as *Napoli Porte Aperte*, was started in 1992 by the Fondazione Napoli '99. Since 1995 it has been sponsored by the Naples city council to encourage the "rediscovery" of historic Naples. May is also the month of the **Vela Longa** regatta, open to any type of sailing boat.

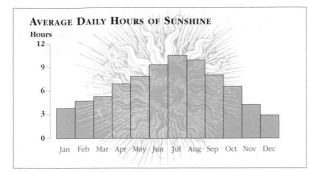

AVERAGE DAILY HOURS OF SUNSHINE

Hours

Sunshine Hours
Naples is famous for its light. The longest days fall in July, when the midday heat can be intense. In autumn the sun can still be quite hot, particularly in the middle of the day.

The Vela Longa regatta is held every May

SUMMER

THIS SEASON can be quite muggy, especially in July, when the temperature sometimes exceeds 40°C (104°F). However, after mid-August the heat is sometimes interrupted by a brief, heavy and often violent thunderstorm that is known all along the coast as the *tropea*.

Summer nights in the city can be spent at the **Estate a Napoli** festival, which from late July to September features various performance art events and films. The week of the Assumption, or *Ferragosto* (15 Aug), is ideal for those who prefer a semi-deserted, if hot, city.

Outside Naples, interesting cultural events are held at the Pompeii amphitheatre *(see p144)*, and the Vesuvian villas *(see p136)* also host various events. For music-lovers, there are the **Estate Musicale Sorrentina** at Sorrento, and the well-known **Festival Internazionale**, which takes place at Ravello *(see p198)*.

JUNE

The feast of **San Giovanni** (24 Jun), linked to the summer solstice, used to be celebrated with magicians and feasting, and night bathing. Out in the countryside people still gather walnuts to make the traditional walnut liqueur called *nocino* that will be ready by late autumn.

From late June to mid-July, the Mostra d'Oltremare *(see p25)* features the **Fiera della Casa**, when furniture, interior furnishings and local handicrafts are on sale or simply on display. The *fiera* gives you the chance to join the busy crowds and makes a change from sightseeing.

JULY

Piazza Mercato *(see p73)* plays host to the feast of the **Madonna del Carmine** (16 Jul), an ancient tradition. The *Madonna Bruna* is kept inside the church of Santa Maria del Carmine: according to legend she miraculously saved the bell tower from a fire.

Fireworks are used to re-enact the miracle wrought by the Madonna; the ceremony ends with the so-called "burning" of the bell tower.

Sant'Anna is celebrated in Ischia on 26 July with a night procession of illuminated boats and a firework display.

AUGUST

August is the traditional holiday month in Italy and you may find many city restaurants, as well as shops, local services and bars, closed until September. Throughout the region the traditional "fast" held on the Eve of the Assumption (the night of 14–15 August) is helped along by helpings of watermelon, eaten on the beach. At Positano, a ceremony in period costume celebrates the landing of the Saracens.

Feast of the Madonna del Carmine

AVERAGE MONTHLY RAINFALL

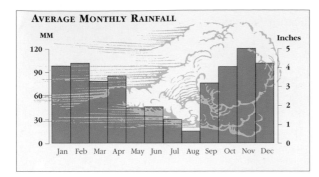

MM — Inches

| | Jan | Feb | Mar | Apr | May | Jun | Jul | Aug | Sep | Oct | Nov | Dec |

Rainfall
The wettest months of the year are November and February. The rainfall does not last for long, but it comes in brief, violent downpours. The driest month is August, but this can also be interrupted by heavy thunderstorms near the end of the month.

AUTUMN

AUTUMN IN NAPLES is quite mild; with September and October perfect for outings and long hikes in the countryside. The sea is warm enough for swimming well into October and even in early November. Nature lovers and amateur photographers will enjoy the splendid soft autumn light and clear days. Then there are popular local feast days, known as *sagre*, in nearby towns, such as the famous wine festivals *(sagra del vino)*, that coincide with the harvesting of the grapes.

Naples itself also comes back to life after the quiet and empty summer months. From September onwards football fans can spend Sunday afternoons in the stadium, following the Neapolitans' favourite sport.

SEPTEMBER

The **Madonna di Piedigrotta** feast is held in the first half of the month. The ancient cave next to the sanctuary *(see p118)*, which has been closed for many years, was once the venue for popular rituals. Today, the festival has once again become fashionable. According to an old proverb, the date of the festival of Piedigrotta marks the beginning of the rainy season.

An increasingly popular festival is the **Settembrata Anacaprese**. Throughout the month of September, shows, games and gastronomic contests are held in Anacapri, Capri's second town.

The Piedigrotta feast in a 1930s photograph

The 19th marks the second celebration of the miracle of the blood of **San Gennaro** in Naples' Duomo. For centuries this ceremony, in which the congealed blood of the saint becomes liquid, has attracted scholars, tourists, local worshippers and city authorities. Some aspects of the ritual, such as the violent supplications uttered in dialect, are today considered to be too pagan and are no longer practised.

OCTOBER

The **Classical music season** begins at the Teatro San Carlo.

NOVEMBER

On **All Souls' Day** (2 Nov), also called the Day of the Dead, families take flowers to the graves of their loved ones. This was traditionally followed by a family meal at a trattoria outside town. This is the time of year when confectioners make the delicious *torrone dei morti* almond nougat.

Aerial view of the San Paolo football stadium

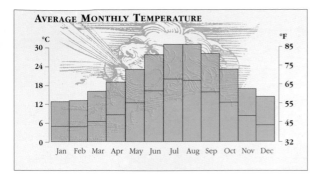

AVERAGE MONTHLY TEMPERATURE

°C / °F

Jan Feb Mar Apr May Jun Jul Aug Sep Oct Nov Dec

Temperature
This chart gives the average minimum and maximum temperatures for each month. July and August are the hottest months, February the coldest. During the winter, relatively cold days may alternate with a spell of very mild and sunny days.

WINTER

THE MONTH OF DECEMBER and the holiday season may sometimes be accompanied by a bit of snow. However, December and January are not usually especially cold, and the days can be bright and sunny. February sometimes brings rain and cold. Although the rainfall is not persistent, heavy showers may occur. The "land of the sun" is not in fact warm all year around, as many think, and the few cold days can be really cold.

DECEMBER

The day of the **Immacolata** (Immaculate Conception, 8 Dec) opens the Christmas holiday season.

A bagpipe player, a tradition at Christmas

People prepare the *presepe* (nativity scene) in their homes with moss and statuettes of figures such as Mary, the ox and donkey, the Wise Men and Jesus in the crib. The Cardinal and Mayor of the city lay wreaths on the Guglia dell'Immacolata *(see p65)*.

Christmas is celebrated with dinner and presents on Christmas Eve followed by midnight mass. The streets are illuminated and the stands on Via San Gregorio Armeno have crib figures on display *(see p39)*. A few days before New Year's Day the fireworks stalls start to appear and the traditional bagpipers add colour to the street scene.

JANUARY

New Year's Eve is celebrated with an impressive display of fireworks. For an enjoyable midnight outdoors, go and join in the merrymaking in the central Piazza del Plebiscito.

Traditionally the year begins with **Sant'Antuono** (Sant' Antonio Abate, 17 Jan) and in the old centre *cippi* or old things are thrown in bonfires.

On **Epiphany** (6 Jan) the Befana witch arrives in Piazza del Plebiscito. This is a feast for children and stalls sell sweets and "gifts from the Befana", particularly in Via Foria. Naughty children are brought (sweet) "lumps of coal".

FEBRUARY

Masked festivities for **Shrove Tuesday** and **Carnival** are accompanied by lasagna dishes. The **Galassia Gutenberg** book and multimedia fair opens, and the **Mostra d'Oltremare** offers exhibits, lectures and cultural events.

Pulcinella, the protagonist of the Naples Carnival

PUBLIC HOLIDAYS

New Year's Day (1 Jan)
Epiphany (6 Jan)
Easter Sunday and Monday
Liberation Day (25 Apr)
Labour Day (1 May)
Ferragosto (15 Aug)
All Saints' Day (1 Nov)
Immaculate Conception (8 Dec)
Christmas Day (25 Dec)
Santo Stefano (26 Dec)

A Christmas feast in a square illuminated with fairy lights

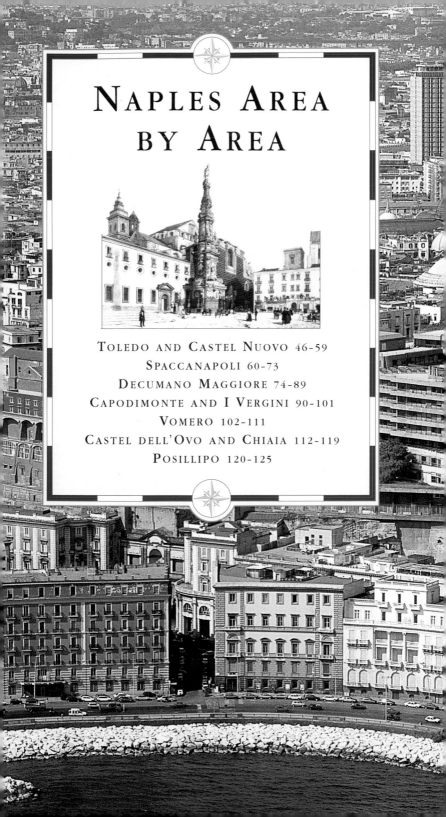

NAPLES AREA BY AREA

TOLEDO AND CASTEL NUOVO

ASTEL NUOVO CASTS its impressive shadow on an area that is both the commercial and administrative centre of modern Naples and the heart of the old capital. This zone extends as far as the harbour, the boarding point for ferry trips. Centuries of history are concentrated in the area – from the ancient archaeological ruins on the hill of Pizzofalcone to 19th-century buildings such as the Galleria Umberto I. Near the Royal Palace and

Cannonballs at Castel Nuovo

fortress of Castel Nuovo, opposite the basilica of San Francesco di Paola, is the majestic Palazzo Reale, a palace built by the Spanish viceroys. Running north from here is a long and famous 16th-century road, Via Toledo, the main artery of Naples. It is still better known by this name (after the man who built it, Viceroy Don Pedro of Toledo) than its newer, official name, Via Roma. Lining the thoroughfare are elegant buildings, stately churches and shops.

SIGHTS AT A GLANCE

Historic Buildings
Castel Nuovo pp54–5 **8**
Palazzo delle Poste e Telegrafi **14**
Palazzo Reale pp50–51 **1**
Palazzo Serra di Cassano **19**

Churches
Santa Brigida **12**
San Ferdinando **4**
San Francesco di Paola **2**
San Giacomo degli Spagnoli **11**
Santa Maria degli Angeli **17**
Santa Maria Egiziaca a Pizzofalcone **18**
Santa Maria Incoronata **10**
Nunziatella **20**

Historic Streets and Squares
Galleria Umberto I **6**
Piazza Giovanni Bovio **15**
Quartieri Spagnoli **13**
Via Chiaia **16**
Via Toledo **5**

Historic Theatres
Teatro Mercadante **9**
Teatro San Carlo **7**

Museums
Museo dell'Appartamento Reale *(see Palazzo Reale)*
Museo Artistico Industriale **21**
Museo Civico *(see Castel Nuovo)*

Historic Landmarks
Caffè Gambrinus **3**

GETTING THERE

Piazza del Plebiscito and part of Via Toledo are closed to traffic, but a number of city buses run nearby. Route R2 comes from Napoli Centrale railway station, while R3 comes from Mergellina railway station. Bus 24 is on the same route as Capodimonte and the Museo Archeologico. The V1 route links Vomero with the funicular at Montesanto and Toledo. Route C80 comes from the airport.

KEY

▨	Street-by-Street map *See pp48–9*
🅿	Parking
⛴	Ferry port
🚠	Funicular

0 metres 350
0 yards 350

◁ **The Scalone d'Onore in Palazzo Reale**

Street-by-Street: Toledo and Castel Nuovo

NAPLES IS A CITY of contrasting moods: the quiet solemnity of Piazza del Plebiscito, a symbol of the city's rebirth, is very different from the animation – you might even call it confusion – of the surrounding streets. It is a pleasure to mingle with the crowd in Via Toledo, drop in at the Caffè Gambrinus or Galleria Umberto I, pause in the shade of the historic church of San Francesco di Paola, or visit the museums at Palazzo Reale and Castel Nuovo. In addition to the rich history and art treasures in this area, Via Toledo is good for shopping.

Galleria Umberto I
The iron and glass dome was built in the late 1800s by Boubée **6**

Via Toledo
This street, named after a Spanish viceroy, borders the Quartieri Spagnoli **5**

Teatro San Carlo
Richly decorated in gilded stucco, the theatre seats 3,000 and the acoustics are excellent **7**

San Ferdinando
Every year on Good Friday there is a performance of the Stabat Mater *composed by Pergolesi for the confraternity based here since 1837* **4**

Caffè Gambrinus
Gabriele d'Annunzio wrote the lyrics to the Neapolitan song "A vucchella" in this café **3**

PIAZ TRIES TREN

PIAZZA PLEBISCITO

★ **San Francesco di Paola**
This Neo-Classical church was designed by Lugano architect Pietro Bianchi in 1817 **2**

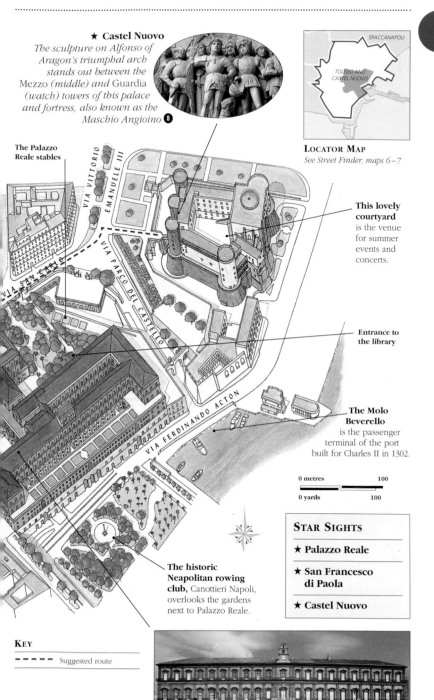

★ Castel Nuovo
The sculpture on Alfonso of Aragon's triumphal arch stands out between the Mezzo *(middle) and* Guardia *(watch) towers of this palace and fortress, also known as the* Maschio Angioino ❽

LOCATOR MAP
See Street Finder, maps 6–7

The Palazzo Reale stables

VIA VITTORIO EMANUELE III

VIA PARCO DEL CASTELLO

VIA SAN CARLO

This lovely courtyard
is the venue for summer events and concerts.

Entrance to the library

VIA FERDINANDO ACTON

The Molo Beverello
is the passenger terminal of the port built for Charles II in 1302.

0 metres	100
0 yards	100

STAR SIGHTS

★ **Palazzo Reale**

★ **San Francesco di Paola**

★ **Castel Nuovo**

The historic Neapolitan rowing club, Canottieri Napoli, overlooks the gardens next to Palazzo Reale.

KEY

– – – – – Suggested route

★ Palazzo Reale
This palace was begun in 1600 for a visit by Philip III of Spain, which never took place ❶

Palazzo Reale ●

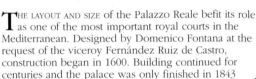

THE LAYOUT AND SIZE of the Palazzo Reale befit its role as one of the most important royal courts in the Mediterranean. Designed by Domenico Fontana at the request of the viceroy Fernández Ruiz de Castro, construction began in 1600. Building continued for centuries and the palace was only finished in 1843 by Gaetano Genovese. The Ala delle Feste wing, used in the 19th century for entertaining, now houses the Biblioteca Nazionale, the library named after King Vittorio Emanuele III, who donated the wing.

Maria Carolina's Revolving Lectern
This unusual Neo-Classical piece is based on models from monastery libraries.

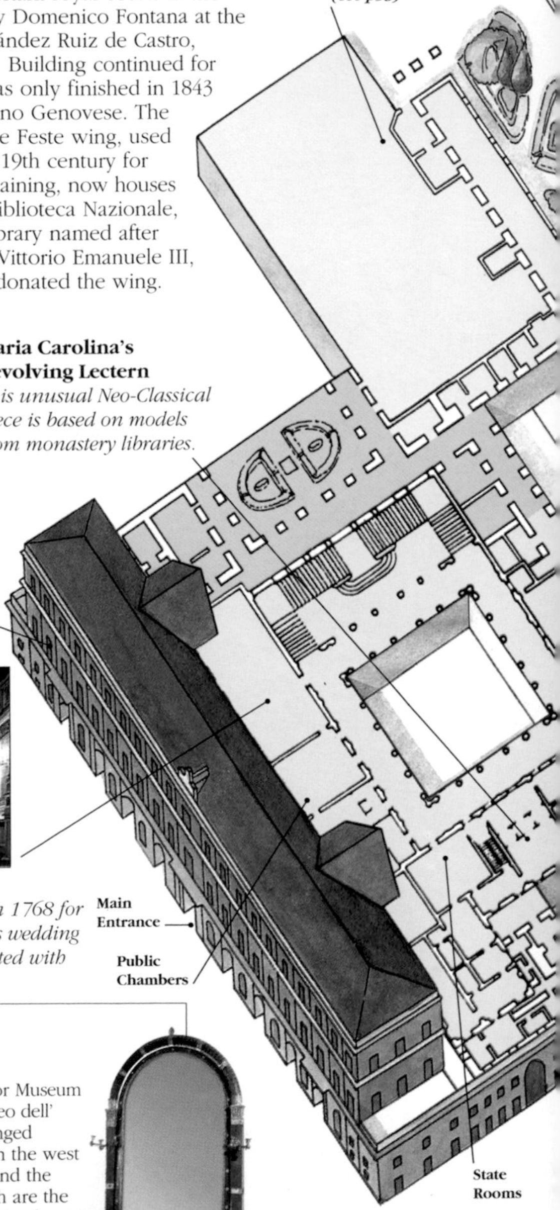

The façade, 169 m (555 ft) long, was altered in the 18th century by Luigi Vanvitelli, who created the niches which now house statues of Neapolitan kings.

Teatro San Carlo
(see p53)

★ Teatrino di Corte
The court theatre was built in 1768 for Maria Carolina of Hapsburg's wedding to Ferdinand IV, and decorated with papier-mâché sculpture.

Main Entrance

Public Chambers

State Rooms

MUSEUM OF THE ROYAL APARTMENTS

The 30 rooms in the first-floor Museum of the Royal Apartments (Museo dell' Appartamento Reale) are arranged around a central courtyard. In the west wing are the Court Theatre and the public chambers; in the south are the private chambers. The east wing houses the Cappella Palatina and the Sala di Ercole. The sumptuous decoration, objets d'art and interior furnishing are of the highest quality. The rooms in the State Rooms house 16th- to 19th-century paintings.

A mirror in the Museo

STAR FEATURES

★ Biblioteca Nazionale

★ Teatrino di Corte

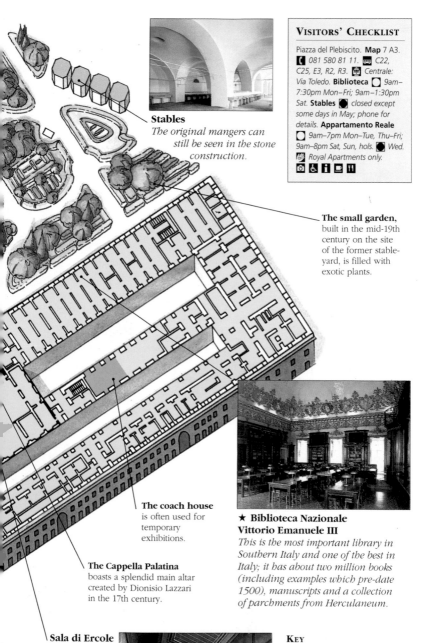

Stables
The original mangers can still be seen in the stone construction.

VISITORS' CHECKLIST

Piazza del Plebiscito. **Map** 7 A3.
081 580 81 11. C22, C25, E3, R2, R3. Centrale: Via Toledo. **Biblioteca** 9am–7:30pm Mon–Fri; 9am–1:30pm Sat. **Stables** closed except some days in May; phone for details. **Appartamento Reale** 9am–7pm Mon–Tue, Thu–Fri; 9am–8pm Sat, Sun, hols. Wed. Royal Apartments only.

The small garden, built in the mid-19th century on the site of the former stable-yard, is filled with exotic plants.

The coach house is often used for temporary exhibitions.

★ Biblioteca Nazionale Vittorio Emanuele III
This is the most important library in Southern Italy and one of the best in Italy; it has about two million books (including examples which pre-date 1500), manuscripts and a collection of parchments from Herculaneum.

The Cappella Palatina boasts a splendid main altar created by Dionisio Lazzari in the 17th century.

Sala di Ercole
This hall was named after the plaster copies of statues in the Real Museo Borbonico (now the Museo Archeologico Nazionale) – including the Farnese Hercules *(see p87) – which were placed here in the 19th century.*

KEY

- ☐ Royal Apartments (first floor)
- ☐ Teatro San Carlo
- ☐ Ala delle Feste
- ☐ Coach house
- ☐ Stables
- ☐ Non-exhibition space

19th-century print of a riding competition at San Francesco di Paola

San Francesco di Paola ❷

Piazza del Plebiscito. **Map** 7 A3.
📞 *081 764 51 33.* 🚌 *C22, C25, E3, R2, R3.* 🚊 *Centrale: Via Toledo.*
🕐 *8–12 noon, 3:30–5:30pm Mon–Sat; 8am–1pm Sun.* ✝ 📷

JOACHIM MURAT, Napoleon's brother-in-law, ruled the city of Naples from 1808 to 1815. Dissatisfied with the chaotic jumble of buildings opposite the Palazzo Reale, he decided to rebuild the whole area. The Largo di Palazzo, now called the Piazza del Plebiscito, was meant to play a major role in city life and was used for festivities, ceremonies and military parades.

The first buildings to go up were the palace built for the Prince of Salerno, and the palazzo that is now the home of the Prefecture. Both were laid out symmetrically. Murat did not see the final results of his scheme, only managing to see Leopoldo Laperuta's design for the Doric colonnade and the initial construction work before the French were driven out of Naples.

In 1815 Ferdinand of Bourbon was reinstated to the throne, and, having fulfilled his vow of reconquering the Kingdom of Naples, completed the project begun by Murat. He commissioned the architect Pietro Bianchi to design the central royal basilica, which was dedicated to San Francesco di Paola. Inspired by the Pantheon in Rome, the church has a circular plan with radiating chapels, a large cupola 53 m (174 ft) high and 34 m (112 ft) wide, complete with rosettes.

The sculpture and paintings inside the church are almost all Neo-Classical except for the high altar, which was rebuilt in 1835 with semi-precious stones and multi-coloured marble, and lapis lazuli taken from a 17th-century altar in the church of Santi Apostoli *(see p96)*. The cool, formal interior can have a rather chilling effect on visitors. According to architectural historian Renato De

Statue of Charles III by Canova

Fusco: "Despite the large size of the interior and the rich marble, stucco and garlanding decoration, the overall impression is not that of Neo-Classical rigour, but rather a lack of harmony between man and the setting, a funereal coldness compared to the exterior". The sobering effect is soon dispelled by emerging into the lovely open space of Piazza del Plebiscito, which is pedestrianized. The two equestrian statues of Charles III and Ferdinand I are the work of Antonio Canova and Antonio Calì.

Caffè Gambrinus ❸

Piazza Trieste e Trento. **Map** 7 A3.
📞 *081 41 75 82.* 🚌 *C22, C25, E3, R2, R3.* 🚊 *Centrale: Via Toledo.*
🕐 *8am–1.30am Mon–Fri, Sun; 8am–2.30am Sat.* 📷

THE CAFÉ dates from 1860; its walls decorated by the leading Neapolitan painters of the time. It soon became the haunt of politicians, artists and writers, including Guy de Maupassant and Oscar Wilde, as well as the local composers Roberto Murolo and Giovanni Bovio. When the literary café also became popular with opponents of the Fascist regime, the prefect closed it down, initiating a long period of decline and neglect. Fortunately, its lavish Belle Epoque decor has been restored and this historic landmark is once again a favourite. Neapolitans drop in for coffee and cakes, or for iced tea and ice cream.

Interior of the historic Caffè Gambrinus

San Ferdinando ❹

Piazza Trieste e Trento 5. **Map** 7 A3.
📞 081 40 05 43. 🚌 C22, C25, E3,
R2, R3. 🚇 Centrale: Via Toledo.
🕐 8am–noon, 5–7pm Mon–Sat;
9:30am–1pm Sun. 🔔

THIS CHURCH was founded in
1622 as San Francesco
Saverio. In 1769 Ferdinand I
dedicated it to his namesake
saint. The Baroque interior
contains frescoes by Paolo
De Matteis as well as sculptures by
Vaccaro as well as the tomb of
Lucia Migliaccio, the Duchess
of Floridia. Ferdinand gave
her his estate on the Vomero
hill, which became Villa La
Floridiana (see p106). Until
1919 the square was called
Piazza San Ferdinando.

Gay Odin shop in Via Toledo

Via Toledo ❺

Map 3 A5, 7 A1 (9 B4). 🚌 C57, E2,
E3, R1, R2, R3, R4, 27. 🚇 Centrale:
Via Toledo.

IN THE 1600s travellers were
equally struck by the lively
crowds in the most famous
street in Naples and by its
amazing length. Via Toledo
owes its name to the Spanish
viceroy Don Pedro de Toledo,
who commissioned its
construction alongside the
Aragonese city walls in 1536.
Fine buildings alternate with
shops and churches.
   Shopping in Via Toledo
caters to all tastes and budgets.
Locals like to stop at Gay Odin
to sample the exquisite home-
made chocolates and at
Pintauro's for the excellent
sfogliatelle pastry (see p181).

The marble floor of the Galleria Umberto I

Galleria Umberto I ❻

Via San Carlo, Via Verdi, Via Santa
Brigida, Via Toledo. **Map** 7 A2.
🚌 C22, E3, R2, R3.
🚇 Centrale: Via Toledo.

THE GALLERIA was built as
part of the Urban Renewal
plan, drawn up after the
cholera epidemic which
struck the city in 1884 (see
pp24–5). The impressive iron
and glass roof and elegant
patterned marble pavement
fill the large open space with
light. The arcade soon
became the favourite haunt
of local composers and
musicians. From the galleria it
was possible to gain entry to
the Salone Margherita, which,
until 1912, was a famous café
chantant, and considered the
heart of cabaret entertainment in Naples.

Teatro San Carlo ❼

Via San Carlo 101–3. **Map** 7 A3.
📞 081 797 21 11. 🚌 C22, C25, R2,
R3, 24. 🚇 Centrale: Via Toledo. 🕐
May: 2–4pm; Jul: noon–2pm. Other
opening times vary; ring in advance.
📷 except during rehearsals, Via San
Carlo 98f, **Season** Oct–Jun. See
Entertainment in Naples p196, p199.

THIS IS ONE of the oldest
remaining opera houses
in the world. Designed by
Giovanni Antonio Medrano
for the Bourbon Charles I, it
was built in a few months
and officially opened on 4
November 1737, 40 years
before La Scala in Milan, on
the king's saint's day. It soon
became one of the most
important opera houses in
Europe, known for its
magnificent architecture and
excellent productions. For
many years, a performance at
the San Carlo was considered
the high point in the career of
a singer or composer.
   A fire in 1816 severely
damaged the interior, which
was immediately rebuilt by
Antonio Niccolini, the architect who a few years earlier
had modified the façade by
adding the foyer and balcony.
The focal point of the
magnificent auditorium, with
its six tiers of boxes, is the
royal box, surmounted by the
crown of the Kingdom of the
Two Sicilies.
   Many great musical figures,
including Gioacchino Rossini
and Gaetano Donizetti, were
at one time artistic directors
here. The world premieres of
Donizetti's Lucia di Lammermoor and Rossini's Mosè were
performed here. Founded in
1812, the San Carlo ballet
school vies with La Scala for
the title of the oldest ballet
school in Italy.

**The Teatro San Carlo façade,
remodelled by Niccolini in 1810**

Castel Nuovo ❽

THE CASTLE WAS called *nuovo* (new) to distinguish it from two earlier ones, dell'Ovo and Capuano *(see pp116 and 81)*, which were too small to accommodate the entire Angevin court. Charles I of Anjou began construction in 1279, but the Cappella Palatina is the only part remaining of the original building. Alfonso V of Aragon (who later became Alfonso I, King of Naples and Sicily) began to rebuild it completely in 1443, the year that marked his triumphant entry into Naples. To celebrate this event, Alfonso later ordered the construction of the superb Arco di Trionfo, one of the most significant expressions of early Renaissance culture in Southern Italy. The castle, with its five impressive cylindrical towers, is designed on a trapezoidal plan facing onto a beautiful central courtyard. From here you can gain access to the most famous chamber in the castle, the Sala dei Baroni (Barons' Hall), now used by the town council. Since 1990 a small but fine art collection, the Museo Civico, has occupied three floors of the west wing.

The Renaissance doorway of the Cappella Palatina

Cappella Palatina

This is the only surviving part of the 13th-century building. An elegant Renaissance doorway leads to the chapel, which is dedicated to St Barbara. The portal itself is crowned with an elaborate rose window typical of the Catalan style of its creators. The portal is also adorned with a Madonna executed by Francesco Laurana (c.1425–1502) in 1474.

The walls inside the chapel were once decorated with frescoes by Giotto and his workshop; today, only small fragments on the splays of the lofty Gothic windows remain.

Sala dei Baroni

Next to the chapel, the Barons' Hall, which is reached by means of an outer stairway, owes its name to the grim events that took place there in 1486. Then, the great barons who had plotted a conspiracy against Ferdinand I of Aragon, were arrested and subsequently executed.

The imposing Castel Nuovo, with its stunning Renaissance triumphal arch

TIMELINE

1279 Charles I of Anjou begins construction of Castel Nuovo	**1443** Alfonso V's total rebuilding plan	**1443–68** Building of Arco di Trionfo	**1547** Popular revolt against the Inquisition	**1647** Signing of pact between the viceroy and Masaniello after popular uprising		
1200	**1300**	**1400**	**1500**	**1600**	**1700**	**1800**
	1329 Giotto and his assistants paint the Cappella Palatina frescoes	**1486** The Barons' conspiracy	**1509–37** Reconstruction of the defence system with new battlements and moats			*The* Barricades at San Ferdinando during the 1848 uprisings *(detail of a painting in the Museo Civico)*

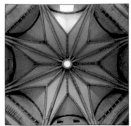

Sala dei Baroni: the splendid Spanish Gothic vault

This elegant, yet grand and austere hall, 26 m (85 ft) wide and 28 m (92 ft) high, was built by the Spanish craftsman Guglielmo Sagrera, who was summoned to Naples for the purpose in 1446. It is now the main meeting room of the town council. Its principal features are the magnificent Catalan-inspired ribbed vault with intersecting ribs in the shape of a huge star, the monumental fireplace, and the large rectangular "cross windows".

Caprile's *Vecchia Napoli* (Old Naples), depicting the famous Zizze fountain in its original state – offer views of a city that no longer exists.

Arco di Trionfo

The combination of white marble against the grey volcanic stone of Castel Nuovo is immediately striking to the visitor, as is the contrast between the ornamental reliefs and the severe geometric form of the towers. The structure, with its two superimposed arches, takes its inspiration from ancient Roman architecture.

The monumental gateway of the *Arco di Trionfo* (Triumphal Arch) was built in 1443 in honour of Alfonso V of Aragon. The bas relief depicting the *Trionfo di Alfonso* (Triumph of Alfonso) lies above the lower section, while the upper arch, which was once intended to house a statue of the sovereign, now holds allegorical figures representing the Four Virtues (looking from left to right, Temperance, Justice, Fortitude and Magnanimity). On the tympanum, supporting two large symbolic statues of rivers, stands a figure

VISITORS' CHECKLIST

Largo Castello. **Map** 7 B2. 081 795 20 03. C25, C55B, C57, C82, R1, R2, R3, R4, 24, 149. Centrale: Via Toledo. 9am–7pm Mon–Sat. see attendants for assistance.

Upper section of Arco di Trionfo

of the archangel St Michael. A number of Italian artists contributed to the final building of the arch, the most significant among them being the Neapolitan artist Francesco Laurana, who also worked on the Cappella Palatina and sculpted the statues of Justice and the bas relief of Alfonso I on his chariot. Another artist of note was Laurana's pupil and assistant Domenico Gagini.

19th-century Neapolitan painting, Museo Civico

Museo Civico

A large part of the west wing of Castel Nuovo and part of the Cappella Palatina are occupied by the Museo Civico (civic museum). Before visiting the museum, do not miss the opportunity to take in the splendid panoramic views of the Bay of Naples and Mount Vesuvius from the upper floors of the castle.

The museum houses paintings, sculptures and objets d'art that come from the castle itself, from neighbouring churches and other Neapolitan monuments. These works date from the 14th to the 19th century, but by far the largest section consists of 19th-century Neapolitan paintings. Some of these – such as Vincenzo

Castel Nuovo in a painting by Antonio Joli

Teatro Mercadante **❾**

Piazza Municipio 74. **Map** 7 B2.
📞 081 551 33 96. 🚌 C22, C25, R2,
R3, R4. 🚇 *Centrale: Via Toledo. See*
Entertainment in Naples, *p196, p199.*

BUILT IN 1778 to a design by Francesco Securo, this theatre was originally known as *"del Fondo"* because money for its construction came from a fund created by the sale of confiscated Jesuit property. The three-tier façade, with eight caryatids supporting the cornice, was added in 1892. The theatre opened in 1779 with *L'Infedeltà Fedele* by Cimarosa, a leading Neapolitan composer.

Late 19th-century façade of the Teatro Mercadante

Santa Maria Incoronata **❿**

Via dell'Incoronata. **Map** 7 B2. 🚌 C22,
C57, R2, R3, R4, 24. 🚇 *Centrale: Via*
Toledo. ◯ *9am–12:45pm Mon–Sat.*

IT IS IMMEDIATELY obvious that this church is at a lower level than Via Medina. The reason goes back to the 16th century, when Charles V built the new moats for Castel Nuovo. Earth had been dug out to make room for the ditches and when it was tipped nearby it partially buried this small mid-14th century church. Santa Maria Incoronata was originally built for Joan I of Anjou to celebrate her coronation and also to house a fragment of Jesus's crown of thorns. The two fresco cycles in the first bay of the main nave, for years attributed to Giotto, are in fact the work of a pupil of his, Roberto Oderisi.

Detail of the portico of Santa Maria Incoronata

San Giacomo degli Spagnoli **⓫**

Piazza Municipio. **Map** 7 B2. 📞 081
552 37 59. 🚌 C22, C25, C55, C80,
C85, R2, R3, R4. 🚇 *Centrale: Via*
Toledo. ◯ *7:30–11:15am Mon–Sat.*

PART OF THE 19th-century Palazzo San Giacomo (now the town hall), the church of San Giacomo dominates Piazza Municipio. In 1540 Don Pedro Alvarez de Toledo, the vice-roy responsible for the present appearance of the city centre, built the church and adjoining hospital for the Spanish community. This was the church of the local aristocracy and although rebuilt in 1741, it still belongs to the Real Hermandad de Nobles Hespanoles de Santiago, a confraternity founded more than four centuries ago.

San Giacomo contains tombs of Spanish nobles, including that of Don Pedro and his wife Maria. They were never buried in their sumptuous tomb however: Don Pedro died in Florence and is buried there in the cathedral.

The marble tomb of Don Pedro Alvarez de Toledo in San Giacomo degli Spagnoli

Santa Brigida **⓬**

Via Santa Brigida 72. **Map** 7 A2.
📞 081 552 37 93. 🚌 C57, E2, R2, R3,
24. 🚇 *Centrale: Via Toledo.* ◯ *8am–*
12:30pm, 5–7pm daily.

THE CURIOUS aspect of this 17th-century church is the dome, which could not be more than 9 m (30 ft) high because it would have obstructed artillery fire from Castel Nuovo. However, the fresco of a vivid sky created by Luca Giordano (1632–1705) on the cupola makes the most of boldly conceived perspective and creates a feeling of immense space.

The artist, nicknamed Luca Fapresto (Luca the Swift) because he worked so rapidly, painted the dome in exchange for his tomb, which can be found in the left transept.

Quartieri Spagnoli **⓭**

Map 7 A1. 🚌 E2, E3. 🚇 *Centrale:*
Via Toledo.

THE SPANISH QUARTER is one of the city's working class districts; densely populated and rather run-down (tourists should take care when visiting the area). Built in the 17th century to the west of Via Toledo to house Spanish troops, its origins live on in the name, but today it is difficult to appreciate the original grid layout. Alleys are festooned with laundry, shielding the streets from the light.

Despite the state of neglect, there is still some fine architecture, such as the church of Montecalvario (founded in

A stall laden with fish in the atmospheric 17th-century Quartieri Spagnoli district

1560), which gives its name to one of the area's districts, and Santa Maria della Concezione, a Baroque masterpiece by Domenico Antonio Vaccaro.

The great Italian poet Leopardi once lived at No. 24 Via Santa Maria Ognibene, and the local playwright Eduardo De Filippo *(see p36)* used the area as a setting for his plays.

Entrance to the Palazzo delle Poste e Telegrafi

Palazzo delle Poste e Telegrafi ⑭

Piazza Matteotti 3. **Map** 7 B1 (9 B5). **(** 081 551 19 47. **▦** C57, E2, E3, R1, R4, 24, 149. **◯** 7am–7:20pm Mon–Sat. **◯**

THE POST OFFICE building was designed in 1935 by Giuseppe Vaccaro as part of an Urban Renewal and Development plan that resulted in the demolition of the San Giuseppe quarter. The bombastic style of the civic architecture of this period (also found in

the police headquarters, the tax office and the provincial administration building) is typical of buildings constructed during the Fascist era. The Post Office combines these emphatic features with other innovative elements of the European Modern Movement.

The curvilinear façade and broad staircase make this one of the most interesting examples of 20th-century Neapolitan architecture. In striking contrast to the Post Office is the nearby cloister of Monteoliveto *(see p64)*, sadly now very dilapidated.

Piazza Giovanni Bovio ⑮

Map 7 B1 (9 C5). **▦** C25, C55, R1, R2, R4.

NEAPOLITANS call this square Piazza della Borsa after the former Stock Exchange *(Borsa)* that dominates it. Built in 1895 when taste was eclectic, the old exchange is reminiscent of 16th-century

buildings in the Veneto. It is now the home of the Chamber of Commerce. Incorporated into the left side of this building is the small church of Sant'Aspreno al Porto, originally medieval but totally rebuilt in the 1600s.

The square marks the beginning of Corso Umberto I, also known as the *Rettifilo*. This grand avenue was built after slum clearance around the harbour, to connect the city centre and the central railway station, giving a new look to early 20th-century Naples *(see pp26–7)*. Like a splendid traffic island, the 17th-century Fountain of Neptune towers over the middle of the square. Frequently altered, the fountain was moved several times before finding its final home in Piazza Bovio in 1898. It was the work of three artists: the statue of Neptune was sculpted by Michelangelo Naccherino, the balusters and lions were by Cosimo Fanzago, and the monsters at the base by Pietro Bernini.

The Fountain of Neptune

Via Chiaia  ⑯

Map 7 A3. 🚌 C22.

IN NEAPOLITAN DIALECT, *chiaia* means "beach", and in fact this street was opened in the 16th century to connect Largo di Palazzo (now Piazza del Plebiscito) with the coast. Together with Via Toledo *(see p53)*, Via dei Mille *(see p113)* and Via Calabritto this is one of Naples' smartest shopping streets. While browsing, it is worth stopping to see the Ponte di Chiaia, a 17th-century gateway restored in the 1800s. Nearby is Palazzo Cellamare, built in the 16th century and enlarged in the 18th century, when it became known for the magnificent banquets and receptions held there. The impressive portal was designed by Ferdinando Fuga. Near the Ponte, a lift affords easy access to Piazza Santa Maria degli Angeli and the Pizzofalcone hill.

The portal of the church of Santa Maria degli Angeli

Santa Maria degli Angeli ⑰

Piazza Santa Maria degli Angeli. **Map** 6 F2. 📞 081 764 49 74. 🚌 C22, E3. ⏰ 7:30–11:30am, 5:30–7pm Fri–Wed; 7:30am–2pm Thu. ♿ 📷

CONSTRUCTION of this church began in the 17th century on land donated to the devout Theatine religious order by Donna Costanza del Carretto Dira, the Princess of Melfi. The building was designed by the Theatine cleric Francesco Grimaldi, and it is clearly visible from any point overlooking the city. The three-nave

Via Chiaia and Ponte di Chiaia

interior is so well designed that Francesco Milizia, the author of an 18th-century guide to Naples, said that it "is perhaps the most well-proportioned church in the city".

The frescoes on the vaults, which depict episodes from the life of the Virgin Mary in vivid and luminous colour, are the work of Giovan Battista Beinaschi (1638–88).

Santa Maria Egiziaca a Pizzofalcone ⑱

Via Egiziaca 30. **Map** 7 A3. 📞 081 764 51 99. 🚌 C22, E3. ⏰ 9:30am–1pm, 5–6:30pm daily. ♿ 📷

THE PORTAL on Via Egiziaca opens out onto the area in front of this Baroque church.

Its construction began in 1661 at the request of the closed order of nuns who lived nearby in the Sant'Agostino convent. The building's design was entrusted to Cosimo Fanzago (1593–1678), a Lombard architect and sculptor who was to become one of the most prestigious creators of the local Baroque style. Its octagonal plan was greatly admired by contemporaries of Fanzago. The paintings in the main chapels are by Paolo De Matteis (1662–1728), while the sculptures are by Nicola Fumo. The high altar is in pure Rococo style.

Palazzo Serra di Cassano ⑲

Via Monte di Dio 14–15. **Map** 6 F2. 📞 081 764 26 52. 🚌 C22, E3. ⏰ 4–7pm Mon–Sat. 📷

THE MAIN DOORWAY to Prince Aloisio Serra di Cassano's palace is no longer the main entrance to one of the most beautiful examples of 18th-century Neapolitan civic architecture. To express his grief over the execution of his son Gennaro – one of the leaders of the 1799 revolution in Naples – the prince ordered the original entrance (at No. 67 Via Egiziaca) to be

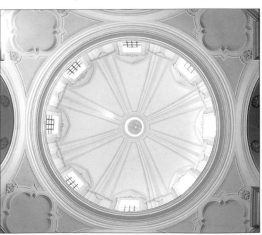

Interior of the cupola of Santa Maria Egiziaca a Pizzofalcone

The impressive double staircase in Palazzo Serra di Cassano

closed that same year. The originality of this building, which was designed by one of the leading architects of the time, Ferdinando Sanfelice (1675–1748), lies in the majestic staircase with its double flight of steps. Set in the entrance hall that opens on to the courtyard, it is decorated with white marble that contrasts beautifully with the building's imposing, grey volcanic stone.

The *piano nobile* (upper floor) of the palazzo is now the home of the Istituto Italiano per gli Studi Filosofici, a leading international cultural institution.

Nunziatella ⑳

Via Generale Parisi. **Map** 7 A4. [081 764 15 20. C22. ask for the military college chaplain (cappellano).

THE FAÇADES of the church and former convent of the Nunziatella, which has been occupied since 1787 by the military college of the same name, converge at a right angle to form a beautiful little square. At the beginning of the 18th century, the Jesuits at the Nunziatella asked architect Ferdinando Sanfelice – who was working on the nearby Palazzo Serra di Cassano at the time – to build the church and restore the convent, which dates from the 16th century.

Entering the little church, the first thing to strike the visitor is the harmonious balance Sanfelice established between the architectural space and the pictorial and sculptural decorative elements. The most important frescoes were painted by Neapolitan artist Francesco de Mura (1696–1782); in the apse is the *Adoration of the Magi*, the *Assumption of the Virgin* is on the ceiling, and on the inside of the façade is *Rest during the Flight to Egypt*. The altar, the work of Giuseppe Sanmartino (1720–93), is one of the most important examples of Neapolitan Baroque in existence.

Museo Artistico Industriale ㉑

Piazzetta Demetrio Salazar 6. **Map** 7 A3. [081 764 74 71. C22, E3. by appointment only. make inquiries at Art Institute.

FOUNDED IN 1878 by Gaetano Filangieri, who also founded the Filangieri Civic Museum *(see p70)*, and Demetrio Salazar,

Scroll decoration on the Nunziatella façade

this was the school where young artists were educated following past examples. The most important works of art are the ceramics. Among these are two large ceramic tile panels designed by the important 19th-century Neapolitan artists Domenico Morelli and Filippo Palizzi.

Façade of the Museo Artistico with its decorative tiles

THE BIRTHPLACE OF PARTHENOPE

Ancient ruins on Pizzofalcone

In the 7th century BC, Greek colonists from Rhodes founded the first urban settlement in Naples on the hill of Pizzofalcone: Parthenope, renamed Palaepolis (old city) three centuries later when Neapolis (new city) was founded to the east. The old city was later abandoned and by the Middle Ages the area had reverted to farmland. The site of ancient Naples was revived however in the 16th century, when it became a residential neighbourhood favoured by aristocrats and important officials, who were attracted by the beauty of the site and its proximity to the Royal Palace. In the 18th century Via Monte di Dio was one of the most important residential streets in Naples, and to this day it retains some of its original character.

SPACCANAPOLI

THE STRAIGHT STREET called Spaccanapoli corresponds to the lower *decumanus*, one of the three main thoroughfares in Greco-Roman Naples; the other two being present-day Via Anticaglia *(see p84)* and Via dei Tribunali *(see pp76–7)*. At the end of the 13th century, after the construction of Castel Nuovo *(see pp54–5)*, the administrative hub of the city began to shift towards the seafront. Commercial activity developed in the Piazza Mercato zone,

Bust-reliquary of San Bartolomeo, Santa Chiara

while in the old centre there was a concentration of churches and convents, notably Santa Chiara. When the city expanded around the newly built Via Toledo *(see p53)* during the era of the Spanish viceroyalty, the area which is now Piazza del Gesù Nuovo became the junction point between the old and modern cities. Subsequent development in the 19th century, including the opening up of Corso Umberto I, led to the demolition of part of the city's medieval fabric.

SIGHTS AT A GLANCE

Historic Buildings
Archivio di Stato ⑰
Monte di Pietà ⑭
Palazzo Carafa Santangelo ⑬
Palazzo Filomarino ⑦

Churches
Cappella Sansevero ⑩
Gesù Nuovo ③
Gesù Vecchio ⑳
Sant'Angelo a Nilo ⑪
Sant'Anna dei Lombardi ②
Santissima Annunziata ㉓
Santa Chiara pp66–7 ⑤
San Domenico Maggiore ⑨
Sant'Eligio Maggiore ㉕
San Giorgio Maggiore ⑮
San Giovanni dei Pappacoda ㉒
Santi Marcellino e Festo ⑲
Santa Maria del Carmine ㉔
Santa Maria La Nova ①
Santa Marta ⑥
Santi Severino e Sossio ⑱

Historic Streets and Squares
Corso Umberto I ㉑
Piazza San Domenico Maggiore ⑧

Spires and Statues
Guglia dell'Immacolata ④
Statue of the Nile ⑫

Museums
Museo Civico Filangieri ⑯

GETTING THERE
Spaccanapoli is partly closed to traffic. The red bus lines R1 (from Vomero), R2 (from the central railway station), R3 (from the Mergellina station) and R4 (from Capodimonte) stop in Via Toledo, a short walk away from the district. Piazza Mercato can be reached by trams 1 and 4. You can also get to Spaccanapoli by underground (Montesanto, Dante and Cavour-Museo stations) and, from Vomero, via the Centrale and Montesanto funicular railways.

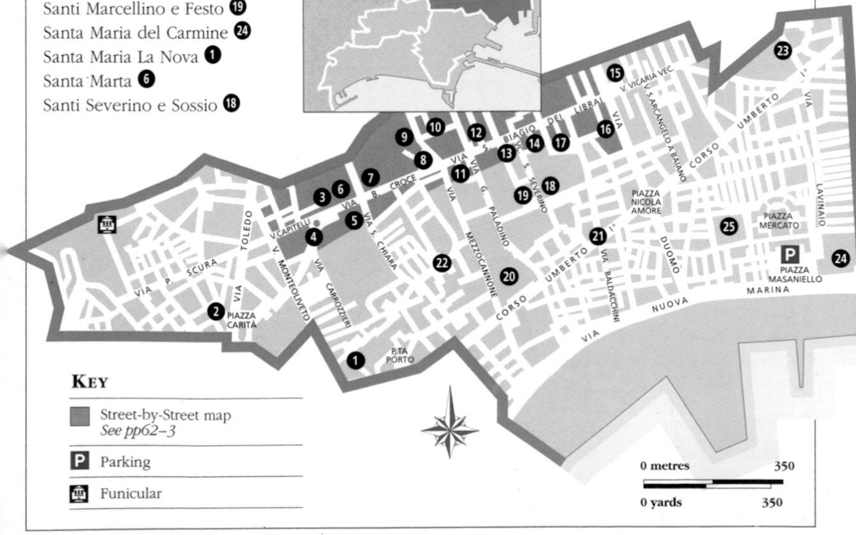

KEY

Street-by-Street map
See pp62–3

P Parking

Funicular

0 metres 350
0 yards 350

◁ **View over Spaccanapoli, once a major thoroughfare in ancient Naples**

Street-by-Street: Spaccanapoli

THE LONG STREET commonly known as Spaccanapoli is divided into seven sections bearing different names. Because of its rich array of churches, squares and historic buildings it has been called an "open-air museum", like nearby Via dei Tribunali. It is also one of the most lively and atmospheric places in Naples, with shops, crafts and cafés. Piazza San Domenico, near the University, is always crowded with young people. Those with a sweet tooth can enjoy the excellent pastries at the Scaturchio pasticceria.

Piazza San Domenico
An unusual siren with two tails is sculpted on the base of the spire **8**

San Domenico Maggiore
This church was built in 1283 by Charles I of Anjou **9**

★ Gesù Nuovo
The rusticated façade of the church was once part of Palazzo Sanseverino **3**

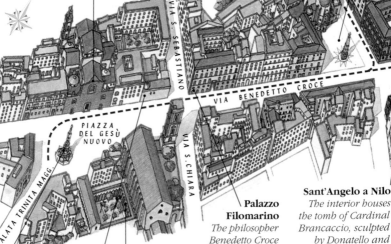

Sant'Angelo a Nilo
The interior houses the tomb of Cardinal Brancaccio, sculpted by Donatello and Michelozzo **11**

⚘ Palazzo Filomarino
The philosopher Benedetto Croce died here in 1952 **7**

Guglia dell'Immacolata
Erected in the 1700s, this spire was named after the statue of the Virgin at its pinnacle **4**

★ Santa Chiara
Robert of Anjou was responsible for building this church. The tiled cloister was designed by Domenico Antonio Vaccaro in 1742 **5**

Santa Marta
This small church dates from the 15th century **6**

PIAZZA DEL GESÙ NUOVO

VIA S. SEBASTIANO

VIA BENEDETTO CROCE

VIA S. CHIARA

CALATA TRINITA MAGG.

★ Cappella Sansevero
This moving Veiled Christ *is the only work of art by a Neapolitan artist (Giuseppe Sanmartino) in the di Sangro family chapel* ⑩

LOCATOR MAP
See Street Finder, maps 4, 5, 7

Statue of the Nile
This statue, erected in honour of the Egyptian god Nile, gives its name to the square in which it stands ⑫

Palazzo Marigliano

Ospedale delle Bambole, the dolls' hospital, is a unique place where dolls and puppets are repaired.

San Nicola a Nilo

VIA S. BIAGIO DEI LIBRAI

VIA PALADINO

VIA GRANDE ARCHIVIO

Palazzo Carafa Santangelo
Diomede Carafa designed this palazzo in the 15th century ⑬

Archivio di Stato
The state archive contains documents dating back to the Angevin period ⑰

Museo Civico Filangieri
Prince Filangieri's art collection in elegant Palazzo Como includes detailed mosaic floor tiles like these ⑯

Monte di Pietà
This majestic building and the adjoining chapel were designed by Giovan Battista Cavagna ⑭

0 metres   100
0 yards   100

KEY

- - - - - Suggested route

STAR SIGHTS

★ **Gesù Nuovo**

★ **Santa Chiara**

★ **Cappella Sansevero**

Santa Maria La Nova ❶

Largo Santa Maria La Nova 1. **Map** 7 B1 (9 C5). [081 552 32 98. C25, C57, CD, E1, E3, R1, R3, R4, 24. Centrale: Via Toledo. M Dante, Cavour-Museo. ◐ closed for restoration. ◻ cloisters open 9am–6:30pm daily.

IN ORDER TO MAKE ROOM for Castel Nuovo *(see pp54–5)* a Franciscan church devoted to the Virgin Mary had to be demolished. In exchange, Charles I of Anjou gave the friars a nearby plot of land and had a new church built at his own expense, Santa Maria La Nova. The richly decorated wooden ceiling was painted by the leading artists of the time (Santafede, Curia, Imparato and Corenzio), creating a gallery of 16th- and 17th-century Neapolitan painting. In the fourth chapel on the right is Giovanni da Nola's altarpiece of Sant' Eustachio. Other chapels contain works by Caracciolo, Teodoro d'Errico and Santacroce. In the former monastery, now the seat of the provincial government, there are two cloisters; the smaller one (No. 44) has Renaissance frescoes and marble tombs, while the other (No. 43) contains a garden. Nearby, at 11 Piazza Tommaso Monticelli, is the 15th-century façade of Palazzo Penna.

Sant'Anna dei Lombardi ❷

Piazza Monteoliveto 3. **Map** 7 A1 (9 B5). [081 551 33 33. C25, C57, CD, E1, E3, R1, R3, R4, 24. Centrale: Via Toledo. M Dante, Cavour-Museo. ◻ 9am–noon Tue–Sat. †

FOUNDED IN 1411 as Santa Maria di Monteoliveto, this was the favourite church of the Aragonese kings, who summoned the leading artists of the time to decorate it. Its name changed when it was assigned to the Confraternity of Lombards (to whom it still belongs), whose church had collapsed in the 1805 earthquake. The roof was damaged during World War II and has not been restored, but the interior contains some fine examples of Renaissance sculpture.

Cappella Piccolomini, altarpiece decoration

The marble altarpiece in the Cappella Piccolomini, by Antonio Rossellino (1475), has dancing angels on the top, the work of Benedetto da Majano. The latter also executed the altarpiece in the Terranova chapel (1489). The Tolosa chapel was decorated by the della Robbia workshop in Florence. To the right of the presbytery is Guido Mazzoni's *Lamentation over the Dead Christ* (1492), an amazingly realistic tableau of eight life-size terracotta figures surrounding Christ. Their grief-stricken faces are said to be modelled on the Aragonese kings.

At No. 3 Via Monteoliveto is the 16th-century Palazzo Gravina, now occupied by the Faculty of Architecture.

Detail of the reliquary in Gesù Nuovo

Gesù Nuovo ❸

Piazza del Gesù Nuovo. **Map** 3 B5 (9 B4). [081 551 86 13. C57, CD, E1, E3, R1, R3, R4, 24. M Dante, Cavour-Museo. Montesanto. ◻ 6:30am– 12:45pm, 4:15–7:30pm Mon–Sat; 6:30am– 1:30pm Sun. †

THE FAÇADE, COVERED IN diamond point rustication, was once part of 15th-century Palazzo Sanseverino. It was retained by the Jesuits when they bought the building and in 1584 transformed it into the large church seen today. The 17th-century doorway incorporates the original Renaissance entrance to the palazzo. The Baroque interior is richly decorated with multi-coloured marbles and ornate works of art including statues, a reliquary and vivid frescoes.

The smaller cloister in the former monastery of Santa Maria La Nova

In the chapel of St Ignatius of Loyola, founder of the Society of Jesus, are two of Cosimo Fanzago's finest works: the sculptures of *David* and *Jeremiah*. The cupola, frescoed by Lanfranco, collapsed in the 1688 earthquake; the only survivors were the corbels showing the four Evangelists in flight. Above the main entrance is Francesco Solimena's huge fresco, *Expulsion of Heliodorus from the Temple* (1725). The statue of the Virgin, on a lapis lazuli globe above the altar, dates from the mid-19th century. The second chapel on the right houses the remains of San Giuseppe Moscati, canonized in 1987.

Guglia dell'Immacolata ❹

Piazza del Gesù Nuovo. **Map** 3 B5 (9 B4). 🚌 C57, CD, E1, E3, R1, R3, R4, 24. Ⓜ Dante, Cavour-Museo. 🚋 Montesanto.

THE JESUITS commissioned this gigantic marble spire as a symbol of devotion to the Virgin Mary, and as a tangible sign of the their power. The monument, modelled on ancient Egyptian obelisks and designed by Giuseppe Genuino, was begun in 1743. The complex stone ornamentation, depicting the Jesuit saints and stories of Mary, was sculpted by Francesco Pagano and Matteo Bottigliero and is regarded as a key work of 18th-century Neapolitan sculpture. The statue of the Madonna is the centre of festivities on the Feast of Immaculate Conception.

Guglia dell'Immacolata

Façade of Gesù Nuovo

Santa Chiara ❺

See pp66–7.

Santa Marta ❻

Via San Sebastiano 42. **Map** 3 B5 (9 B3). 📞 081 726 04 95. 🚌 C57, CD, E1, E3, R1, R3, R4, 24. Ⓜ Dante, Cavour-Museo. 🚋 Montesanto. ◯ 8:30am–noon Sun.

THIS SMALL CHURCH, was founded by Margherita di Durazzo in the 15th century and became the headquarters of one of the city's most important confraternities, whose members included kings, viceroys and high-ranking officials. The church stands opposite the bell tower of Santa Chiara *(see pp66–7)*. The doorway still retains its original depressed arch structure. On the high altar is a painting by Andrea and Nicola Vaccaro (1670), depicting Santa Marta, to whom the church is dedicated. The *Codice di Santa Marta (Codex of St Martha)*, with its valuable miniatures, came from this church and is now kept in the Archivio di Stato, or state archive *(see p70)*. You can get to the underground cemetery from the room next to the sacristy.

Palazzo Filomarino ❼

Via Benedetto Croce 12. **Map** 3 B5 (9 C5). 🚌 C57, CD, E1, E3, R1, R3, R4, 24. Ⓜ Dante, Cavour-Museo. 🚋 Montesanto. **Library** ◯ 9am–12 noon Tue, Fri.

THIS IS THE first of many noble buildings you will see in the Spaccanapoli and Decumano Maggiore areas. These mansions and palaces are often in a bad state of preservation yet have retained an air of splendour and stateliness, and still bear traces of the lives of the generations of aristocrats who built and lived in them. The original Palazzo Filomarino dates back to the 14th century, but the building was substantially altered in the 16th century. It then underwent restoration in the following century after being damaged during Masaniello's uprising *(see p73)*. The 18th-century doorway is the work of the architect Sanfelice. Philosopher Benedetto Croce, a leading figure in Italian culture and politics in the first half of this century *(see p24)*, lived in this palazzo in the latter part of his life. The Italian Institute of Historical Studies, founded by Croce, takes up the whole of the first floor with its 40,000-volume library. At No. 45 on the same street is the impressive Baroque doorway of Palazzo Carafa della Spina.

The library of philosopher Benedetto Croce on the first floor of Palazzo Filomarino

Santa Chiara ❺

IN 1310 ROBERT OF ANJOU laid the first stone of the convent and church that the Angevin rulers later chose as the site for their tombs. Santa Chiara was where the kingdom's assemblies were held, as well as ceremonies, such as the one celebrating the miracle of San Gennaro's blood *(see p40)*. In the mid-1700s, the church's Gothic lines were obscured by the addition of elaborate Baroque ornamentation. After the church was totally destroyed by fire in 1943, restoration work tried to recover as much as possible of the original; the present interior is simple and austere, typical of a Franciscan church. Near the apse are the fine sculpture groups of the royal Angevin tombs; a beautiful wooden 14th-century crucifix executed by an unknown artist is on the altar. The lovely cloisters are an oasis of calm and a convenient meeting place for Neapolitans.

★ Poor Clares' Choir
Built by Leonardo Di Vito, this choir is one of the best examples of Neapolitan Gothic. It was frescoed by Giotto and his assistants, but only fragments of the original have remained intact.

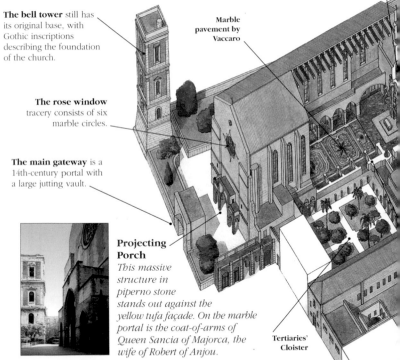

The bell tower still has its original base, with Gothic inscriptions describing the foundation of the church.

Marble pavement by Vaccaro

The rose window tracery consists of six marble circles.

The main gateway is a 14th-century portal with a large jutting vault.

Projecting Porch
This massive structure in piperno stone stands out against the yellow tufa façade. On the marble portal is the coat-of-arms of Queen Sancia of Majorca, the wife of Robert of Anjou.

Tertiaries' Cloister

TIMELINE

Detail of the cloister

1340 Santa Chiara consecrated and declared royal church	**1742** Building of the tiled cloister	**1943** 4 Aug: fire caused by bomb destroys church
		1995 Museo dell'Opera opens to the public

1300	1700	1900
1310 Robert of Anjou lays the first stone	**1343** Giovanni and Pacio Bertini sculpt Tomb of Robert of Anjou	**1769** Church totally rebuilt in Baroque style
		1953 4 Aug: restored church reopens for worship

Royal Tombs
The tombs of Charles of Calabria (shown here) and his wife Mary of Valois are by Tino da Camaino (c.1285–1337). In the centre of the rear wall is the tomb of Robert of Anjou, one of Italy's greatest medieval funerary monuments.

VISITORS' CHECKLIST

Via Benedetto Croce. **Map** 3 B5.
081 552 62 80. C25, CD, E1, E3, R1, R3, R4. M Dante, Cavour-Museo, Montesanto.
Church 8:30am–12:30pm, 4:30– 8pm; Cloister & Museum 9:30am–1pm, 2:30–5:30pm Mon–Sat; 9:30am– 1pm Sun and hols. museum only.

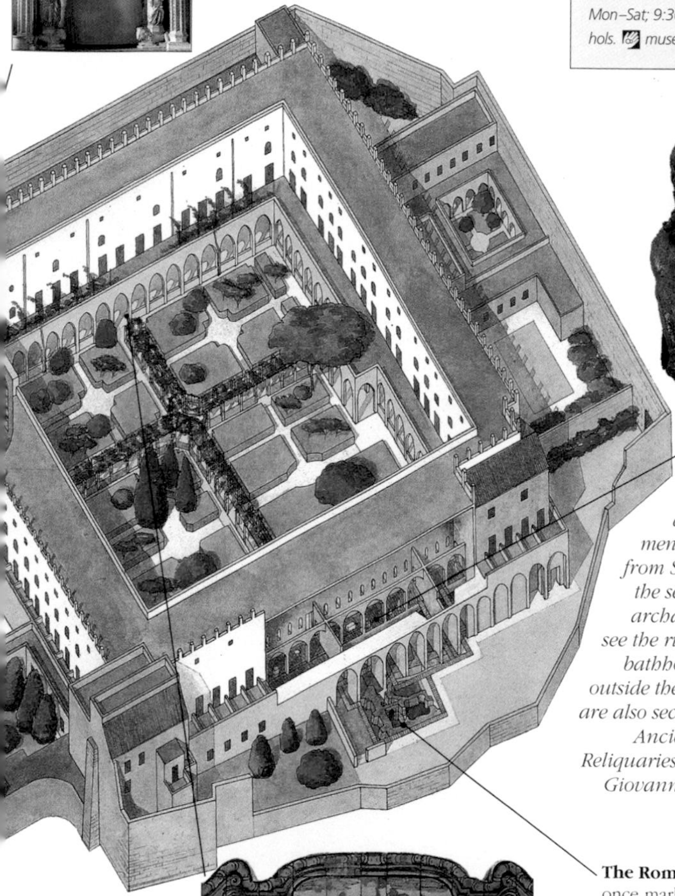

★ Museo dell'Opera
This museum houses objects, decorative ornaments and sculptures from Santa Chiara. In the section devoted to archaeology, you can see the ruins of a Roman bathhouse that extend outside the museum. There are also sections on History, Ancient Marbles and Reliquaries. This last boasts Giovanni da Nola's Ecce Homo *(1519).*

The Roman baths, which once marked the city's western limit, lie between the first two rooms of the Museo dell'Opera and the outer courtyard.

The Tomb of Philip of Bourbon, the idiot son of Charles III who died in 1777, is found in the last chapel on the right. Designed by Ferdinando Fuga, it is one of the few 18th-century works that survived the fire in 1943.

★ Tiled Cloister
The simple arches of the 14th-century cloister frame the garden redesigned by Domenico Antonio Vaccaro in 1742. The 72 octagonal pillars are punctuated by seats at intervals, and every surface is decorated with majolica tiles painted by Donato and Giuseppe Massa.

STAR FEATURES

★ Royal Tombs

★ Poor Clares' Choir

★ Tiled Cloister

★ Museo dell'Opera

Guglia di San Domenico

Piazza San Domenico Maggiore **8**

Map 3 B5 (9 C3). CD, E1, R2. M Dante, Cavour-Museo, Montesanto. Montesanto.

THIS PIAZZA was the result of a rare Renaissance town-planning project in Naples. In the 1500s the area, once crossed by the Greek city walls, was still being used for kitchen gardens. Rebuilding by the Aragonese rulers transformed the zone into a setting appropriate for the church of San Domenico, which had been chosen to house the royal tombs. They also wanted to improve the area around the statue of the Nile, the aristocratic residential district. The top of the piazza is dominated by the apse of San Domenico; next to this is the lovely 14th-century portal of the church of Sant'Arcangelo a Morfisa. Imposing buildings line the other sides of the square. Opposite the church (at No. 17) is the 17th-century Palazzo Sangro di Casa-calenda; to the left (No. 3) is Palazzo Petrucci with its 15th-century portal; to the right (Nos. 12 and 9) are Palazzo Corigliano and Palazzo Sangro di Sansevero. In the centre stands the Guglia di San Domenico, built in gratitude for release from the plague of 1656. The spire was designed by Cosimo Fanzago and finished only in 1737 by Domenico Antonio Vaccaro.

San Domenico Maggiore **9**

Piazza San Domenico Maggiore 8/a. **Map** 3 B5 (9 C3). 081 557 32 04. CD, E1, R2. M Dante, Cavour-Museo, Montesanto. Montesanto. 7:30am–noon (9am–1pm Sun), 4:30–7pm.

IN 1283 CHARLES I OF ANJOU ordered the construction of a new church and monastery for the powerful Dominican order. The Gothic three-nave building was built onto the medieval church of Sant'-Arcangelo a Morfisa, whose 14th-century doorway still remains. The appearance of today's church is the result of radical reconstruction. In 1506 a fire almost totally destroyed the basilica. In 1850–53 Federico Travaglini rebuilt the interior in Neo-Gothic style, removing much of the original spirit of this monument. However, in the second chapel on the right there are 14th-century frescoes ascribed to Pietro Cavallini, a pupil of Giotto. The tombs of 45 rulers and dignitaries at the Aragonese court are arranged along a balcony in the sacristy. The ceiling fresco was painted by Francesco Solimena in 1706.

Cappella Sansevero **10**

Via Francesco de Sanctis 19. **Map** 3 B5 (9 C3). 081 551 84 70. CD, E1, R2. M Dante, Cavour-Museo, Montesanto. Montesanto. 10am–4:40pm Wed–Mon (10am–1pm Sun).

THE LAVISH decoration in the family chapel was planned by Raimondo di Sangro, Prince of Sansevero, in the second half of the 18th century. In each sculpture group a member of the powerful family is represented by an allegorical figure. Antonio Corradini's *Modesty* (to the left of the altar) is set on the tomb of the prince's mother. On the tomb of his father, said to be a dissolute man who later repented his ways, is Francesco Queirolo's *Deception* (to the right of the altar). The focal point of the chapel is the extraordinary *Veiled Christ*, the masterpiece of Neapolitan sculptor Giuseppe Sanmartino (1720–93). Sculpted from a single block of marble, the recumbent figure of Christ lies draped with the thinnest of translucent veils. In the chapel crypt, two "anatomical machines", perhaps creations of the mysterious Raimondo di Sangro himself, are on display. The stories about the famous prince – inventor, alchemist, lover of science and the occult, and Masonic Grand Master – have engendered legends depicting him as a demon or a sorcerer.

Corradini's *Modesty* in the Cappella Sansevero

Fresco by Francesco Solimena in the sacristy of San Domenico Maggiore

Sant'Angelo a Nilo ⑪

Piazzetta Nilo. **Map** 3 B5 (9 C3).
█ 081 551 62 27. ▦ CD, E1, R2.
Ⓜ Dante, Cavour-Museo, Montesanto.
▦ Montesanto. ◻ 8:30am–1pm,
4:45–7pm Mon–Sat; 8:30am–1pm
Sun. █

B UILT IN THE late 1300s by
Cardinal Brancaccio next
to his family palace, this church
was remodelled four centuries
later by Arcangelo Guglielminelli. It houses the earliest
Renaissance work in Naples:
the cardinal's funerary monument, sculpted in Pisa by
Donatello and Michelozzo in
1426–7 and sent to Naples by
ship. On the front of the
sarcophagus, in the bas relief
representing the *Assumption of
the Virgin*, Donatello created
one of the first examples of
his revolutionary "stiacciato"
technique – the relief receding
gradually from the foreground
to give the illusion of depth.
From the church you can visit
the courtyard of Palazzo
Brancaccio where, thanks to
the family's patronage, the
first public library in Naples
was founded in 1690.

Statue of the Nile ⑫

Largo Corpo di Napoli. **Map** 3 B5.
▦ CD, E1, R2. Ⓜ Dante, Cavour-
Museo, Montesanto. ▦ Montesanto.

A N 18TH-CENTURY inscription
informs the reader that
the Alexandrian merchants
who worked in this area of
the Greco-Roman city had
this statue sculpted in honour
of the Egyptian god Nile. The
statue disappeared after the
merchants left Naples; and
although it was found in the
1400s, its head was missing. At
that time the recumbent putti
next to the god, symbols of the
many tributaries of the river
god, were interpreted as
babies at their
mother's
breast, so

The frescoed ceiling in the Monte di Pietà chapel

that the sculpture was called
"the Body of Naples", the
mother-city suckling her
children. The statue has
kept this name despite the
addition of a bearded head
in the 17th century.

Palazzo Carafa Santangelo ⑬

Via San Biagio dei Librai 121. **Map** 3
C5 (10 D3). ▦ CD, E1, R2. Ⓜ Dante,
Cavour-Museo, Montesanto.
▦ Montesanto. ◻ 7am–1pm,
4–7pm Mon–Sat.

T HIS IMPORTANT example of
Neapolitan Renaissance
architecture is known as
Palazzo della Capa di Cavallo
because of the terracotta copy
of a horse's head (now in the
courtyard). This was a gift from
Lorenzo de' Medici to his friend
Diomede Carafa in 1471 to em-
bellish his new palace. The
original sculpture, a Roman
bronze, has been in the Museo
Archeologico (see pp86–9)
since 1809.

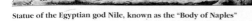

Statue of the Egyptian god Nile, known as the "Body of Naples"

The marble portal, similar to
that of Palazzo Petrucci in
Piazza San Domenico (see p68),
and the façade with its shallow
rustication are examples of
the new Renaissance style. In
late 15th-century Naples this
look merged with the late
Gothic style, as can be seen
in the form of the arches and
pilasters and the inlay in the
wooden doors with the
Carafa family coats of arms.
Opposite the palace is the
animated Baroque façade of
the church of San Nicola a
Nilo, which is also the site of
a second-hand dealer's stall.

Monte di Pietà ⑭

Via San Biagio dei Librai 114. **Map** 3
C5 (10 D3). █ 081 551 70 74. ▦
CD, R2. Ⓜ Dante, Cavour-Museo,
Montesanto. ▦ Montesanto.
◻ 9am–2pm Sat.

T HIS MAJESTIC BUILDING was
built in the late 1500s for
the charitable institute set up
to grant loans to people in
debt to moneylenders. The
Cappella della Pietà at the
end of the courtyard has a
late Renaissance façade with
sculptures by Pietro Bernini
(at the sides of the entrance)
and Michelangelo Naccherino
(on the tympanum). The
church interior was frescoed
by Belisario Corenzio and the
young Battistello in the early
1600s. Today this is the main
office of the Banco di Napoli.

San Giorgio Maggiore **⑮**

Via Duomo 237/a. **Map** 3 C5 (10 E3).
081 28 79 32. C5, C55, E1,
R2. 8am–noon, 5–7:30pm
Mon–Sat; 8:30am–1:30pm Sun.

One of the cloisters in the Archivio di Stato

SAN GIORGIO MAGGIORE, originally an early Christian basilica, is one of the city's oldest churches. It was completely rebuilt in the mid-1600s to a design by Cosimo Fanzago. The only surviving part of the original church is the semi-circular apse with Corinthian columns at the entrance of the 17th-century church, originally built facing a different direction. The right-hand nave of the rebuilt church was demolished in the late 19th century to make room for the extended Via Duomo. The frescoes in the third chapel are by Francesco Solimena. Before visiting the church, pause for a moment at Palazzo Marigliano (at No. 39 Via Duomo). Though run-down, it is one of the most important examples of 16th-century Neapolitan civic architecture.

Museo Civico Filangieri **⑯**

Via Duomo 288. **Map** 3 C5 (10 E3).
081 20 31 75. E1, R2, C5,
C55. for restoration.

THE BUILDING now occupied by the Civic Museum was built in the late 15th century as the Como family residence in the Florentine Renaissance style. It became a monastery in the late 1500s, was demolished during work on Via Duomo (1879) and then faithfully rebuilt 20 m (66 ft) from its original site.

In 1882 Prince Gaetano Filangieri established his fine art collection there and donated it to the city in 1888. Much of the collection was scattered during World War II and was reassembled through private donations. Today it consists of objects from various sources, including weapons, furniture, paintings, medallions, porcelain, coins and costumes. The spiral staircase leads from the ground floor to the Sala Agata (named after the founder's mother), which in turn leads to the prince's library via a suspended passageway.

Archivio di Stato **⑰**

Piazzetta Grande Archivio 5.
Map 3 C5 (10 E3). C5, C55B, CD,
E1, R2. 9am–1pm Mon–Fri;
8am–1pm Sat.

IN 1835 FERDINAND II decided to use the former Benedictine monastery of Santi Severino e Sossio to house the enormous quantity of documents relating to the administration of the kingdom that had accumulated since the Angevin period. The old monastery, built in the 9th century and enlarged in 1494, was remodelled to allow for its new function.

The huge complex has four cloisters and a number of rooms containing numerous works of art. One cloister is known as the *Chiostro del platano*, named after an ancient plane tree (felled in 1959 because it was dying) which, according to tradition, had been planted by St Benedict himself. The mid-16th century frescoes depicting the life of the saint are the work of Antonio Solario, known as Lo Zingaro or "gypsy". The State Archive contains over a million files, registers, documents and parchments, and is one of the most important in Europe.

By the entrance to the former monastery is the 17th-century Fontana della Selleria.

The Sala Agata in the Museo Civico Filangieri, Palazzo Como

Santi Severino e Sossio ⑱

Via Bartolomeo Capasso 22. **Map** 3 C5
(10 D4). 📞 *081 563 81 11.* 🚌 *C5,
C55B, CD, E1, R2.* ⏰ *8–10am
Mon–Sat; 9am–12:30pm Sun.* ✚

Marco Pino, *Adoration of the Magi*

FOUNDED IN THE 9th century together with the adjoining monastery (which became the Royal Archives in 1835), this church was rebuilt from the late 1400s on, and finished in 1571. The façade is the result of restoration effected after the 1731 earthquake. In the interior there are some excellent works of art. Among the paintings are beautiful canvases by the Sienese painter Marco Pino (first, third and sixth chapels on the right). The sculptures include the tomb of Andrea Bonifacio (who died at the age of six), a masterpiece by the Spanish sculptor Bartolomeo Ordoñez, in the vestibule of the sacristy. From here you can go down to the lower church, which is undecorated.

Santi Marcellino e Festo ⑲

Largo San Marcellino 10. **Map** 3 C5
(10 D4). 📞 *081 551.61 77.* 🚌 *C5,
C55B, CD, E1, R2.* ⏰ *8am–8pm
Mon–Fri; 8am–2pm Sat.*

THE TWO ADJACENT monasteries of Santi Marcellino e Pietro and of Santi Festo e Desiderio, date from the 8th century. In the

A NUMBER FOR EVERY OCCASION

At noon every Saturday life stands still for a few minutes in the streets and alleyways of Old Naples in anticipation of an important event – the lottery draw. In the hall of the lottery office (Ufficio Lotto e Lotterie) at No. 17 Via del Grande Archivio, a crowd will be waiting impatiently for the result. Devised in Genoa in the 16th century, the lottery was legalized the following century and grew rapidly in popularity in the 1800s. Neapolitans were immediately hooked. As Matilde Serao wrote in the late 19th century: "Even Neapolitans who can't read know *La Smorfia* by heart

The lottery in a 19th-century print

and immediately apply it to any dream or real-life event whatsoever". *La Smorfia* is a guide to the significance of numbers and is the lottery "bible". It can be found in any Lotto office. There are about 60,000 entries in alphabetical order, and each entry has a corresponding number. The book was first published in the 19th century and is regularly updated in order to offer readers interpretations of even the most modern events and dreams. For example, should you dream of owning a computer, you will find that the number to choose is 45.

mid-15th century they were combined to create a single large complex. The church, built the following century, is adorned with refined 18th-century marble inlay. Unfortunately, it is now in a state of almost total abandon and has been closed to the public for many years. The spacious cloister with piperno stone arches has a pretty garden in

the centre; from the south-facing side there is a splendid panoramic view of the Bay of Naples. By royal decree, the complex became the property of the University of Naples in 1907. The building next to the church is occupied by the Museum of Palaeontology, which has a fine painted majolica floor and over 50,000 artefacts on display.

The airy cloister of the San Marcellino monastery

Courtyard of Gesù Vecchio, part of the University of Naples

Gesù Vecchio ⑳

Via Giovanni Paladino 39. **Map** 3 C5 (10 D4). **Library** 081 551 70 25; **Anthropology Museum** 081 552 78 07; **Zoology Museum** 081 552 70 89; **Mineralogy Museum Library** 081 552 77 37. C5, CD, E1, R2. 9am–6:45pm Mon–Fri. **Museums** 9am–2pm Mon–Fri; 10am–1pm Sat–Sun. museums.

THE HOME OF the University of Naples since 1777, this late 16th-century building was the first Jesuit college in the city. In the late 19th century, thanks to the Urban Renewal plan (see pp24–5), the university expanded with the addition of a large factory building looking out over Corso Umberto I. One part remaining of the original college is the lovely Cortile delle Statue (courtyard of statues), from which you can visit the upstairs rooms occupied by the university library since 1808, and home to 850,000 volumes. In 1801 the large

hall that was once the Jesuits' library was turned over to the Mineralogy Museum, the most important in Italy and one of the most famous in the world. Other sections house the Anthropology Museum and the Zoology Museum, founded in 1811 by Joachim Murat, then ruler of Naples.

Back in Via Paladino, look out for the sumptuous Baroque interior of the college church (at No. 38), begun in 1564, and containing works by Solimena and Fanzago.

Corso Umberto I ㉑

Map 4 D5 & 7 C1 (10 E4). C5, C55B, CD, E1, R2.

THIS WIDE straight street, known to Neapolitans as the Rettifilo, connects the central railway station (Stazione Centrale) with the city centre and Piazza Giovanni Bovio (see p57). It was built in the late 19th century as part of the Urban Renewal plan (see pp24–5). The most important building is the University of Naples, with its impressive Neo-Renaissance façade.

Cappella Pappacoda ㉒

Largo San Giovanni Maggiore. **Map** 7 B1 (9 C4). 081 552 69 48 (Istituto Universitario Orientale). C5, CD, C55B, E1, R2. apply at the Istituto or during temporary exhibitions.

IN THE EARLY 15th century Artusio Pappacoda, Grand Seneschal and councillor in the Angevin court, founded

this small church. The original late Gothic doorway, like marble embroidery on the austere tufa façade, is the work of Antonio Baboccio (1351–1435), a sculptor, architect and goldsmith who also sculpted the main portal of the cathedral (see pp82–3). The campanile is particularly interesting because of the colour contrast created by the different materials – marble, tufa and piperno. The church is now deconsecrated and is used as the Great Hall by the nearby Istituto Universitario Orientale (Oriental Institute).

Portal of Cappella Pappacoda

Santissima Annunziata ㉓

Via dell'Annunziata 35. **Map** 4 D4 (10 F3). 081 20 74 55. C5, C55B, CD, E1, R2 8–12am, 5–7pm Mon–Sat; 8am–1pm Sun.

THE SANTA CASA dell'-Annunziata was a charitable institution that existed as long ago as the

The façade of the University in Corso Umberto I after expansion of the site

Painting of the *Madonna Bruna* in Santa Maria del Carmine

early 1300s to offer help to abandoned children. The church was destroyed by fire in 1757 and rebuilt by Luigi and Carlo Vanvitelli, who designed the cupola and light-filled, one-nave interior with 44 Corinthian columns and three chapels on each side. Among the parts untouched by the fire is the sacristy, with frescoes by Corenzio (1605) and 16th-century inlaid wooden cupboards. To the left of the church, an impressive marble doorway leads to the former foundling hospital, now used as a hospital.

Santa Maria del Carmine ㉔

Piazza del Carmine. **Map** 4 E5.
📞 081 20 11 96. 🚃 1, 2.
🚋 C82. ⏰ 6:30am–12:30pm,
5–7:30pm Mon–Sat;
6:30am–1:30pm Sun. ✝

NEAPOLITANS are devoted to this church because of its many works of art but in particular because of the *Madonna Bruna*, a 14th-century painting kept behind the altar. This famous effigy, the object of deeply felt veneration, is celebrated annually on 16 July at the feast of the Madonna del Carmine (*see p41*), during which the miracle of the Madonna is re-enacted.

Except for the cross dome in the presbytery, little remains of the original Angevin construction. Instead the church displays typical 18th-century architectural forms

PIAZZA MERCATO

Thanks to their position near the harbour, the churches of Sant'Eligio and Santa Maria del Carmine and the area around them became the focal point of commercial life in late 13th-century Angevin Naples. The lively market quarter around Piazza Mercato in the heart of Naples was also the setting for significant events in the city's history. In 1268, Corradino, the last Hohenstaufen king of Naples, was beheaded at the tender age of 16 in front of the Carmine church and the new Angevin rulers

View of Piazza Mercato, with Santa Maria del Carmine

decreed that in future all executions were to be carried out in the square. In 1647 the uprising against the Spanish headed by Tommaso Aniello d'Amalfi, known as Masaniello (*see pp20–21*), began here. Ten years on, the square was used for the graves of those who had died during the plague epidemic. But the most dramatic events occurred in 1799, when the short-lived, glorious Parthenopean Republic was crushed and all its leaders were executed in Piazza Mercato.

both inside and out. The interior was decorated by Tagliacozzi Canale; the ceiling, destroyed in World War II, has been completely rebuilt in keeping with the original. To the left of the nave is the tomb of Corradino, Duke of Swabia, who was beheaded in 1268 in Piazza Mercato opposite the church (*see above*). The medieval wooden crucifix placed in a tabernacle under the triumphal arch is also the object of devout worship. There are frescoes and canvases by Solimena in the wings of the transept. The 75-m (246-ft) campanile, completed by Fra Nuvolo in 1631, is the tallest in Naples.

Sant'Eligio Maggiore ㉕

Largo Sant'Eligio. **Map** 4 D5 (10 F4).
📞 081 553 84 29. 🚃 1, 2. 🚋 C82.
⏰ 8am–1pm Mon–Wed; 8am–1pm,
5–6:30pm Thu–Sun. ✝

THE HISTORY of Sant'Eligio has parallels with Santa Chiara (*see pp66–7*). This church, the first to be founded by the Angevin dynasty in Naples, was destroyed in World War II and in the process of reconstruction none of the later Baroque additions were restored. Go through the side doorway with the pointed arch to enter the austere Gothic three-nave interior with its impressive raised transept. The left-hand nave leads to a cross-vaulted area decorated with 14th-century frescoes by artists of the Giotto school.

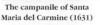

The campanile of Santa Maria del Carmine (1631)

DECUMANO MAGGIORE

I N THE HEART of Greco-Roman Naples, part of the ancient grid plan with three parallel east-west roads (Roman *decumani*), intersected at right angles by the north-south *cardines*, is present-day Via dei Tribunali. It was once called Decumano Maggiore (or Massimo) because it was so vital a part of the city structure. In the late 13th and early 14th centuries the area was significant for its

One of the lions at the Duomo entrance

Gothic religious architecture. Today, the churches of San Lorenzo, San Pietro a Maiella and especially the Duomo (cathedral), reveal this past.

The Duomo is a stupendous blend of art and architectural styles from the 4th to 19th centuries. Outside the city walls, past 18th-century Piazza Dante, lies the Museo Archeologico Nazionale, home of one of the world's richest classical archaeological collections.

SIGHTS AT A GLANCE

Historic Buildings
Accademia di Belle Arti **20**
Castel Capuano
  and Porta Capuana **14**
Palazzo Spinelli di Laurino **5**
Pio Monte della Misericordia **13**

Churches
Cappella Pontano **3**
Duomo pp82–3 **11**
Gerolamini **10**
Santa Caterina a Formiello **15**
San Gregorio Armeno **9**
San Lorenzo Maggiore **8**
Santa Maria delle Anime
  del Purgatorio ad Arco **6**
Santa Maria di
  Donnaregina Nuova **17**
Santa Maria di
  Donnaregina Vecchia **16**
Santa Maria Maggiore
  della Pietrasanta **4**
San Paolo Maggiore **7**
San Pietro a Maiella **2**

Historic Streets and Squares
Piazza Bellini **1**
Piazza Dante **21**
Via Anticaglia **18**

Spires
Guglia di San Gennaro **12**

Museums
*Museo Archeologico
  Nazionale pp86–9* **19**

GETTING THERE
Via dei Tribunali allows limited traffic and no buses cross it. The red bus lines R1 (from Vomero), R2 (from the Centrale railway station), R3 (from the Mergellina railway station) and R4 (from Capodimonte) stop in Via Toledo, Via Diaz and Via Monteoliveto. The R2 bus runs along Corso Umberto I, which crosses Via Duomo at Piazza Nicola Amore. R1 passes by the Museo Archeologico Nazionale. You can take the Metro (Montesanto station) and, from Vomero, the Montesanto funicular. The Metro goes to the Museo Nazionale (Cavour-Museo station) and Piazza Dante.

KEY

Street-by-Street map
See pp76–7

P Parking

M Metro station

0 metres   500
0 yards   500

◁ **Interior of the Duomo, with its Mannerist paintings set into the carved, gilded wooden ceiling**

Street-by-Street: Via dei Tribunali

VIA DEI TRIBUNALI was named after Castel Capuano, visible in the distance at the end of this long avenue, when it became the home of the civil courts *(tribunali)* in the 1500s. One of the streets crossing the Decumano Maggiore is Via San Gregorio Armeno, among the loveliest streets in Old Naples, where art and handicrafts flourish. The craftsmen in San Gregorio Armeno still carve shepherds and other figures for the traditional Neapolitan nativity scenes *(see p39)*, just as they did four centuries ago – to the delight of visitors and Neapolitans alike.

San Paolo Maggiore
The sacristy was frescoed by Solimena in 1689–90 **7**

Piazza Bellini
This is one of the liveliest spots in the centre **1**

Sant'Antonio a Port'Alba Monastery

Croce di Lucca

Santa Maria delle Anime del Purgatorio ad Arco
Funerary motifs adorn the area in front of the church and its interior **6**

Palazzo Firrao

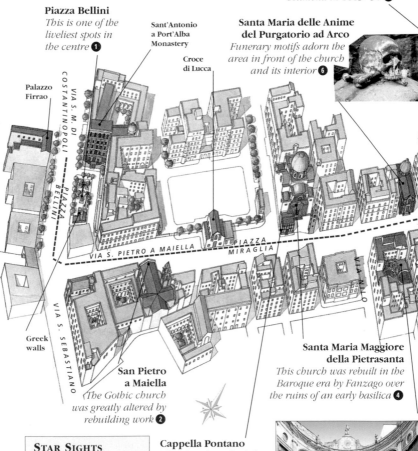

VIA S. M. DI COSTANTINOPOLI

PIAZZA BELLINI

VIA S. PIETRO A MAIELLA

PIAZZA MIRAGLIA

VIA S. SEBASTIANO

Greek walls

San Pietro a Maiella
The Gothic church was greatly altered by rebuilding work **2**

Santa Maria Maggiore della Pietrasanta
This church was rebuilt in the Baroque era by Fanzago over the ruins of an early basilica **4**

STAR SIGHTS

★ San Lorenzo Maggiore

★ San Gregorio Armeno

★ Duomo

Cappella Pontano
This chapel was built for the humanist Pontano **3**

Palazzo Spinelli
Created in the 1700s by merging two 16th-century palaces, Palazzo Spinelli has an original oval courtyard with stuccoes **5**

Guglia di San Gennaro
The spire was erected to thank the saint for saving the city from Vesuvius in 1631 **12**

Gerolamini
The façade of the monastery church was designed by Ferdinando Fuga **10**

★ Duomo
The cathedral was built over the ruins of two early Christian basilicas **11**

Statue of San Gaetano

VICO CINQUESANTI

VIA DUOMO

VIA DEI TRIBUNALI

VIA S. GREGORIO ARMENO

VIA DUOMO

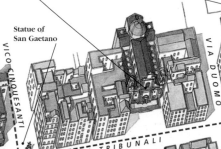

Santa Maria della Colonna

Pio Monte della Misericordia
A portico was built onto the façade to shelter the needy **13**

★ San Lorenzo Maggiore
San Lorenzo contains many layers of history: an 18th-century façade, Gothic interior and ancient ruins under the cloister **8**

★ San Gregorio Armeno
The lavish decoration of this monastery is immediately apparent in the vestibule **9**

KEY

- - - - - Suggested route

| 0 metres | 100 |
| 0 yards | 100 |

Piazza Bellini ❶

Map 3 B5. 🚌 C5, C57, CD, E1, R3, R4. Ⓜ *Dante, Cavour-Museo, Montesanto.* 🚇 *Montesanto.*

THIS SQUARE, at the southern end of Via Santa Maria di Costantinopoli, is one of the most interesting places in Old Naples. The area now occupied by the piazza and street lay outside the city proper until the mid-16th century, when the viceroy Pedro de Toledo extended the city walls. The remains of part of the ancient Greek walls of Neapolis were brought to light in the piazza after excavations carried out in 1954. The walls are visible in the middle of the square, at the foot of the monument to the composer Vincenzo Bellini. Overlooking the square is the monastery of Sant'Antonio a Port'Alba, which incorporates the 15th-century Palazzo Conca. On the opposite side is Palazzo Firrao (No. 99 Via Santa Maria di Costantinopoli), an important example of 17th-century Neapolitan civic architecture. The façade is adorned with busts of the Spanish royal family.

San Pietro a Maiella ❷

Via San Pietro a Maiella 4. **Map** 3 B5. 📞 081 45 90 08. 🚌 C5, C57, CD, E1, R3, R4. Ⓜ 🚇 *Montesanto.* 🕐 7:30am–noon, 5:30–7:30pm Mon–Sat; 8:30am–1pm Sun. 🚻

THE FOUNDER OF this church, the nobleman Pipino da Barletta, dedicated it to Pietro da Morrone, the hermit friar from Maiella who became Pope Celestine V in 1294. The original Gothic architecture, modified by the numerous additions over the centuries, was restored between 1888 and 1927. The restoration uncovered some 14th-century frescoes in two of the chapels. The removal of the Baroque decoration also revealed splendid gilded

An outdoor café in Piazza Bellini

wooden ceilings in the nave and transept with paintings by Mattia Preti (1656–61), regarded as among the supreme examples of 17th-century Neapolitan painting.

Since 1826 the monastery (at No. 35) annexed to the church has been occupied by one of Italy's major music conservatoires. The courtyard is well worth visiting.

Cappella Pontano ❸

Via Tribunali (no street number, opposite No. 376). **Map** 3 B4. 🚌 C5, C55, CD, E1, R3. Ⓜ *Dante, Cavour-Museo, Montesanto.* 🚇 *Montesanto.* 🕐 9am–2pm Mon–Sat.

THE FAMOUS HUMANIST Giovanni Pontano, secretary to King Ferdinand of Aragon, commissioned this small, elegant chapel in 1492. Based on a design for a pagan temple, the harmonious proportions make it one of the most significant works produced in Renaissance Naples. The chapel contains a frescoed triptych by Francesco Cicino da Caiazzo – restored in 1792 – and a 15th-century pavement of coloured tiles, which is in a good state of preservation. The numerous Latin epigraphs were written by Giovanni Pontano himself.

Bust of Giovanni Pontano

Santa Maria Maggiore della Pietrasanta ❹

Via Tribunali (opposite No. 376). **Map** 3 B5. 🚌 C5, CD, E1, R3. Ⓜ 🚇 *Montesanto.* 🕐 9am–2pm Mon–Sat.

The interior of Santa Maria Maggiore della Pietrasanta

THE CHURCH WAS named after a holy stone *(pietrasanta)* with an inscribed cross, which was kept here until recently and was popular with worshippers. This majestic, centrally planned church was built by Cosimo Fanzago over the ruins of an early Christian basilica. Traces of the original church have been discovered in the crypt. The campanile *(see p18)* also belonged to the basilica; dating from the 10th–11th centuries, it is the sole example of early medieval architecture in Naples. Many fragments of even older buildings, from the Roman age on, were inserted into the lower part of the campanile. In the Middle Ages the road was lower and passed under the bell tower arch.

Palazzo Spinelli di Laurino ❺

Via Tribunali 362. **Map** 3 B5. ▦ C5, CD, E1, R2, R3. Ⓜ Dante, Cavour-Museo, Montesanto. 🚋 Montesanto. ◯ 8am–7pm Mon–Sat.

I N THE 18TH CENTURY, the architect Ferdinando Sanfelice carried out radical changes to this 16th-century palazzo. He also created the oval courtyard and the building beyond, where the chatter from the crowded Via dei Tribunali could be clearly heard by the dukes of Laurino. The double-flight monumental staircase is another of Sanfelice's designs. Similar examples can be seen in the Palazzo Serra di Cassano (see p58), Palazzo dello Spagnolo and Palazzo Sanfelice (see p94).

Santa Maria delle Anime del Purgatorio ad Arco ❻

Map 3 B4. Via Tribunali 39. ▦ C5, CD, E1, R2, R3. Ⓜ Dante, Cavour-Museo, Montesanto. **Church** ◯ 9am–2pm Mon–Sat. **Cemetery** ◯ 11:30am–12:30pm Mon–Sat. 🚻

T HIS CHURCH STILL belongs to the confraternity of the same name founded in 1604 to collect alms to pay for the masses for the souls of the dead. Evidence of the importance attached to worship of the dead in 17th-century Naples is shown by the many skulls, bones and other funerary motifs on the small stone columns in front of the façade, on the façade itself, and in the interior. The church has a single nave and lavish Baroque decoration. In the apse area there is a disturbing relief with a winged skull by Cosimo Fanzago, who also designed the church. Steps lead to the underground cemetery, which is still used for the worship of

Interior of the church of Purgatorio ad Arco

souls in Purgatory, a ritual not altogether appreciated by the Christian church.

San Paolo Maggiore ❼

Piazza San Gaetano. **Map** 3 C4. 📞 081 45 40 48. ▦ C5, CD, E1, R2, R3. Ⓜ Dante, Cavour-Museo, Montesanto. 🚋 Montesanto. ◯ 9am–1:20pm Mon–Sat; 9am–2pm Sun.

I N GRECO-ROMAN NAPLES, present-day Piazza San Gaetano was the site of the Greek Agora and later, of the Roman Forum. The Romans built a Temple of the Dioscuri here, which was converted into a Christian basilica in the 8th century. This ancient church was then remodelled from 1583 to 1603 by Francesco Grimaldi. The new

church, with a three-nave Latin cross plan, also incorporated the pronaos of the pagan temple; but only two Corinthian columns of the latter survived the 1688 earthquake.

In the richly decorated interior there are fine frescoes by Massimo Stanzione on the vault over the central nave. Sadly, they were damaged by water seepage and bombardments during World War II. The Cappella Firrao, on the left side of the apse, has many 17th-century tombs, sculptures and frescoes. The marvellous paintings in the sacristy are by Francesco Solimena (1689–90). A stairway leads down to the crypt (also accessible from outside the church).

Façade of San Paolo Maggiore

UNDERNEATH THE CITY

Underneath Naples there is another world to be explored, just as fascinating as the city above. Since its early days the city has been built out of material quarried from the ground – the local yellow tufa is excellent for building. Over the years, caves and tunnels were left in this way, and became catacombs, aqueducts, passageways, and escape and shelter areas during

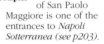

Entrance to underground Naples

World War II bombing raids. The caves were extended to their current size during Spanish rule (see pp20–21), when it was forbidden to import raw material for building houses and palazzi. Today you can descend into the bowels of Naples: on the left-hand side of San Paolo Maggiore is one of the entrances to Napoli Sotterranea (see p203).

San Lorenzo Maggiore ❽

Via dei Tribunali 316. **Map** 3 C4 (10 D3). *081 454 948. E1. Dante, Cavour-Museo, Montesanto. Montesanto.* **Church** *8:30am–noon, 5–7pm.* **Excavations** *10am–1:30pm Mon–Sat. Aug.*

THE CONSTRUCTION of one of Naples's oldest and richest monumental complexes was begun in 1265, for Charles I of Anjou, on the site of a 6th-century church *(see p33)*. The façade was totally rebuilt by Sanfelice in 1742, but the large 14th-century portal and original wooden doors are intact. The single-nave Gothic interior has an apse, designed by French architects, with nine chapels placed around the ambulatory. Here is the tomb of Catherine of Austria, a fine sculpture by Tino da Camaino (c.1323) and, in the sixth chapel from the right, frescoes by a Neapolitan pupil of Giotto. It was in this church that the writer Boccaccio first saw the girl he celebrated in his writings as Fiammetta.

To the right of San Lorenzo is the monastery, where you can visit the cloister, the chapterhouse and the refectory which, from 1442 on, was the assembly hall of the royal Parliament. The cloister affords access to the excavation site that has revealed important remains of the Greco-Roman city. These include a *macellum* (market) and a vast area below this where you can see the building that housed the *aerarium* (public treasury) and a street of workshops.

The Baroque interior of the church of San Gregorio Armeno

San Gregorio Armeno ❾

Convent: Piazzetta San Gregorio Armeno 1; **Church**: Via San Gregorio Armeno 44. **Map** 3 C5 (10 D3). *081 552 01 86. E1. Dante, Cavour-Museo, Montesanto. Montesanto.* **Convent and Church** *9:30–12 noon daily.*

THIS IS ONE OF the most important religious sites in Naples. San Gregorio was founded in the 8th century by a group of nuns who had fled Byzantium with the relics of St Gregory to escape religious persecution. The monastery was rebuilt in the 1500s and enlarged the following century. The lovely campanile was erected in 1716 on a footbridge that connected two parts of the complex. The decoration of the sumptuous Baroque interior – a "room of Paradise on Earth", as Carlo Celano wrote in his guide to Naples – was designed in the mid-18th century by Niccolò Tagliacozzi Canale. Notable works include the late 16th-century wooden ceiling, the two organs and, above the entrance, Luca Giordano's frescoes of *The Embarkation, Journey and Arrival of the Armenian Nuns with the Relics of St Gregory* (1671–84).

There is a lovely fountain in the cloister with a statue of Christ and the Samaritan, sculpted in 1733 *(see p21)*. From here you can visit the Cappella della Madonna dell'Idria, decorated by Paolo De Matteis in 1712.

Cloister of San Lorenzo Maggiore

Gerolamini ❿

Church: Piazza Gerolamini 107; **Cloisters, Library & Gallery**: Via Duomo 142; **Cappella dell'Assunta**: Via Duomo 144. **Map** 3 C4 (10 D2). **Library** *081 29 44 44.* **Oratorio dell'Assunta** *081 44 91 39. CD, E3, R3. Dante, Cavour-Museo, Montesanto. Montesanto.* **Church, Cloisters & Gallery** *9:30am–1pm Mon–Sat.* **Library** *10:30am daily except Sat (11:15am).*

THE MONASTERY of the Gerolamini was founded in the late 16th century by the Oratorio di San Filippo Neri congregation, also called "dei Gerolamini" because they came from San Girolamo alla

The cloister in the Gerolamini

Carità in Rome. The church was built in Tuscan Renaissance style; the interior was rebuilt in the early 1600s, and the façade was modified by Ferdinando Fuga in 1780. Luca Giordano, Pietro da Cortona and Guido Reni decorated the Baroque interior.

Alongside the church there are two cloisters. The first, designed by Giovanni Dosio, shares features with the cloister he created at the Certosa di San Martino *(see pp108–11)*. There are fine paintings in the Quadreria (art gallery). The 60,000-volume library has 18th-century furnishings and decoration.

Duomo ⓫

See pp82–3.

Guglia di San Gennaro ⓬

Piazza Riario Sforza. **Map** 3 C4 (10 D2). 🚌 C5, C57, CD, E1, R2. Ⓜ *Dante, Cavour-Museo.*

THIS SCULPTED marble spire is dedicated to San Gennaro, the patron saint of Naples, for having protected the city during the 1631 eruption of Vesuvius. The *guglia*, the oldest of the three spires in Naples, was designed by Cosimo Fanzago in 1636, the same artist who later worked on the Guglia di San Domenico *(see p68).* The bronze statue at the top of the spire was sculpted by

Guglia di San Gennaro

Tommaso Montani. Behind the spire in the small square you can glimpse the stairway of the side entrance to the Duomo *(see pp82–3)* and, higher up, the dome of the Cappella del Tesoro di San Gennaro.

Pio Monte della Misericordia ⓭

Via Tribunali 253. **Map** 3 C4. 📞 *081 44 69 73.* 🚌 *C5, C57, CD, E1.* Ⓜ *Cavour-Museo.* **Church** 🕘 *9:30am–1:30pm Mon–Sat.* **Art gallery** 🕘 *9am–1pm Thu–Sat.* 📷 *by appt.*

***The Seven Acts of Mercy,* a masterpiece by Caravaggio**

PIO MONTE is one of the most important charitable institutions in Naples. It was founded in 1601 to aid the poor and ill and to free the Christian slaves in the Ottoman Empire. The entire complex was designed by Francesco Antonio Picchiatti in the second half of the 17th century. After passing through the five-arch loggia (where pilgrims could shelter) decorated with sculptures by Andrea Falcone (1666–71), you enter the church. The eye is immediately drawn to the extraordinary altarpiece, *The Seven Acts of Mercy,* a masterpiece by Caravaggio (1571–1610), one of Italy's greatest artists. The art gallery on the first floor of the building houses the

fine Pio Monte collection. Pio Monte is still active as a charitable institution today.

Castel Capuano and Porta Capuana ⓮

Piazza Enrico De Nicola and Via Concezio Muzy. **Map** 4 D4 (10 F2). 📞 *081 223 72 44.* 🚌 *C5, C57, CD, E1, R2.* Ⓜ *Cavour-Museo.* **Cappella Sommaria** 🕘 *by appt.*

A PALACE AND FORTRESS built by the Normans in 1165 to defend the nearby city gateway, Castel Capuano remained a royal residence for the Angevin and Aragonese rulers even after the construction of Castel Nuovo *(see pp54–5)*. In 1540 Don Pedro de Toledo turned the castle into law courts, a function it maintains to this day. On the first floor is the huge frescoed Court of Appeal, which leads to the splendid Renaissance Cappella della Sommaria, decorated by the Spanish painter Pietro Roviale.

A short distance away from the courts stands the gateway of Porta Capuana. Although much older in origin, its present appearance is the result of late 15th-century reconstruction by Giuliano da Maiano. The two towers, called Honour and Virtue, enclose the marble arch, repeating the pattern established in the Arco di Trionfo in Castel Nuovo.

The marble arch of Porta Capuana, rebuilt in the 1400s

Duomo ⓫

The bust of San Gennaro

THIS GREAT CATHEDRAL was built for Charles I of Anjou in the late 1200s–early 1300s. The church incorporated older Christian buildings and has been altered substantially over the centuries. The left-hand nave leads to the early medieval basilica of Santa Restituta, radically changed in the 17th century, and the San Giovanni in Fonte baptistry. The Cappella Minutolo has retained its original Gothic structure and decoration; the mosaic pavement and 13th-century frescoes are by Montano d'Arezzo. The Crypt of the Succorpo was built under the apse in the 1500s to house the relics of San Gennaro, until then in the Montevergine sanctuary. In the early 1600s the Cappella del Tesoro di San Gennaro was erected after the ending of the 1527 plague epidemic.

★ Baptistry
This is the oldest baptistry in the Western world, built around AD 550. The mosaics date from the same period.

★ Santa Restituta
The structure of the early Christian basilica was changed in the Angevin period (when it became a side chapel in the new cathedral) and its decoration was replaced in the late 1600s. In the last chapel on the left is the beautiful mosaic Madonna and Saints Gennaro and Restituta, executed by Lello da Orvieto in 1322.

The archaeological area, which can be entered from the left-hand nave, reveals layers of buildings from three successive periods: Greek, Roman and early Middle Ages.

The three portals were the work of Antonio Baboccio da Piperno (1407); the middle one still bears two 14th-century lions and Tino da Camaino's *Virgin and Child* in the lunette.

TIMELINE

400	1300	1500	1600	1900
c.450 The Santa Restituta and Santa Stefania basilicas built	**1300** Duomo built on the site of the two basilicas	**1497** Work begins on crypt to house relics of San Gennaro	**1876** The façade is rebuilt in Neo-Gothic style	**1969** Digs begin in archaeological area
	c.550 The San Giovanni in Fonte baptistry added to Santa Restituta	**1349** An earthquake destroys the façade of the Duomo	**1608–37** Cappella del Tesoro di San Gennaro erected	**1621** Old ceiling replaced by present-day one in gilded wood

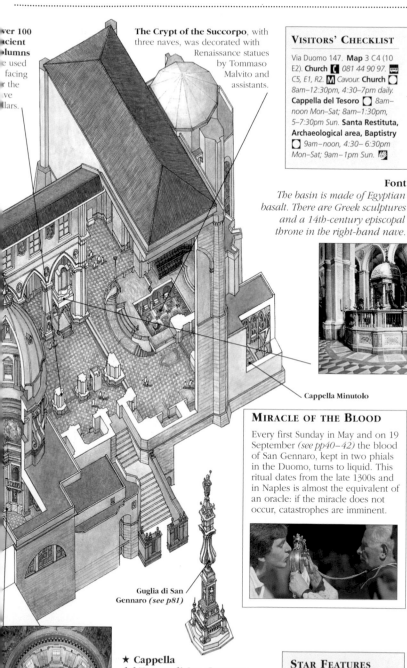

ver 100
cient
lumns
e used
facing
r the
ve
lars.

The Crypt of the Succorpo, with three naves, was decorated with Renaissance statues by Tommaso Malvito and assistants.

VISITORS' CHECKLIST

Via Duomo 147. **Map** 3 C4 (10 E2). **Church** 📞 081 44 90 97. 🚌 C5, E1, R2. Ⓜ Cavour. **Church** ⏰ 8am–12:30pm, 4:30–7pm daily. **Cappella del Tesoro** ⏰ 8am–noon Mon–Sat; 8am–1:30pm, 5–7:30pm Sun. **Santa Restituta, Archaeological area, Baptistry** ⏰ 9am–noon, 4:30– 6:30pm Mon–Sat; 9am–1pm Sun. 📷

Font
The basin is made of Egyptian basalt. There are Greek sculptures and a 14th-century episcopal throne in the right-hand nave.

Cappella Minutolo

MIRACLE OF THE BLOOD

Every first Sunday in May and on 19 September *(see pp40–42)* the blood of San Gennaro, kept in two phials in the Duomo, turns to liquid. This ritual dates from the late 1300s and in Naples is almost the equivalent of an oracle: if the miracle does not occur, catastrophes are imminent.

Guglia di San Gennaro *(see p81)*

★ Cappella del Tesoro di San Gennaro
The dome with its depiction of Paradise was frescoed by Lanfranco in 1641–3. The most precious object in the chapel is the reliquary bust of San Gennaro, a masterpiece of Gothic craftsmanship in gold.

STAR FEATURES

★ Cappella del Tesoro di San Gennaro

★ Baptistry

★ Santa Restituta

The monumental façade of Santa Maria di Donnaregina Nuova

Santa Caterina a Formiello ⓯

Piazza Enrico De Nicola. **Map** 4 D4 (10 F1). **[** 081 44 42 97. **▦** C5, E1, R2. **M** Cavour-Museo. **◯** 9am–5pm Mon–Sat. **◐** Sun.

THE DOME OF Santa Caterina a Formiello dominates the surrounding area. The church was called *formiello* because it was built next to *formali*, the ancient city aqueducts. The 16th-century building has delightful Baroque decoration in the interior. Luigi Garzi and Guglielmo Borremans executed the frescoes (1695–1709). The marble tombs of the Spinelli family are in the apse area.

Santa Maria di Donnaregina Vecchia ⓰

Vico Donnaregina 25. **Map** 3 C4 (10 D1). **[** 081 29 91 01. **▦** C5, E1, R2. **M** Cavour-Museo. **◯** 9am–noon Sat.

THE MONASTERY and the church of Santa Maria di Donnaregina Vecchia were founded in the 8th century and then totally rebuilt in 1293, at the request of Marie of Hungary, wife of Charles II of Anjou. The interior of the church, with one nave that

ends in a pentagonal apse, was built on two levels to create a separate area for nuns. The lower part boasts an elegant marble tomb of the queen who founded the complex, sculpted by Tino da Camaino in 1325–6. In the upper section – reached via a stairway to the right of the entrance – is the

Detail of the 13th-century fresco cycle in Donnaregina Vecchia

largest 14th-century cycle of frescoes in Naples, which was painted by Roman artists and local pupils of Giotto from 1332 to 1335 *(see p19)*.

Santa Maria di Donnaregina Nuova ⓱

Largo Donnaregina 7. **Map** 3 C4 (10 D1). **[** 081 29 91 01. **▦** C5, E1, R2. **M** Cavour-Museo. **◐** for restoration.

IN THE EARLY 1600s the Poor Clares in the Santa Maria Donnaregina convent decided to build a new church, incorporating part of the old church in the new construction. The two churches, connected by the apse areas, were separated during restoration work in 1928–34. The original 14th-century features were rediscovered and the plan of the 17th-century construction was modified. The single-nave interior is richly decorated in multi-coloured marble with floral motifs, and there are fine frescoes by Francesco Solimena (1657–1747) in the nuns' choir.

Via Anticaglia ⓲

Map 3 C4 (10 D2). **[** 081 779 41 11. **▦** C5, E1, R2. **M** Cavour-Museo.

THE THIRD, northernmost *decumanus* (east–west major road) in Greco-Roman Naples today has four official sections (Via Sapienza, Via Pisanelli, Via Anticaglia and

The elegant interior of the pharmacy in the Ospedale degli Incurabili

Foro Carolino, present-day Piazza Dante, the 18th-century palace and hemicycle designed by Luigi Vanvitelli

Via Santi Apostoli), as does Spaccanapoli, the lower *decumanus* (see p61).

The name "Anticaglia", meaning ruins, derives from the remains of the brick walls of a Roman building in this stretch of the street. These walls connected the ancient theatre, on the left as you go towards Via Santa Maria di Costantinopoli, and the bath-house on the opposite side of the street. The theatre, where Emperor Nero is known to have acted, had a seating capacity of about 8,000. Nearby was the *odeion*, or ancient roofed theatre, used for concerts and poetry readings.

On the corner of Via Duomo and the third *decumanus*, there is a fine marble and piperno double stairway – from here you can visit the atrium of the church of San Giuseppe dei Ruffi, which was added in the early 18th century. Once past the Roman ruins, a right-hand turn at Via Armanni takes you to the Ospedale degli Incurabili. Inside is the unusual *Farmacia* (pharmacy) with about 400 brightly coloured majolica vases on shelves of inlaid wood – a positive art gallery of Neapolitan ceramics. However, visits are allowed only during the month of May for the "Maggio dei Monumenti" *(see p40)*.

Museo Archeologico Nazionale ⓲

See pp86–9.

Accademia di Belle Arti ⓴

Via Vincenzo Bellini 36. **Map** 3 B4 (9 B2).
☎ 081 44 18 87. ⬚ C5, C57, R1, R4, 24, 149. Ⓜ Dante, Cavour-Museo, Montesanto. ◯ 9am–1pm Mon–Sat.

Aᴿᴄʜɪᴛᴇᴄᴛ Enrico Alvino transformed the 18th-century convent of San Giovanni delle Monache into the Academy of Fine Arts in the 1840s. The Neo-Renaissance style reflects the prevailing fashion of the time. A broad staircase with plaster casts of ancient sculptures leads to the first floor, which still bears traces of the convent cloister. There is an important collection of modern painting, especially works by 19th-century Neapolitan and southern Italian artists.

The Accademia di Belle Arti staircase

Piazza Dante ㉑

Map 3 A5 (9 B3). ⬚ C5, C57, E1, R1, R4, 24, 149. Ⓜ Ⓜ Dante.

Tʜᴇ ɴᴀᴍᴇs given to this square over the centuries sum up its history. Until the 1700s it lay outside the city walls and was used as a marketplace, hence the name Largo del Mercatello. In the

18th-century print of Largo del Mercatello

second half of the 18th century it took on its present form and was called Foro Carolino, after King Charles III, who commissioned the new layout. The semicircular façade with its colossal columns was designed by Luigi Vanvitelli as a setting for the king's statue, which was intended for the central niche but was never sculpted. The 26 figures on the cornice are allegories of the sovereign's qualities. Following the unification of Italy, a statue of Dante was placed in the middle of the square, hence its present name. To the left of the piazza is Port'Alba, the gateway built in 1625 to connect the city with outlying districts.

Museo Archeologico Nazionale ⑲

THIS BUILDING, housing one of the world's most important archaeological museums, started life in the late 1500s as the home of the royal cavalry and was rebuilt in the early 17th century as the seat of Naples university. In 1777, when Ferdinand IV transferred the university to the former monastery of Gesù Vecchio *(see p72)*, the building was again adapted to house the Real Museo Borbonico and library. In 1860 it became public property. Restoration and reorganization of exhibits still continue in the museum.

Sacrifice of Iphigenia
In this Pompeiian fresco, Iphigenia, daughter of Agamemnon, is about to be sacrificed to Artemis, who saves her by taking a deer instead.

Bust of "Seneca"
Found in the Villa dei Papiri (see p140) in Herculaneum, this 1st-century BC bronze head was long thought to represent the philosopher Seneca the Elder. Today, however, its identity is less certain.

★ The Battle of Alexander
The splendid mosaic from the House of the Faun in Pompeii (see p146) depicts Alexander the Great's victory over Persian emperor Darius III (333 BC).

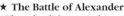

The Secret Cabinet
The erotic works from Pompeii and Herculaneum housed here caused embarrassment at the time of the Bourbons. Today, however, they are available for public viewing.

KEY TO FLOORPLAN

- ☐ Basement
- ☐ Ground floor
- ☐ Mezzanine
- ☐ First floor
- ☐ Second floor
- ☐ Non-exhibition space

Blue Vase
This wine vessel found in a Pompeii tomb was made with the so-called glass-cameo technique: a layer of opaque white paste was placed over coloured glass and then engraved with decorative motifs.

VISITORS' CHECKLIST

Piazza Museo 19. **Map** 3 B4.
081 44 01 66. Cavour-Museo. C64, C83, E1, R1, R4, 24, 110, 47, 135. 9am–7pm Wed–Mon. 25 Dec, 1 Jan, 1 May.

Spring Fresco
The fresco removed from the Villa Stabia in the Varano plain is a masterpiece of grace and elegance; the female figure rendered with soft, delicate colours.

Stairs down to Egyptian Collection

★ Farnese Bull
Excavated in the Baths of Caracalla in Rome, this is the largest sculptural group (c.200 BC) to have survived from antiquity. The best-known piece in the Farnese Collection, it shows the punishment of Dirce who, having ill-treated Antiope, was tied to an enraged bull by the latter's sons.

★ Farnese Hercules
Made by Glykon of Athens, this statue is an enlarged copy of a sculpture by the Greek master Lysippus. Napoleon is said to have regretted leaving it behind when he removed his booty from Italy in 1797.

Temporary entrance

STAR FEATURES

★ The Battle of Alexander

★ Farnese Hercules

★ Farnese Bull

Exploring the Museo Archeologico

THE REAL MUSEO BORBONICO, as the museum was known, held the Farnese Collection of paintings, ancient artefacts and books, and archaeological finds from sites in Campania and Southern Italy. In 1925 the books moved to the Palazzo Reale *(see pp50–51)* and in 1957 the Farnese Collection paintings returned to Capodimonte *(see pp98–101)*. The remaining material consisted of ancient finds, and the museum became the Archaeological Museum. The impressive Farnese Collection and sculpture from Herculaneum, Pompeii and other Campanian cities can be seen on the ground floor, the mezzanine level, and the first floor. Pompeiian mosaics, on the mezzanine level, and domestic items, weapons and murals, on the first floor, show daily life in the ancient cities. A lower ground floor level houses the Egyptian Collection. The arrangement aims to display the exhibits in context.

Wild goat from Edessa

Funerary stela of the scribe Huy

SCULPTURE

THE FINE collection of Greco-Roman sculpture consists mostly of works found in excavations around Vesuvius and the Phlegraean Fields, as well as the treasures from the Farnese Collection. The sculptures – most of which are the only existing Roman copies of lost Greek originals – are displayed on the ground floor. Among the numerous fine works are the statues of *Harmodios and Aristogeiton*, or the "tyrannicides", young Athenians who killed the 6th-century BC tyrant, Hipparchos, and the bronze and alabaster *Artemis of Ephesos*, whose many breasts symbolize fertility. The *Doryphoros* carrying a spear is a copy of a famous Greek original, as is the impressive *Farnese Hercules*. The *Farnese Atlas*, holding up the world, is a Hellenistic statue, while the huge *Dioscuri* statues, discovered in the Roman baths of Baia *(see p133)*, and the harmonious *Farnese Flora* are copies by Roman sculptors.

Cameo with Dionysus and satyr

INCISED GEMS

THIS PRECIOUS collection, begun by Cosimo de' Medici, contains Greek, Roman and Renaissance gems. The highlight is the veined sardonyx *Farnese Cup*, a large and beautiful cameo carved in Egypt around the 2nd and 1st centuries BC. Another stunning agate and sardonyx cameo shows the infant Dionysus playing with a satyr.

THE EGYPTIAN COLLECTION

VALUABLE works of Egyptian art from the Ancient Kingdom (2700–2200 BC) to the Roman age are exhibited here. The black basalt *Farnese Naophorous*

The Farnese Flora

represents a kneeling official. These were the intermediaries between men and gods. The limestone funerary stela of Huy (1320–1200 BC) retains some of its original colouring.

As well as human and animal mummies, the Egyptian section includes Canopic vases, containers for the internal organs of the deceased with lids in the shape of animal heads. The collection of *shabti* comprises wood, stone and faience statuettes representing workers for the deceased in the afterlife.

MOSAICS

THE MAJORITY of the mosaics on display in the museum come from Pompeii, Stabiae, Herculaneum and Boscoreale and date from the 2nd century BC to AD 79. The realistic images, such as the female portraits from Pompeii, are particularly fascinating.

Mosaic of a female from Pompeii

Among the many pavement mosaics made of tiny tesserae and often derived from Greek paintings, is *La Fattucchiera* (the Sorceress). This interesting example of the Hellenistic tradition depicts a scene from *Synaristoi*, a comedy by the Greek playwright Aristophanes. Another masterpiece is the *Battle of Alexander* found at Pompeii. This large, detailed mosaic was based on a Hellenistic painting and depicts Alexander the Great leading his cavalry against Darius III, the Persian Emperor, seen fleeing in his chariot.

Some rooms in the museum have reconstructions of large mosaic paved floors.

observatory. A large sundial *(meridiana)*, decorated with the signs of the zodiac, was created for the spacious hall which had originally been destined to be the Bourbon library (Biblioteca Borbonica).

The idea of the observatory, however, was discarded when experts realized that the location of the building meant that it was impossible to have a total view of the sky. A few years later the observatory was built elsewhere *(see p97)*. As originally planned, the Salone della Meridiana was opened to the public in 1804 as a library.

There are also numerous fragments of frescoes which depict landscapes, portraits and mythological scenes and characters, such as the *Sacrifice of Iphigenia*. These show the variety and quality of Roman painting from this period.

TEMPLE OF ISIS

THE PAINTINGS, sculptures and furnishings from the Temple of Isis in Pompeii are presented in such a way as to recreate the sanctuary as it appeared to the first archaeologists in

Head of Isis

1764. *The Portrait of Io at Canopos* was uncovered on 18 November of the same year in the presence of King Ferdinand IV, and shows the nymph Io being welcomed to Egypt by Isis. The marble head of the goddess, to whom the temple was dedicated, dates from the 1st century AD.

VILLA DEI PAPIRI

THIS VILLA in Herculaneum *(see p140)*, still partly buried today, was an art gallery in its own right. The rich array of artworks found here during the excavations in 1750–61 are exceptional: this ancient private collection has been handed down to us intact. A map of the villa shows where every object was found.

Statue of a faun, Villa dei Papiri

Among the pieces on display are life-size statues and small sculptures in marble and bronze, such as the *Dancing Faun* which greeted visitors in the atrium of the villa. Most of the pieces were inspired by Greek figurative art. A vast library of around 1,700 papyrus scrolls was also found in the villa. An apparatus used to unroll the charred scrolls is on display. The original scrolls are now kept in the Biblioteca Nazionale *(see p51)*.

FRESCOES

MOST OF THE frescoes in the collection were removed from buildings in cities buried by the eruptions of Vesuvius, and assembled here from the mid-1700s onwards. The most important came from the Basilica in Herculaneum (such as the painting of *Achilles and Chiron*). Others were taken from the Villa di Fannio Sinistore at Boscoreale, where one wall was decorated with illusionistic architectural perspective, and from the extensive landed property of Julia Felix in Pompeii *(see p147)*. The frieze from her house, with a still life of apples and grapes and scenes from the forum, gives a fascinating glimpse of everyday life in a 1st-century AD city.

SALONE DELLA MERIDIANA

WHEN THE BUILDING was being reorganized and fitted out as a museum in the late 18th century, the architects had the idea of adding an

The famous fresco *Achilles and Chiron* from Herculaneum

THE MODEL OF POMPEII

Model of Pompeii

PAPER, CORK AND WOOD were all used in the making of this extensive scale model of the Pompeii excavations. The archaeologist Giuseppe Fiorelli had the original idea and the model was constructed in various stages between 1861 to 1879. The extraordinarily exact reproduction of every detail found in the ruins (including paintings and mosaics done in watercolour), make this an extremely important historical document. In some cases, when detailed records of Pompeiian decoration are needed, this model is the only useful source that remains.

CAPODIMONTE AND I VERGINI

LTHOUGH THE SPANISH viceroys had forbidden construction outside the city walls, from the 17th century onwards suburban development continued. In the early 19th century, building began in the northern suburbs. The avenue leading to the Capodimonte palace, now the home of one of Europe's most important museums, was created as an extension of Via Toledo. The

Porcelain at Capodimonte

square next to the Museo Archeologico was redesigned and Via Foria, on which the Botanic Garden and, from 1751, the huge Albergo dei Poveri were being built, was widened. The old Sanità, Vergini and Fontanelle districts have retained the character of a lively working quarter. On the streets leading to the early Christian cemeteries, tenements alternate with historic churches and buildings.

SIGHTS AT A GLANCE

Churches and Cemeteries
Cimitero delle Fontanelle **6**
Santi Apostoli **8**
San Gennaro Catacombs **12**
San Giovanni a Carbonara **7**
Santa Maria degli Angeli
  alle Croci **9**
Santa Maria della Sanità and
  San Gaudioso Catacombs **5**
San Severo and Catacombs **4**

Historic Buildings
Albergo dei Poveri **11**
Osservatorio Astronomico **14**
Palazzo Sanfelice **3**
Palazzo dello Spagnolo **2**

Historic Gate
Porta San Gennaro **1**

Museums and Galleries
*Museo Nazionale and Park of
Capodimonte pp98–101* **13**

Parks and Gardens
Orto Botanico **10**

GETTING THERE
The Capodimonte museum and Catacombs of San Gennaro can be reached via bus routes 24 and R4, which start from Piazza del Municipio and Piazza Bovio. You can walk to the Vergini and Sanità districts from the Metro station at Piazza Cavour. Many buses run along Via Foria. Bus C51 serves the Fontanelle.

| 0 kilometres | 250 |
| 0 miles | 250 |

KEY

Street-by-Street map
See pp92–3

P Parking

M Metro station

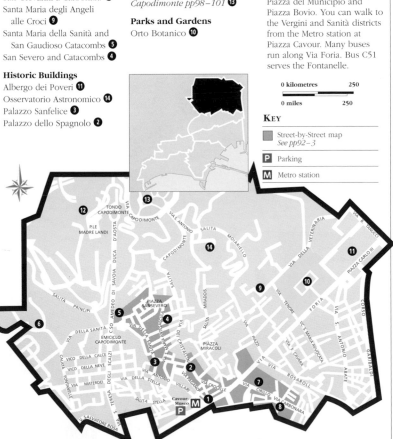

◁ **Caravaggio's** *Flagellation of Christ* **(1610), on display in the Museo di Capodimonte**

Street-by-Street: North of the Ancient Walls

THE AREA NORTH OF THE CITY WALLS has been used for
burials and worship of the dead since it was first
inhabited. A visit to the catacombs (which were underground cemeteries and not hiding places), first created
in the early Christian era, is an unforgettable experience.
The area outside the walls was also used to dump
rubbish. The district known today as Via San Giovanni
a Carbonara was once called the Fosso Carbonario
(literally, "coal ditch"), and this is how the street and
the beautiful 14th-century church acquired their
current names.

**The church of
Santa Maria dei
Vergini**, built in the
14th century, was
badly damaged in
World War II.

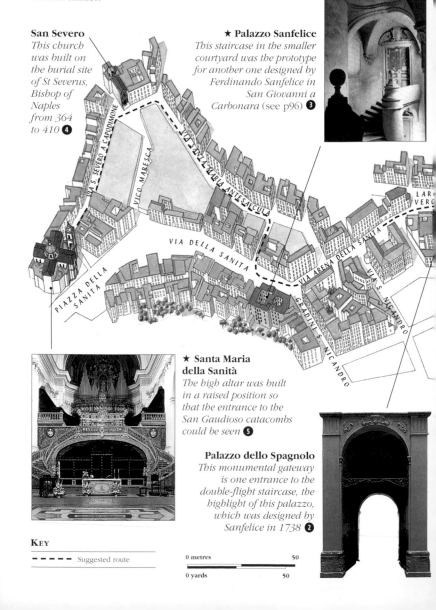

San Severo
*This church
was built on
the burial site
of St Severus,
Bishop of
Naples
from 364
to 410* **4**

★ Palazzo Sanfelice
*This staircase in the smaller
courtyard was the prototype
for another one designed by
Ferdinando Sanfelice in
San Giovanni a
Carbonara (see p96)* **3**

**★ Santa Maria
della Sanità**
*The high altar was built
in a raised position so
that the entrance to the
San Gaudioso catacombs
could be seen* **5**

Palazzo dello Spagnolo
*This monumental gateway
is one entrance to the
double-flight staircase, the
highlight of this palazzo,
which was designed by
Sanfelice in 1738* **2**

KEY

– – – – – Suggested route

0 metres   50

0 yards   50

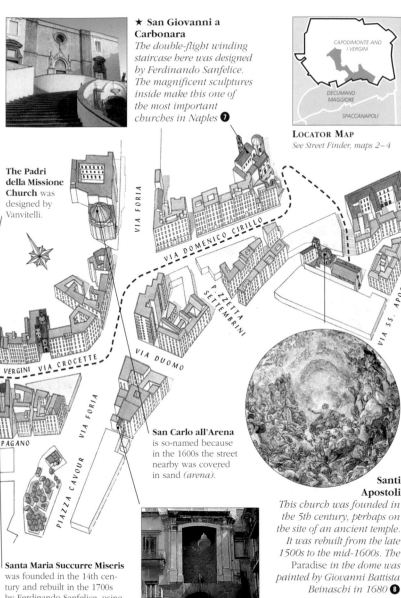

★ San Giovanni a Carbonara
The double-flight winding staircase here was designed by Ferdinando Sanfelice. The magnificent sculptures inside make this one of the most important churches in Naples ❼

LOCATOR MAP
See Street Finder, maps 2–4

The Padri della Missione Church was designed by Vanvitelli.

San Carlo all'Arena is so-named because in the 1600s the street nearby was covered in sand *(arena)*.

Santa Maria Succurre Miseris was founded in the 14th century and rebuilt in the 1700s by Ferdinando Sanfelice, using Baroque motifs throughout.

Santi Apostoli
This church was founded in the 5th century, perhaps on the site of an ancient temple. It was rebuilt from the late 1500s to the mid-1600s. The Paradise in the dome was painted by Giovanni Battista Beinaschi in 1680 ❽

Porta San Gennaro
In the mid-15th century the city walls were extended and this gateway was rebuilt in its present location ❶

STAR SIGHTS

★ Palazzo Sanfelice

★ Santa Maria della Sanità and San Gaudioso Catacombs

★ San Giovanni a Carbonara

The double-flight staircase in Palazzo dello Spagnolo

Porta San Gennaro ❶

Map 3 C3. 🚌 C5, CD, 47, 110. Ⓜ Cavour-Museo.

THIS GATEWAY was named after San Gennaro, the patron saint of Naples, because it marked the beginning of the street that leads to the catacombs where he was buried (see p97). After the plague of 1656, Mattia Preti painted a fresco on each city gate as an ex voto from those who survived. Porta San Gennaro is the only one that still has traces of the artist's work. On the inner façade is a bust of San Gaetano with a dedication and the date – 1658.

Palazzo dello Spagnolo ❷

Via Vergini 19. **Map** 3 B3. 🚌 C5, C51, C52, CD, 47, 110. Ⓜ Cavour-Museo. ⏱ 7:30am–2pm, 3:30–8pm Mon–Fri; 7:30am–1pm Sat.

BUILT IN 1738 by Ferdinando Sanfelice (1675–1748) for the Marquis Nicola Moscati, this building became the property of the Spanish nobleman Tommaso Atienza in the 19th century and was renamed the Palace of the Spaniard. In addition to his work as an architect, Sanfelice also designed temporary staging and scenery for outdoor feasts, organized by the court in order to win the Neapolitans' favour. This theatrical aspect of his work can be clearly seen in the two palazzi he designed for the Sanità district.

Once through the majestic doorway of the Palazzo dello Spagnolo, you will notice a feature taken from the Palazzo Sanfelice: the magnificent double-flight external staircase. This type of staircase, which effectively separates the main courtyard from the smaller one, is one of the most notable features of Neapolitan palaces.

Palazzo Sanfelice ❸

Via Sanità 2–4. **Map** 3 B3. 🚌 C5, CD, 47, 110. Ⓜ Cavour-Museo. ⏱ 8am–1pm, 3–7pm Mon–Fri; 8:30am–1pm Sat.

FERDINANDO SANFELICE built this large palazzo for his own family in 1728, as can be seen in the inscription on the top of the right-hand doorway. It is one of the finest palazzi in Naples and it was here that the famous Neapolitan architect first created the unusual external staircase he subsequently adopted, with some variations, in Palazzo dello Spagnolo ten years later. This type of strikingly original staircase became Sanfelice's

Painting by Giovan Battista Spinelli in San Severo

trademark. His contemporaries likened it to a large bird with outspread wings, and it became known as a stair ad ali di falco – a "falcon's wing" staircase.

The best way to grasp the beauty of the design is to walk up the steps; from the first landing you can see the garden behind. On the far side of the second courtyard (at No. 2 Via Sanità), which has unfortunately lost its original decoration, there is yet another elliptical staircase.

San Severo and Catacombs ❹

Piazza San Severo 81. **Map** 3 B2. 🕿 081 45 46 84. 🚌 R4. Ⓜ Cavour-Museo. ⏱ 9am–noon, 5–9pm Mon–Sat; 9am–noon Sun. 🔓 by appt only.

Fresco of San Pietro in the catacombs of San Severo

SAN SEVERO was the Bishop of Naples from 364 to 410. This site was chosen for his tomb and, as was the usual practice among early Christians, a large underground cemetery grew up around it. The basilica over the catacombs was abandoned in the 9th century when the saint's relics were transferred to San Giorgio Maggiore (see p70). The building was only restored in the 16th century and again more comprehensively in the late 17th century. In the third chapel on the left is the entrance to the catacombs. In the same chapel there is a cell with three arched niches hewn out of the stone to house sarcophagi. The niches are decorated with frescoes which, despite their poor condition, are good examples of catacomb painting.

Central nave of Santa Maria della Sanità

Santa Maria della Sanità and San Gaudioso Catacombs ❺

Via Sanità 124. **Map** 3 A2. ☎ *081 544 13 05.* Ⓜ *Cavour-Museo.* ◯ *8am–noon, 5–8pm daily (except Thu & Sun pm).* ⚑ **Catacombs** ☑ *every 45 mins 9:30–12:30am Mon–Sat.* ◨

View of Santa Maria Sanità from the Ponte della Sanità

THE HEART of the working-class Sanità quarter is the basilica of Santa Maria. Confusingly, the church is also known as the church of San Vincenzo because it houses a much revered image of the popular saint, known locally as 'o munacone (the big monk). Designed by Fra Nuvolo, the church was built on a Greek cross plan in 1603–13, with 24 columns supporting one central dome and 12 lateral domes (a reference to Christ and the Apostles). The central tiled dome is overlooked by the 19th-century Ponte della Sanità, linking the city centre to Capodimonte.

Inside, the main altar was raised to allow worshippers to see the space that serves as a kind of atrium for the underground cemetery. The entrance to the catacombs can be clearly seen.

Tradition has it that in 452, the African bishop Settimio Celio Gaudioso died in exile in Naples, and was buried in the Sanità valley. The catacombs grew up around his tomb and were named after him. The many corridors still bear traces of frescoes and mosaics (4th–6th centuries AD). The catacombs remained in use for centuries. Evidence for this includes some rather gruesome early 17th-century tombs, each with a skeleton drawn on the wall and a skull set into the surface in a realistic depiction of the deceased.

Cimitero delle Fontanelle ❻

Via Fontanelle 77. **Map** 3 A3. ☎ *081 544 77 46 (Church of Maria Santissima del Carmine).* 🚌 *C52.* Ⓜ *Cavour-Museo.* ● *for restoration.*

A WALK ALONG Via Fontanelle through an area that is more like a country village than a city district, leads to the church of Maria Santissima del Carmine, from which you can visit the Fontanelle cemetery (cimitero). The huge rock-hewn caverns on the hill of Materdei were already being used as the city ossuary when they were selected as the final resting place for the thousands of victims of the devastating 1836 cholera epidemic.

Some people may find the place upsetting, as did the tourist played by Ingrid Bergman in Rossellini's film Viaggio in Italia, which made the cemetery famous.

The ossuary of the Fontanelle Cemetery

San Giovanni a Carbonara ❼

Via San G. a Carbonara 5. **Map** 3 C3.
📞 081 29 58 73. ⭘ Mon–Sat.

Cappella Caracciolo di Vico, San Giovanni a Carbonara

T HE IMAGINATIVE double-flight staircase designed by Ferdinando Sanfelice in the early 1700s leads to the 14th-century Chapel of Santa Monica. Left of the chapel is the doorway to San Giovanni a Carbonara. Founded in 1343 by Augustinian monks, this church was restored and enlarged at the end of the century by King Ladislas to make it a worthy burial site for the Angevin rulers.

When the king died in 1414, his tomb, the work of anonymous Tuscan and Lombard sculptors *(see p18)*, was erected at the request of his sister, Joan II, who succeeded him to the throne. The grandiose funerary monument, with seated statues of Ladislas and Joan, dominates the single-nave interior. Through a small doorway beneath the monument is the circular Cappella Caracciolo del Sole, built in 1427 and paved with coloured Tuscan tiles. Behind the altar is the tomb of Ser Gianni Caracciolo, Joan's lover and Grand Seneschal at the court, who died in 1432.

To the left of the presbytery is the harmonious Cappella Caracciolo di Vico, built in the Renaissance style in 1517 by Giovan Tommaso Malvito following a design by Bramante. Another work by Malvito is the richly decorated tomb of the Miroballo family opposite the entrance of the church.

Santi Apostoli ❽

Largo Santi Apostoli 9. **Map** 3 C4.
📞 081 29 93 75. 🚌 CD, E3. Ⓜ Cavour-Museo. ⭘ 8am–noon, 5:30–8pm Mon–Sat; 8:30am–1pm Sun.

T O REACH the church of Santi Apostoli you have to go along a short stretch of Via Pisanelli, which turns into Via Anticaglia *(see p84)*. The church was founded in the 5th century and restructured at the beginning of the 17th century by Francesco Grimaldi (1610) and, after 1627, by Giovanni Conforto. The church is best known for a wonderful fresco cycle by Giovanni Lanfranco (1638–46). This masterpiece influenced artistic development in Naples. The artist also frescoed the cupola of the Cappella del Tesoro di San Gennaro *(see pp82–3)*.

Santa Maria degli Angeli alle Croci ❾

Via Veterinaria 2. **Map** 3 C2. 📞 081 44 07 56. 🚌 47. Ⓜ Cavour-Museo. ⭘ 7am–1:30pm, 5–7pm Mon–Sat; 7am–2pm Sun. 🚫 .

T HE NAME of this church refers to the Stations of the Cross, once marked by wooden crosses *(croci)* alongside the ascent to the church. Santa Maria was founded at the end of the 16th century by Franciscans and rebuilt in 1638 by Cosimo Fanzago. The façade is simply decorated with white and grey marble.

The white and grey marble façade of Santa Maria degli Angeli alle Croci

This plain design was a daring shift from the usually lavish architecture of Neapolitan Baroque. The interior houses a magnificent marble pulpit sculpted by Cosimo Fanzago. The eagle supporting it symbolizes St John the Evangelist. The extraordinary bas relief of the dead Christ on the altar was sculpted by Carlo Fanzago, Cosimo's son.

Cactus plants in the Orto Botanico

Orto Botanico ❿

Via Foria 223. **Map** 4 D2. 📞 081 44 97 59. 🚌 47. Ⓜ Cavour-Museo. ⭘ 9am–2pm Mon–Fri by appt; Apr–Jun: Wed–Thu.

E STABLISHED IN 1807 by Joseph Bonaparte, the "Royal Plant Garden" is today one of the leading Italian botanical gardens for the high quality of its collections as well as its sheer size, covering 12 hectares (30 acres). It has a rich stock of tree and shrub specimens from all latitudes and examples of many plant species, as well as several glasshouses with varying climatic conditions. The temperate house is an early 19th-century Neo-Classical building. The collections of citrus trees, desert plants and tree ferns are particularly interesting. Even though you may not be a botanical enthusiast, a walk along the paths of this green oasis, in the heart of one of the busiest areas in Naples, can make a very pleasant break from the city.

Albergo dei Poveri ⓫

Piazza Carlo III. **Map** 4 E2.
47, C55B. **M** Cavour-Museo.

THE ENORMOUS BUILDING you see today is only one-fifth of the large-scale complex that King Charles III wanted to build to provide a refuge for "the poor of the entire kingdom". Construction of the "Hotel of the Poor" began in 1751 according to a design by Ferdinando Fuga. Work continued until 1829, but the project was never finished. For many years it has been in a state of neglect (the 1980 earthquake further damaged an already dilapidated building) and restoration plans have yet to proceed.

San Gennaro Catacombs ⓬

Via Capodimonte 13. **Map** 3 A1.
081 741 10 71. R4, 24.
9:30, 10:15, 11, 11:45am.

THE ORIGINAL nucleus of this large subterranean cemetery may have been the tomb of a pagan aristocrat donated in the 2nd century to the growing Christian community. The catacombs began to grow in importance in the 3rd century after acquiring the tomb of Sant'Agrippino, but it was as the burial site of the saint, bishop and martyr Gennaro, brought here in the

The Neo-Classical façade of the Osservatorio Astronomico

5th century, that the catacombs became famous. The cemetery also housed the tombs of Neapolitan bishops up to the 11th century. The vast size and two-level layout of this holy site distinguish it from other catacombs of the same era and make it the most important complex in Southern Italy. Remains of precious 2nd- to 10th-century mosaics and frescoes (including the oldest known portrayal of San Gennaro, dating from the 5th century) adorn the walls of the catacombs. Don't miss the Bishops' Crypt on the upper floor and the Sant'Agrippino Oratory and baptistry on the lower level. The basilica of San Gennaro extra Moenia was erected over the catacombs in the 5th century but was greatly modified by subsequent rebuilding in the 11th century and then again in 1932.

Museo Nazionale and Park of Capodimonte ⓭

See pp98–101.

Osservatorio Astronomico ⓮

Salita Moiariello 16. **Map** 3 B1.
081 557 51 11. 24.
Mon–Fri by appt. the museum.

SITUATED IN THE MIDDLE of a large park on top of the hill of Miradois, 150 m (490 ft) above sea level, the observatory benefits from a splendid vantage point with fine panoramic views of the city and the bay. Founded in 1819 by Ferdinand IV, this was the first scientific facility of its kind in Europe. The Bourbon court had always been keenly interested in astronomic studies, and it was Charles III who established the first university chair of astronomy in Naples in 1735. The observatory was originally planned for the Museo Archeologico, and in fact construction of a new observatory began there in 1791 (see p89), but the project was discarded. A few years later the elegant Neo-Classical building that now houses the observatory was built by the Gasse brothers. Today part of the observatory is occupied by a museum with a fine collection of clocks, telescopes and old scientific instruments.

Watercolour of the Catacombs of San Gennaro by Giacinto Gigante

Museo Nazionale and Park of Capodimonte 🏛

FROM THE BEGINNING Capodimonte was both a royal palace and a museum because Charles III wanted a home for the works of art he had inherited from his mother Elizabeth Farnese. Construction began in 1738 under architect Antonio Medrano, but the palace was only completed a century later, despite the fact that a large part of the Farnese Collection had been on display there since 1759. The collection was dispersed after the French occupation in 1799 *(see p23)*, but following the Bourbon restoration in 1815, was enlarged considerably.

In 1860 Capodimonte became the property of the House of Savoy and was the residence of the Dukes of Aosta until 1947. The museum was opened to the public again in 1957.

In 1996, after restoration, the first floor was reopened, and in 1997 the Neapolitan and contemporary art collections were arranged on the second floor (not shown here).

Pietà
This painting by Annibale Carracci, which dates from around 1600, drew inspiration from Michelangelo and is one of the masterpieces of Carracci's monumental style.

Main Entrance

THE PARK OF CAPODIMONTE

Charles III was drawn to Capodimonte because of hunting, his favourite pastime, and he decided to build an important hunting lodge here. The first section of this large park (over 120 hectares/300 acres), with numerous ancient trees, was laid out by Ferdinando Sanfelice in 1742 into five broad radiating roads, lined with holm-oaks. The buildings used for various court activities can be found in the woods.

The rooms in the Royal Apartments on the first floor reveal the two-fold function as royal palace and museum that Capodimonte fulfilled from the outset.

Ferdinand IV at Capodimonte by Antonio Joli

KEY

- ☐ Farnese Gallery
- ☐ Borgia Collection
- ☐ De Ciccio porcelain collection
- ☐ Farnese and Bourbon Armoury
- ☐ Maria Amalia's Porcelain Parlour
- ☐ Royal apartments
- ☐ Non-exhibition space

Neapolitan Craftsmanship
This is a multi-purpose piece of early 19th-century furniture made in a Neapolitan factory: the lower part contains a glass bowl, which serves as an aquarium, and a table with a bird cage, which serves as a jardinière. The rotating figure of Fortune is perched on top.

VISITORS' CHECKLIST

Via Miano 2 (Porta Piccola), Via Capodimonte (Porta Grande).
Map 3 B1. 081 744 13 07. R4, 24. **Museum** 10am–6pm Tue–Sat, 9am–2pm Sun. **Park** 8am–1 hr before sunset. museum only.

Café

★ **Danaë** *(c.1545)*
Golden light bathes this canvas by Titian, in which the mythical god Jupiter disguises himself as a shower of gold in order to seduce Danaë, daughter of the king of Argos.

★ **Crucifixion** *(1426)*
In this early Renaissance painting by Masaccio, the emotional intensity of faces and gestures emphasizes the drama. The panel was part of an altarpiece for a church in Pisa, now dismantled and scattered in various museums.

First Floor

★ **Maria Amalia's Porcelain Parlour**
This room was built in 1757–9 for the Royal Palace at Portici (see p136); then dismantled and moved here in 1866. The walls and ceiling of the queen's parlour are tiled with about 3,000 pieces of finest Capodimonte porcelain.

STAR EXHIBITS

★ **Crucifixion by Masaccio**

★ **Danaë by Titian**

★ **Maria Amalia's Porcelain Parlour**

Exploring the Museo di Capodimonte

THE FARNESE COLLECTION, which is the core of the Art Gallery, features the major Italian and European schools of painting from the 15th to the 17th centuries. When the Real Museo (now the Museo Archeologico Nazionale, *see pp86–9*) was created in Palazzo degli Studi in the early 1800s, the paintings were transferred from Capodimonte and returned in 1957, along with other works purchased since the 19th century by the Bourbon rulers and the Italian government. Following the completion of recent restoration and rearrangement of the collections, 13th–19th century Neapolitan painting and sculpture is now displayed on the second floor. The 19th-century collection is located in the mezzanine, while the first floor is devoted to the Farnese Collection and the Royal Apartments.

Antea (1531–35) by Parmigianino

PAINTING FROM THE 13TH TO THE 16TH CENTURIES

THE FARNESE COLLECTION did not focus on medieval works, so that paintings from this period are later purchases or come from churches in the Naples region. For example, the beautiful *Santa Maria de Flumine* (c.1290) came from a church of the same name in Amalfi. The most important 14th-century painting is the large altarpiece painted by Simone Martini in 1317 on the occasion of the canonization of St Louis of Toulouse *(see pp18–19)*, *St Louis of Toulouse Crowning Robert of Anjou King of Naples*.

The 15th century is also represented by a superb canvas – Masaccio's *Crucifixion*, actually the upper part of a dismantled polyptych taken from the church of the Carmine in Pisa. The other panels are in Pisa, London, Berlin and Malibu.

Transfiguration by Giovanni Bellini

Giovanni Bellini's masterpiece, *Transfiguration* (c.1480–85), has been considered one of the gems of the Farnese Collection since the 1600s. The *Tavola Strozzi* panel is an extraordinary "snapshot" of 15th-century Naples.

The focal point of the 16th-century paintings are the splendid Titians: *Portrait of Pope Paul III*, *Pope Paul III with His Grandchildren*, and *Danaë (see p99)*, which exemplify the Venetian genius's masterly use of colour. Artists from the region of Emilia Romagna, the home of the Farnese family, are well represented. Major works are Correggio's

masterpiece *Mystic Marriage of St Catherine* and the *Antea* by Parmigianino, a portrait of a young woman with elegant dress and a marten stole. An important group of canvases by the Carraccis includes Annibale Carracci's *Pietà*, inspired by the strong sculptural forms of Michelangelo, and his large allegorical work, *Hercules at the Crossroads*, in which the mythical hero has to choose between pleasure and virtue.

PAINTING FROM THE 17TH TO THE 20TH CENTURIES

AMONG THE 17TH-CENTURY works in the museum, Bartolomeo Schedoni's *Charity* (1611) is one of the most famous, and is greatly admired for its expressive intensity. The myth of *Atalanta and Hippomenes* is depicted in Guido Reni's canvas, which the Bourbon rulers bought in 1802 because they lacked a major work by the Bolognese master.

The astounding *Flagellation of Christ* by Caravaggio *(see p90)* was painted in stages from 1607 to 1609–10, and hung in San Domenico Maggiore until its move to Capodimonte. It is regarded as the linchpin of all 17th-century Neapolitan painting, which is represented here by many leading artists, such as Battistello Caracciolo, Luca Giordano and Mattia Preti. No less astounding is Artemisia Gentileschi's painting of

The *Tavola Strozzi*, a representation of 15th-century Naples (detail)

CAPODIMONTE AND I VERGINI

Judith and Holofernes, a subject she made her own. The artist, who favoured rather violent themes, was an exceptionally gifted painter and remarkably independent for a woman of her times.

Portrait of Ferdinand IV as a Youth was painted by the German artist Anton Raphael Mengs in 1760; the young king, whose luxurious clothes are rendered in great detail, was nine at the time. In addition, there are some fine landscapes by Ferdinand IV's court painter, Jakob-Philipp Hackert.

Capodimonte also has a large body of 19th-century Neapolitan paintings, including works by Anton Pitloo, the Dutch painter who settled in Naples *(see p35)*, and Giacinto Gigante. Don't miss the latter's famous painting of the Cappella del Tesoro in the Duomo. Among the modern works, Andy Warhol's *Mount Vesuvius (see p26)* was painted in 1985 for an exhibition at the museum in the same year.

Judith and Holofernes by Artemisia Gentileschi (1597–1651)

THE COLLECTION OF DRAWINGS AND PAINTINGS

AMONG THE MUSEUM's huge inheritance there are about 2,500 drawings and watercolours and 22,000 prints and engravings. One of the most famous works is a cartoon (a preparatory drawing made with charcoal or chalk) made by Michelangelo around 1546. It was drawn for part of the fresco of *The Crucifixion of St Peter* in the Cappella Paolina in the

Francesco Solimena's *Study of a Young Man's Face* (1728)

Vatican. Perforations (which can still be seen) were made with a needle, and powder was sprinkled over the holes to transfer the lines to the wall where the fresco was to be painted.

Solimena's *Study of a Young Man's Face* is a charming study for a later painting. Another important cartoon is Raphael's *Moses before the Burning Bush*, a preparatory drawing for a detail of a fresco in the Stanza di Eliodoro in the Vatican.

THE DECORATIVE ARTS

THE MAJOR SECTION in the fine Decorative Arts collection is the armoury, which has about 4,000 weapons and is one of the most important of its kind. Many of the objects here

come from the Naples Royal Arms Factory, founded in 1734 by Charles III. There are also over 4,000 ceramic pieces in this part of the museum, including the De Ciccio majolica collection and examples of the superb porcelain manufactured in Naples at the instigation of Charles III. A fine example of this craftsmanship is Queen Maria Amalia's Porcelain Parlour *(see p99)*.

Other decorative arts include objects made of ivory, amber and rock crystal, as well as medallions, semi-precious stones and other pieces such as the 17th-century gilded silver table trophy of Diana by Jacob Miller.

Diana on a Deer, table trophy

THE ROYAL PORCELAIN FACTORY

King Charles III promoted and fostered the manufacture of decorated porcelain in Naples. The "soft-paste" porcelain, produced with the aid of leading chemists and mineralogists in the Kingdom of Naples, allowed the Real Fabbrica to vie with top European manufacturers such as Meissen. A new pavilion for the Royal Factory was opened in the royal park of Capodimonte in

The Biscuit Vendor (1750–51)

1743, and the fame of Neapolitan porcelain continued to grow. By 1759, when the king returned to Spain, the factory had become so important to him that he had it dismantled and took it, as well as its staff, with him. The factory was reopened in 1771 by Ferdinand, and production of top-quality pieces began again. Today the Royal Factory is the home of the Institute for the Porcelain and Ceramics industry.

VOMERO

IN 1885 THE Town Council of Naples approved a plan for a new district to be developed "in the rise between Castel Sant'Elmo, the village of Vomero and Antignano", which, once completed, would accommodate 30,000 inhabitants. So began the story of the district of Vomero, which soon became famous for its scenic beauty and healthy climate. These qualities have since been partly ruined (especially since World War II) by chaotic, uncontrolled property development with total disregard for the natural surroundings. Yet, some interesting areas are preserved. At the top of the hill is one of the most important monuments in Naples, the Certosa di San Martino, with its splendid Baroque church, fine museum and the elegant residence called the Quarto del Priore.

Detail of the cloister, Certosa di San Martino

SIGHTS AT A GLANCE

Historic Buildings
Castel Sant'Elmo ❹
Certosa and Museo Nazionale di San Martino pp108–11 ❺

Parks and Gardens
Villa La Floridiana ❷

Streets and Squares
Pedamentina ❻
Via Luigia Sanfelice ❼
Via Scarlatti ❶

Museums and Galleries
Museo Nazionale della Ceramica Duca di Martina ❸

GETTING THERE
The fastest way to reach Vomero is via the funiculars: the Chiaia route from Parco Margherita, the Centrale from Via Toledo and the Montesanto from the historic centre. To get to Castel Sant'Elmo and the Certosa you can also take the circle bus line V1 from Piazza Fuga, which connects with the Centrale funicular.

KEY

- ▮ Street-by-Street map *See pp104–5*
- 🅿 Parking
- Ⓜ Metro station
- 🚠 Funicular

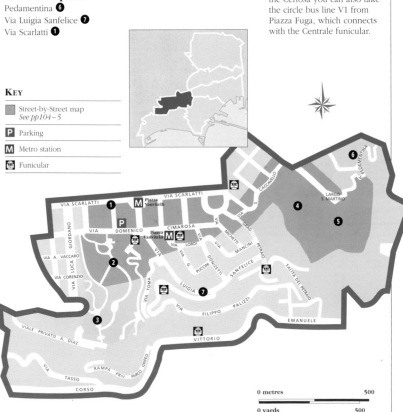

Street-by-Street: Vomero

Take one of the funicular railway lines up the hill to Vomero for fine views of the city centre and the Bay of Naples. Art-lovers will find that Neapolitan masters are well represented in the museums of the Certosa di San Martino and Villa La Floridiana (the Duca di Martina). Meanwhile, a walk along the atmospheric streets in the heart of the district reveals an eclectic range of shops and goods, including the Daniele pasticceria in Via Scarlatti, known for its delectable cakes. In Via Luigia Sanfelice is the villa of the Neapolitan comic Eduardo Scarpetta.

Eduardo Scarpetta

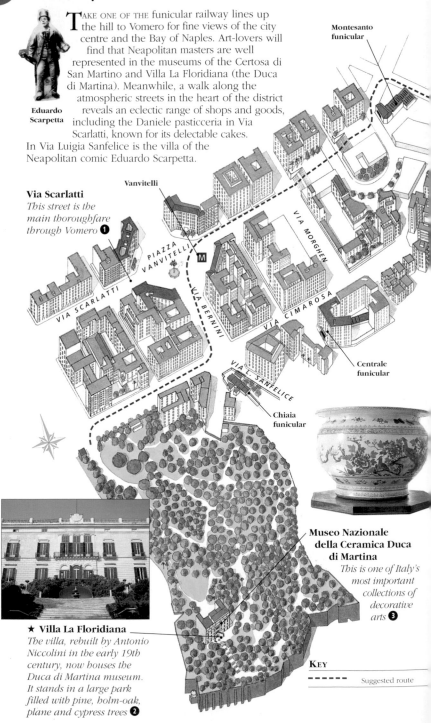

Montesanto funicular

Vanvitelli

Via Scarlatti
This street is the main thoroughfare through Vomero ❶

PIAZZA VANVITELLI   Ⓜ

VIA SCARLATTI

VIA MORGHEN

VIA BERNINI

VIA CIMAROSA

Centrale funicular

VIA L. SANFELICE

Chiaia funicular

Museo Nazionale della Ceramica Duca di Martina
This is one of Italy's most important collections of decorative arts ❸

★ **Villa La Floridiana**
The villa, rebuilt by Antonio Niccolini in the early 19th century, now houses the Duca di Martina museum. It stands in a large park filled with pine, holm-oak, plane and cypress trees ❷

Key

- - - - - -   Suggested route

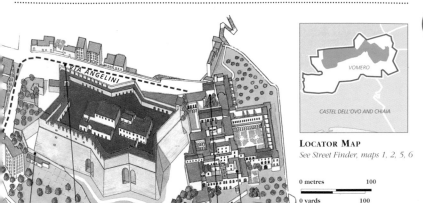

LOCATOR MAP
See Street Finder, maps 1, 2, 5, 6

| 0 metres | 100 |
| 0 yards | 100 |

In Via Tito Angelini are some turn-of-the-century houses, such as Villino Maria (below), which have survived the wave of property development since World War II.

★ **Certosa and Museo Nazionale di San Martino**
After the unification of Italy, this impressive complex – built in the 14th century but drastically restructured later on – became state property and was turned into a museum ⑤

The section of the Museo di San Martino given over to Neapolitan painting and sculpture of the 19th century includes Vincenzo Gemito's expressive *Head of a Peasant Woman*.

★ **Castel Sant'Elmo**
The patriots of the Parthenopean Republic (see p23) conquered the castle in 1799, but when the revolution was crushed they were imprisoned there ④

STAR SIGHTS

★ **Certosa and Museo Nazionale di San Martino**

★ **Villa La Floridiana**

★ **Castel Sant'Elmo**

Via Scarlatti **❶**

Map 2 D5. 🚇 *Centrale: Piazza Fuga; Chiaia: Via Cimarosa.* 🚌 *V1.*

THE MOST ELEGANT street in Vomero is lined with tall plane trees and descends from Piazza Vanvitelli towards Via Cilea. Now closed to traffic, Via Scarlatti is the perfect place for a pleasant walk interrupted by the odd break for shopping. If you lift your gaze above the line of shops you will note the striking contrast between the 19th-century buildings and those constructed in the last 30 years in the wave of property development that has radically altered the face of Vomero.

Villa La Floridiana **❷**

Via Domenico Cimarosa 77, Via Aniello Falcone. **Map** 2 C5. 📞 *081 578 55 65.* 🚌 *C28, V1.* 🚇 *Centrale: Piazza Fuga; Chiaia: Via Cimarosa.* ◯ *9am–1 hr before sunset.*

IN 1817 FERDINAND I acquired an estate on the Vomero hill as a present for his second wife Lucia Migliaccio, the Duchess of Florida, whom he had married shortly after the death of Maria Carolina of Austria. The estate, which was named La Floridiana in honour of the duchess, included a park with a magnificent view of the

city. There were two buildings on the property. The Villa La Floridiana was rebuilt as a summer residence in the Neo-Classical style by Antonio Niccolini in 1817–19. It now houses the Duca di Martina Ceramics Museum *(see below).* There was also a "Pompeiian" coffee-house, later called Villa Lucia, also designed by Niccolini, which became private property.

The Italian government purchased the Villa La Floridiana in 1919.

Museo Nazionale della Ceramica Duca di Martina **❸**

Villa Floridiana, Via Domenico Cimarosa 77, Via Aniello Falcone 171. **Map** 2 C5. 📞 *081 578 84 18.* 🚇 *Centrale: Piazza Fuga; Chiaia: Via Cimarosa.* 🚌 *C28, V1.* 📷 *9:30am, 11am, 12:30am daily.* 🎨 🚫

PLACIDO DE SANGRO, the Duke of Martina and member of an illustrious noble family, was an avid, passionate collector of decorative art objects, especially porcelain and ceramics. When he died in 1891, his valuable collection of about 6,000 pieces was inherited by his grandson Placido, who donated them to the city of Naples in 1911.

Since the mid-1920s Villa La Floridiana has been the home of the Duca di Martina National Ceramics Museum, where curators aim to reproduce as closely as possible the arrangement and spirit of the collections in the De Sangro residence. The pleasant and unusual atmosphere of a home-cum-museum has remained unchanged, despite additions and later donations.

The porcelain pieces come from the most important Italian and other

Interior of the Duca di Martina ceramics museum

European factories, while the collection of Oriental art – consisting mostly of 18th- and 19th-century porcelain – is one of the best in Italy.

The museum also contains 15th-century ivory pieces, majolica, Limoges enamel, leather and tortoiseshell objects and drawings by 17th- and 18th-century Neapolitan artists, including Solimena, Giordano and De Matteis.

Castel Sant'Elmo **❹**

Via Tito Angelini. **Map** 2 E5. 📞 *081 578 40 30.* 🚌 *V1.* 🚇 *Montesanto: Via Morghen.* ◯ *9am–5pm Tue–Fri, Sun; 9am–7pm Sat.* ● *Mon.* 🎨 📷

IN THE 1330s the Angevin rulers instigated a flurry of building on the Vomero hill west of Naples – the construction of the Certosa di San Martino and the enlarge-ment and reconstruction of the nearby fortified residence of Belforte, which had been inhabited by Charles I of Anjou's family since 1275.

In the 16th century Pedro Scriba, a leading military architect of the time, completely transformed the 14th-century castle into its present six-pointed star configuration.

Because of its strategic position, Castel Sant'Elmo under viceroy Pedro de Toledo became the focal point of the new defence system for Naples. For centuries it was used as a

Looking across the Floridiana park

prison; among its illustrious "guests" were the great Renaissance philosopher Tommaso Campanella, the 1799 revolutionaries and patriots involved in the 19th-century Risorgimento.

The entrance bears Charles V's coat of arms and a fine epigraph. The complex, which also contains a large lecture hall, has been the venue for temporary exhibitions and cultural events since 1988. From the castle walls there is a spectacular 360-degree view of Naples and the bay.

Certosa di San Martino ❺

See pp108–11.

Pedamentina ❻

Map 2 F5. Montesanto: Via Morghen, Corso Vittorio Emanuele. C16, V1.

THE STEPS CONNECTING Castel Sant'Elmo and the city sprawling below still make for a delightful walk "descending towards the sea amidst the green slopes", as old guidebooks put it, even though the landscape has changed considerably in the meantime. Descent being easier than ascent, you may choose to go down rather than climb the

Castel Sant'Elmo on the top of Vomero hill

414 steps from San Martino to Corso Vittorio Emanuele and take in the glimpses of beautiful panoramic views that change at every stage. The route downwards passes by dilapidated buildings and slum housing, but the views of the bay are rewarding.

Via Luigia Sanfelice ❼

Map 2 D5 & 2 E5. Centrale: Piazza Fuga; Chiaia: Via Cimarosa.

SHOULD YOU ASK for the "Santarella", people will point to Via Luigia Sanfelice. The key to this riddle lies in a curve in the road where there is a villa with a curious

nameplate: "Qui rido io" (this is where I laugh). This was the home, built in 1909, of the well-known Neapolitan author and comic actor Eduardo Scarpetta (the father of Eduardo De Filippo), whose best-known work is *Na santarella (see p37)*. In Via Luigia Sanfelice and nearby Via Filippo Palizzi there are a number of elegant houses which are interesting examples of Neo-Renaissance or Art Nouveau styles.

Nameplate at the villa of comic actor and author Eduardo Scarpetta

---

FROM THE "FERROVIA DI DELIZIA" TO THE FUNICULAR RAILWAY

In 1875 the engineers Bruno and Ferraro designed a rail system to take passengers up the Vomero hill along the Chiaia and Montesanto slopes, using two funiculars, connected so that the ascent of one line caused the descent of the other. The "train of delights",

The present-day funicular railway

as it was called, allowed travellers to admire stupendous views of the bay while crossing the hill, in those days a rural area. The initial scheme gradually evolved into two independent funicular railways which ran through a tunnel, providing a rapid and efficient means of transport between Vomero and the city centre. The Chiaia funicular was opened in 1889, Montesanto in 1891. In order to improve connections with what in the meantime had become the most rapidly expanding district in the city, the Centrale funicular was built in 1928. Centrale was the longest of the three; from its starting point in Via Toledo it reaches a point halfway between the other two. There is also a fourth line, the Mergellina funicular, which connects the seafront with Via Manzoni.

Certosa di San Martino ❺

I**N 1325 CHARLES Duke of Calabria** began construction of what is one of the richest monuments in Naples. The Carthusian monks were forward looking, and from the 16th to the 18th centuries the greatest artists of the time worked at the Certosa (charterhouse) of San Martino.

Procession tray

The original look of San Martino was gradually altered by Mannerist and Baroque rebuilding. The most radical redecoration and enlargement was carried out by the architects Giovanni Antonio Dosio, at the end of the 16th century, and Cosimo Fanzago, who took over in 1623. The 17th and 18th centuries brought further changes.

The French deconsecrated the monastery in 1806, and since 1866 it has housed the San Martino museum, with displays of Neapolitan art and history.

Chiostro dei Procuratori
This cloister was built in the late 16th–early 17th century by Giovanni Antonio Dosio.

Nativity section

Historical section

The Prior's garden

★ **Quarto del Priore**
The Prior's Residence was richly decorated and had a splendid panoramic view over the bay of Naples (see p111).

TIMELINE

Chain of the Order of the Two Sicilies

1325 Construction begun under Charles of Anjou	**1578** Decoration and enlargement by Dosio and Conforto	**1631–56** Complex rebuilt and redecorated by Cosimo Fanzago	**1807** The last monks forced to leave the monastery	
1300		**1600**		**1800**
1368 Consecration of the church	**1623** Cosimo Fanzago begins work on the Chiostro Grande		**1799** Monastery damaged during Parthenopean revolution	**1866** The Certosa becomes state property and part of it is turned into a museum

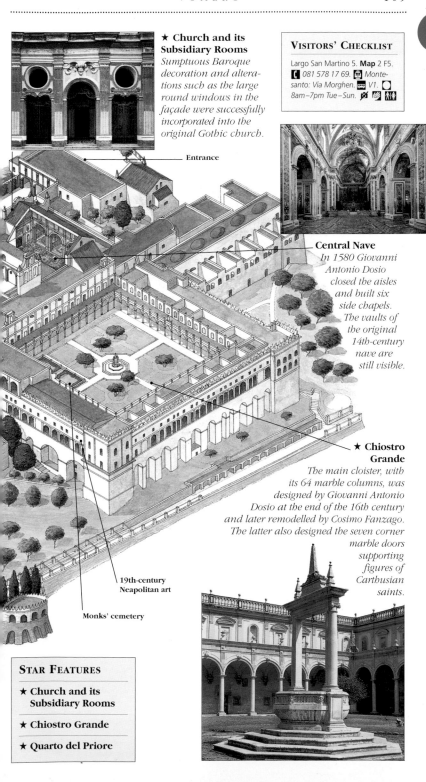

★ **Church and its Subsidiary Rooms**
Sumptuous Baroque decoration and altera-tions such as the large round windows in the façade were successfully incorporated into the original Gothic church.

VISITORS' CHECKLIST

Largo San Martino 5. **Map** 2 F5.
📞 081 578 17 69. 🚋 Monte-santo: Via Morghen. 🚌 V1. ⬜ 8am–7pm Tue–Sun. 🚫 🏷 🏛

Entrance

Central Nave
In 1580 Giovanni Antonio Dosio closed the aisles and built six side chapels. The vaults of the original 14th-century nave are still visible.

★ **Chiostro Grande**
The main cloister, with its 64 marble columns, was designed by Giovanni Antonio Dosio at the end of the 16th century and later remodelled by Cosimo Fanzago. The latter also designed the seven corner marble doors supporting figures of Carthusian saints.

19th-century Neapolitan art

Monks' cemetery

STAR FEATURES

★ Church and its Subsidiary Rooms

★ Chiostro Grande

★ Quarto del Priore

Exploring the Certosa di San Martino and the Museum

FROM THE OUTSET the Carthusian monks intended San Martino to be a storehouse for Neapolitan history and civilization. The collections document the rich and varied forms of artistic expression found in Naples from the 15th to 19th centuries: from paintings to coral jewellery, traditional crib scenes *(presepi)*, porcelain, prints and ivory carvings. There is also a fascinating collection of maps. Other parts of the museum are devoted to Neapolitan costumes, festivals and theatre. The minor arts section contains an interesting collection of glass from Venice and other European sources.

Although a large part of the collections in the San Martino Museum is closed to the public as a result of restoration work, the beauty of the church, the Quarto del Priore (Prior's Residence), the cloisters and the gardens will more than make up for what you miss.

Detail of the inlaid wood panelling in the sacristy (1587–98)

THE CHURCH AND ITS SUBSIDIARY ROOMS

AT THE END OF THE 14th century, the prior Severo Turboli set up an elaborate plan for the complete restructuring of the San Martino charterhouse. The original Angevin church was enlarged and modernized and its Gothic structure almost completely disappeared under the multitude of frescoes, stucco-work and marbles produced by leading artists of the time.

The most radical changes to the building were carried out in the 17th century by architect and sculptor Cosimo Fanzago, who worked at San Martino from 1623 to 1656. He designed the interior of the church and its lavish decoration. Coloured marble adorns the nave and chapels, such as in the Cappella di San Bruno. The rooms adjacent to the church are also richly ornamented. In the sacristy the panels of the beautiful inlaid walnut wardrobes contain 56 intarsia scenes with striking perspective effects (16th century). The fresco of *The Triumph of Judith* on the vault of the brightly-lit Cappella del Tesoro was painted by Luca Giordano in 1704.

HISTORICAL SECTION

THESE INTERESTING rooms dedicated to the history of the Kingdom of Naples are temporarily closed to the public. Paintings, furnishings, sculptures, medallions, arms and memorabilia recreate the key moments in the political, social and cultural history of Naples, from the Aragonese to the Bourbon dynasties. The importance of this valuable collection is exemplified in two famous works that combine historical and artistic

The Cappella di San Bruno, designed by Cosimo Fanzago (1631)

Statue of Charles III of Spain (1754)

documentary significance:
*The Revolt of Masaniello (see
pp20–21)*, painted in 1647,
and *Piazza del Mercatello
during the 1656 Plague*, both
painted by Micco Spadaro.
These dramatic compositions
tell the story of two important
events in the history of 17th-
century Naples. They are also
an accurate and useful
representation of what the
city looked like at that time.

Panorama of Naples Viewed from the Conocchia, by Giacinto Gigante

THE NATIVITY SCENES

ONLY TOWARDS the
end of the 19th
century did the
presepe or nativity
scene start to be
considered an
artistic genre in
its own right,
worthy of a
museum. This
section of the San
Martino museum
has one of the most
important public
collections of its
kind, with displays
of entire nativity scenes as
well as individual figures,
such as Mary and Joseph, the
Three Kings or the shepherds.
Animals and accessories, such
as the crib, are also displayed.

Among the most important
nativity scenes is a creation
by the Neapolitan playwright,
Michele Cucinello. Many of the
statuettes were executed by
famous Neapolitan artists.
*Blind Beggar with
Cataracts* (c.1780), in
the Perrone Collection
(*see p39*), is by the artist
Giuseppe Sanmartino,
who sculpted the *Veiled
Christ* in the Cappella
Sansevero (*see p63*).

***Blind Beggar with Cataracts* by
Giuseppe Sanmartino**

NINETEENTH-CENTURY
NEAPOLITAN ART

THIS COLLECTION of paintings
and sculpture also displays
pieces that are significant from
both an artistic and historical
standpoint. The collection
consists of purchases made
by the Italian government but
owes its strength primarily to
donations of important private
Neapolitan collections.

All the schools of painting
that flourished in this area
during the 19th century are
represented here. A recurring
theme was the Campania
landscape, a favourite with
local artists. The paintings
usually depict a serene and
beautiful landscape, such as
in Giacinto Gigante's
*Panorama of Naples Viewed
from the Conocchia*. Among
the pieces of sculpture, those
by Vincenzo Gemito are not
to be missed. *Il Malatiello*
(The Sick Child) and *Testa
della Popolana* (Head of a
Peasant Woman) portray the
expressive intensity characteristic of this artist's work.

THE QUARTO DEL
PRIORE

The prior, the only person
who was allowed contact
with the outside world,
governed the life of the
monastery from his apart-
ments. This was a fabulous
residence, rich with artistic
treasures and opening onto
lush gardens overlooking
Naples and the sea.

Built in the 17th century
and enlarged the following
century, the luxurious
quarters have undergone
scrupulous restoration.
Originally, this part of the
complex was used to exhibit
the rich art collection of the
Carthusian monks. Following
the restoration, an attempt

**Triptych by Jean Burdichon (c.1414) in the art
gallery of the Quarto del Priore**

has been made to recreate
the Quarto del Priore as it
was when inhabited by the
prior, with paintings, sculpture, fabric and furniture
adorning the rooms.

The art collection
and high-quality
furnishings reflect
the refinement
and great artistic
sensitivity of the
Carthusian monks
as well as their
ability to keep
abreast of the
latest artistic and
architectural
developments.

With its stunning decor,
works of art and sculpture
and spectacular panoramic
views over the city, the
Quarto del Priore is one of
the highlights of a visit to
the Certosa di San Martino.

The Borgo Marinaro and Castel dell'O

Sights at a Glance

Historic Buildings
Castel dell'Ovo **2**

Historic Streets and Sites
Lungomare **3**
Mergellina **11**
Piazza dei Martiri **4**
Santa Lucia **1**

Museums and Galleries
Museo Diego Aragona Pignatelli
    Cortes and Museo delle
    Carrozze in Villa Pignatelli **7**

Churches
Santa Maria del Parto **12**
Santa Maria di
    Piedigrotta **9**
Santa Maria in Portico **8**

Parks and Gardens
Parco Virgiliano **10**
Villa Comunale **5**

Aquarium
Stazione Zoologica **6**

CASTEL DELL'OVO AND CHIAIA

THE CHIAIA AREA grew to its present extent in the 19th century, although there had been buildings along the seafront outside the city walls since the 16th century. In the late 18th century the construction of the Villa Reale (now called the Villa Comunale) along the Riviera di Chiaia changed the face of this part of Naples.

In the meantime, the city was becoming popular with tourists: 8,000 per year were reported by 1838, which is a significant number of

Decorative detail in the Stazione Zoologica

visitors for that time. In the second half of the 19th century, the development of the Amedeo quarter and the elegant streets that radiate from Piazza Amedeo made this the favourite residential area of the upper middle class. The Chiaia area also bears traces of the distant past: Castel dell'Ovo, the fortress jutting into the sea in front of Santa Lucia, and the oldest castle in Naples, and the Parco Virgiliano in Mergellina, said to be the place where the Roman poet Virgil was buried.

GETTING THERE

The fastest way to get to this area is by metro (Mergellina station for Mergellina and the seafront area; Piazza Amedeo station for the Chiaia area). The funicular from the Parco Margarita station takes you from Chiaia to Vomero, while

the Mergellina funicular takes you from Mergellina to Via Manzoni. The R3 bus route, tram 1 and bus 140 run along the Riviera di Chiaia and skirt the Villa Comunale. The circular bus routes C24, C25 and C28 link the whole area.

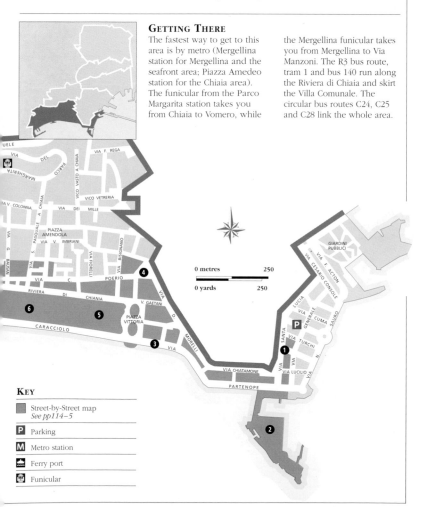

KEY

▨	Street-by-Street map *See pp114–5*
P	Parking
M	Metro station
⛴	Ferry port
🚠	Funicular

Street-by-Street: Lungomare

BESIDES BEING a pleasant way of spending the time, walking along the seafront is a tradition handed down over generations of Neapolitans. However, the sea is not just something to look at here: in the summer, despite the many "no bathing" signs, it is filled with bathers and every day of the year huge quantities of fish are sold on the seafront and in Mergellina, and served in the many neighbouring restaurants. At the Villa Comunale you can combine a walk in the park with a visit to Europe's oldest aquarium. Nearby Villa Pignatelli has stupendous rooms with 19th-century furnishing and decoration.

San Pasquale was built for Charles III in 1749, on the occasion of the birth of his first son.

Villa Comunale
The kiosk, known as the Cassa Armonica or sound box, was built in the gardens during the 19th-century restoration of the villa ❺

Palazzo Pignatelli

VIA RIVIERA DI CHIAIA

VIA FRANCESCO CARACCIOLO

Stazione Zoologica
This aquarium was founded in 1872 as a centre for marine studies ❻

Santa Maria in Portico
The church is built on a Latin cross plan with one nave and its dome is covered with multi-coloured tiles ❽

KEY

- - - - -   Suggested route

0 metres   200

0 yards   200

★ Villa Pignatelli
Originally called Villa Acton, this house was modelled on an ancient Pompeiian design, with the side facing the sea consisting of a loggia supported by Doric columns ❼

Santa Lucia
There are shrines all over Naples, such as this one in Via Santa Lucia, dedicated to St Lucy ❶

LOCATOR MAP
See Street Finder, maps 5–7

Borgo Marinaro is a characteristically lively place to wander around, with its small harbour, cafés and trattorias.

Piazza dei Martiri
The lovely façade of Palazzo Calabritto enlivens this popular square ❹

★ **Castel dell'Ovo**
The unmistakable bulk of the castle dominates the surrounding area ❷

STAR SIGHTS

★ **Castel dell'Ovo**

★ **Lungomare**

★ **Villa Pignatelli**

★ **Lungomare**
This column, taken from a building in Via Anticaglia (see p84), is dedicated to those who died at sea ❸

Santa Lucia ❶

Map 7 A4. 🚌 *C25, 140.*

ONE OF the most famous streets in Naples, Santa Lucia exemplifies the city's striking contrasts. Luxury hotels that were built for the elite in the 19th century and imposing buildings for the regional government rub shoulders with the Pallonetto di Santa Lucia slum area where the poor eke out a living. This quarter is named after the church at the beginning of the street, Santa Lucia a Mare, whose history goes back to the 9th century. It has been rebuilt several times. Before you reach the seafront, on the right, you will see the tall rocky face of the hill of Pizzofalcone, the site of the oldest part of Naples *(see p59).*

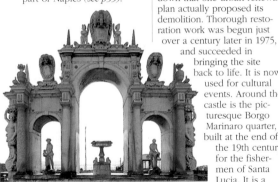

The Immacolatella Fountain

Castel dell'Ovo ❷

Borgo Marinaro. **Map** 7 A5.
📞 *081 41 50 02.* 🚌 *C25, 140.*

THE OLDEST CASTLE in Naples is built on the islet of Megaris, once the site of a villa belonging to the Roman patrician Lucullus. Later, in the 5th century, a community of monks founded the San Salvatore monastery, the only remaining part of which is the church. The oldest part of the castle dates from the 9th century. Under the Norman, Hohenstaufen, Angevin and Aragonese rulers, the castle underwent continuous changes according to the requirements of each dynasty. The present appearance is the result of the rebuilding carried out after 1503, the year the fortress was almost destroyed during a siege by Ferdinand II of Spain.

Despite the rebuilding, there followed a period of decline that lasted until 1871, at which point the castle was so run-down that one urban renewal plan actually proposed its demolition. Thorough restoration work was begun just over a century later in 1975, and succeeded in bringing the site back to life. It is now used for cultural events. Around the castle is the picturesque Borgo Marinaro quarter, built at the end of the 19th century for the fishermen of Santa Lucia. It is a popular place with visitors because of its restaurants, cafés and lively atmosphere.

Castel dell'Ovo with its tall tufa curtain walls

Lungomare ❸

Maps 5 & 6.
🚌 *C25, 140.* 🚇 *1.*

A WALK ALONG the road skirting the coast from Santa Lucia to Mergellina is another experience you must not miss while in Naples. The view of the city and the bay is breathtaking. The first stretch of the seafront – which corresponds to Via Nazario Sauro and Via Partenope – was built in the 19th century, as a result of reclamation along Via Santa Lucia and Via Chiatamone. The two ends of this long and pleasant seafront promenade are marked by two beautiful 17th-century fountains: the Immacolatella, which was built by Michelangelo Naccherino and Pietro Bernini in 1601, and the Sebeto fountain, which was the work of Cosimo Fanzago (1635–7).

THE LEGEND OF THE EGG

Opinions vary as to the origin of the curious name given to Castel dell'Ovo, or Castle of the Egg, which first appears in 14th-century documents. One possible explanation is the shape of the castle. However, popular tradition has it that the name derives from a magic egg hidden in the castle which determined its fate and that of the entire city: as long as the egg remained intact, both would be protected from catastrophes. The magic spell was supposed to have been originally cast on the ancient egg by the Latin poet Virgil, who, according to medieval legends, possessed supernatural powers and the gift of divination.

The castle in the 1800s

Piazza dei Martiri **❹**

Map 6 F2. 🚌 *C25.*

T HE SQUARE OF MARTYRS is the heart of the "chic" commercial centre of Naples. Its focal point is the Monumento ai Martiri Napoletani designed by Enrico Alvino in 1866–8, with four lions at the base symbolizing the anti-Bourbon uprisings of 1799, 1820, 1848 and 1860. Palazzo Calabritto (No. 30), built by Luigi and Carlo Vanvitelli, dominates the square on the seaward side.

Along the streets that radiate from the square, historic palazzi alternate with elegant shops and cafés. Palazzo Portanna (No. 58), built in the 18th century by Mario Gioffredo, was rebuilt by Antonio Niccolini for Lucia Migliaccio, the morganatic wife of Ferdinand IV. Among the Neo-Renaissance and Liberty style buildings along Via Filangieri and Via dei Mille, Palazzo Mannajuolo (No. 36 Via Filangieri) is worth seeing for its beautiful inner staircase. In nearby Via Poerio and Via San Pasquale are the Lutheran and Anglican churches, founded in 1861–2.

19th-century statue at the Villa entrance

Villa Comunale **❺**

Map 6 E2. 🚌 *C18, C19, C24, C28, R3, 140.* 🚋 *1.*

T HE FIRST DESIGN for this park area dates from 1697, during the rule of viceroy Luis de la Cerda, but it was Ferdinand IV who, almost a century later, asked architect Carlo Vanvitelli and landscape gardener Felice Abate to lay out the Real Passeggio di Chiaia as a public park.

The Villa Reale, later the Villa Comunale, was completed in 1781, and was enlarged in the following century. Among the pine, monkey puzzle, palm and eucalyptus trees there are 19th- and early 20th-century sculptures and several fountains, including the so-called *Paparelle,* which in 1825 replaced the famous *Farnese Bull* sculpture group, which is now in the Museo Archeologico *(see p86).* The park, which extends from the Riviera di Chiaia to Via Caracciolo, also boasts the Neo-Classical building occupied by the Stazione Zoologica and the iron and glass kiosk known as the Cassa Armonica, designed in 1877 by Enrico Alvino. Of the many pavilions planned for the park in the 19th-century restoration, this was the only one built.

Façade of the Stazione Zoologica

Stazione Zoologica **❻**

Villa Comunale. **Map** 6 E2. 📞 *081 583 32 63.* 🚌 *C18, C19, C24, C28, R3, 140.* 🚋 *1.* 🕐 *Nov–Feb: 9am–7pm Tue–Sat; 9am–2pm Sun; Mar–Oct: 9am–6pm Tue–Sat; 9:30am–7:30pm Sun.* 🌐

T HIS INSTITUTE, run by the Consiglio Nazionale delle Ricerche (National Research Council), is one of the oldest and best known of its kind in the world. It was established in 1872–4 by the German scientist Anton Dohrn to study marine environments. The building, designed by Adolf von Hildebrandt, was enlarged and remodelled in 1888, 1904 and again in 1957. It contains research labs, a small exhibition and the oldest aquarium in Europe, with specimens from the Bay of Naples. The frescoes of marine and rural scenes in the reading room of the library were painted by Hans von Marées in 1873.

The park area of Villa Comunale with the Riviera di Chiaia along the seafront

Museo Diego Aragona Pignatelli Cortes and Museo delle Carrozze in Villa Pignatelli **❼**

Riviera di Chiaia 200. **Map** 6 D2.
📞 081 761 23 56. 🚌 C18, C19, C28, R3, 140. 🚋 1. 🕐 9am–2pm Tue–Sun. 🚫 ♿

THE NEO-CLASSICAL villa was built in 1826 by Pietro Valente for the illustrious Acton family. The Rothschilds became the new owners 20 years later and changed the furnishings and interior decoration. Prince Diego Aragona Pignatelli Cortes then purchased the villa, which is named after him, and in 1952 his granddaughter donated it to the Italian state. The loveliest rooms are the red hall in Louis XVI style, the smoking room with leather-lined walls and the ballroom with its large, elegant mirrors and magnificent chandeliers. Villa Pignatelli is often used for temporary exhibitions, concerts and other cultural events. A small building nearby is occupied by the **Museo delle Carrozze** (Carriage Museum), which has an interesting collection of Italian and French coaches dating from the late 1800s to the early 1900s.

Presbytery and apse of the Chiesa dell'Ascensione a Chiaia

Santa Maria in Portico **❽**

Via Giuseppe Martucci 17. **Map** 6 D2. 📞 081 66 92 94. 🚌 C18, C19, C28, R3, 140. 🚋 1. Ⓜ Amedeo. 🚗 Chiaia: Parco Margherita. 🕐 8–11am, 5–7pm Mon–Sat; 6–8pm Sun. ✝

IN 1632 THE DUCHESS of Gravina Felice Maria Orsini donated some of her property to the Padri Lucchesi della Madre di Dio congregation so they could build a monastery and church. The name "in Portico" refers to the Roman church of Santa Maria in Campitelli al Portico d'Ottavia, where the Lucca Fathers came from. For years the façade in piperno was attributed to Cosimo Fanzago, but is now known to be the work of Arcangelo Guglielminelli. The interior is decorated with fine 18th-century canvases and stuccoes by Domenico Antonio Vaccaro, who also designed the high altar. There is a crib with 17th-century figures in the sacristy. A short walk down nearby Via Piscicelli takes you to the **Chiesa dell'Ascensione a Chiaia**, with fine paintings by Luca Giordano. The 14th-century church was rebuilt in the 1600s by Cosimo Fanzago.

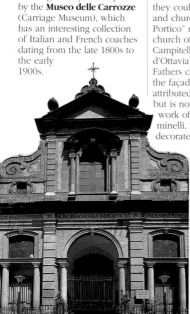

The façade of Santa Maria in Portico

Santa Maria di Piedigrotta **❾**

Piazza Piedigrotta 24. **Map** 5 B3. 📞 081 66 97 61. 🚌 C16, C24. 🚋 1. Ⓜ Mergellina. 🕐 7am–noon, 5:30–8pm Mon–Sat; 7am–1:30pm, 5:30–8pm Sun. ✝

THIS CHURCH is mentioned in a letter written by Giovanni Boccaccio in Neapolitan dialect in 1339, in which he mentions the "Madonna de Pederotta". Much altered over the years, Santa Maria di Piedigrotta is commonly believed to have been rebuilt in 1353 to replace a church founded in 1207. It was again rebuilt in the mid-1400s and in the early 1500s. The orientation of the church, which had faced the "grotta" (cave), was altered the following century.

Fresco by Belisario Corenzio in Santa Maria di Piedigrotta

The present façade is the result of 19th-century restoration by Enrico Alvino. Gaetano Gigante decorated the vault. Inside is the 15th-century wooden panel *Descent from the Cross*, by an unknown Neapolitan artist.

The church's great popularity is linked to a beautiful 14th-century wooden sculpture of the *Madonna and Child*, made by the Siena School, which dominates the church from a high tabernacle. The worship of the Piedigrotta Madonna culminates in the 7 September feast (see p42). In the past, even the royal family took part in the solemn procession. Worshippers did not appreciate the statue's restoration in 1976 to its original state, because the Virgin's large blue mantle and luminous halo were removed.

Parco Virgiliano ❿

Via Salita Grotta 20. **Map** 5 A2.
☎ 081 66 93 90. 🚌 C16, C24. 🚇 1.
Ⓜ Mergellina. ◐ 8am–1:30pm daily.

View of the Parco Virgiliano

MYTH, LEGEND, traces of the past and natural beauty are what make this park one of Naples's most intriguing sites. It officially became a park after restoration work in 1930. In 1939 a monument to the poet Giacomo Leopardi was erected, and his remains were transferred here from Recanati, his home town.

The park is famous mostly because, according to legend, the poet Virgil is buried here. However, the so-called Tomb of Virgil is in fact an anonymous Roman funerary monument and has nothing to do with the great poet.

Another legend involving Virgil is that with a single gesture he created the *Crypta Neapolitana*, a tunnel about 700 m (2,300 ft) long; but this too is belied by historical facts: it was built by the Roman architect Cocceius in the 1st century BC to connect Neapolis and Puteoli. In the 1920s the tunnel caved in and is now inaccessible. The entrance, however, with its medieval frescoes and epigraphs, can still be seen from the park.

Mergellina ⓫

Map 5 B4. 🚌 C16, C21, C24. 🚇 1.
Ⓜ Mergellina.

THE FISHERMEN'S quarter that developed over the inlet at the foot of Posillipo hill, and was hailed by poets and writers for its beauty, was a popular place for pleasure trips from the Angevin age on. The harmony of the landscape was broken by 19th-century land reclamation that extended the coastline further into the sea. However, Mergellina is still enjoyable to walk around. The numerous cafés, called *chalet* by the locals, offer excellent ice cream and fresh fruit.

St Michael and the "Mergellina devil"

Hydrofoil boats for the islands and other destinations in the bay depart from the quays in the harbour.

Santa Maria del Parto ⓬

Via Mergellina 21. **Map** 6 B4.
☎ 081 66 46 27. 🚌 C16, C24.
🚇 1. Ⓜ Mergellina. ◐ by appt only. 🔔

THE HISTORY of the church of Santa Maria del Parto is closely linked with the figure and works of Jacopo Sannazaro (1458–1530), the famous Neapolitan humanist and poet in the service of the Angevin court. The church was built in the 1520s, upon the initiative of Sannazaro, on a plot of land donated by Frederick of Aragon and was named after one of the poet's works, *De Partu Virginis*. Behind the high altar is the tomb of the poet himself, a fine marble group sculpted by Giovan Angelo Montorsoli and Francesco del Tadda in 1537, and probably designed by Sannazaro himself. Before leaving, don't forget to look at the "Mergellina devil" depicted in a wooden panel by Leonardo da Pistoia on the right-hand altar. The panel shows St Michael, who has just vanquished the devil – the devil has assumed the guise of a beautiful woman.

The small harbour of Mergellina, filled with fishing boats and pleasure craft

DIRECTORY

Bagno Elena
Via Posillipo 14.
081 575 35 20.

Bagno Ideal
Via Posillipo 18.
081 575 36 17.

Bagno Sirena
Via Posillipo 357.
081 575 12 55.

Bagno Rocce Verdi
Via Posillipo 68.
081 575 67 16.

Bagno Marechiaro
Discesa Marechiaro.
081 769 12 15.

Marechiaro
*The original name for the water by this fishing village was
Mare planum (calm sea), which was translated literally in
Italian as "Marepiano". With usage it became "Marechiaro",
the name now used for the area as a whole. At weekends
Neapolitans love to come and eat out here (see p184).*

Church of Santa
Maria del Faro

Marinella Beach, with
its parks and lido, is
one of the area's most
popular resorts.

Palazzo degli Spiriti
*The remains of the "palace
of the spirits" are visible only
from the sea. This name was
given to the three-storey
Roman ruins because of
their mysterious appearance.*

SWIMMING AND RELAXING

If sightseeing in Naples in midsummer becomes too much,
take a break at one of the *stabilimenti balneari* (bathing
spots) along the Posillipo coast. Rent a deckchair and an
umbrella and swim in the sea or the pool provided.
Neapolitans started the habit in the 19th century at the
Bagno Elena, first opened 150 years ago. A short distance
away are the **Bagno Ideal** and the **Bagno Sirena**. For those
who prefer cliffs to sand, there are the **Bagno Rocce Verdi**,
with two seawater pools, and **Bagno Marechiaro** *(see p178)*,
with its restaurant overlooking the waters of the bay.

The rocks at Posillipo

POMPEII & THE AMALFI COAST

POMPEII & THE AMALFI COAST

TO THE NORTH OF NAPLES *fertile plains sweep down to the town of Santa Maria Capua Vetere, home to one of the largest remaining Roman amphitheatres in Italy. The remote hinterland to the east is wild, mountainous and lonely country. To the south is the breathtaking Amalfi coast and the dramatic seaboard of the Cilento. Buried Roman towns and Greek ruins reveal the region's ancient history.*

From the 17th century onwards Naples was an increasingly crowded and often tormented metropolis. By contrast, the countryside around the city managed to retain its charm and attracted visitors, especially foreigners, many of whom made Campania their home. "A brief sojourn in Naples", the German historian Gregorovius wrote in the mid-1800s, "is enough to demonstrate that not all life is concentrated in the city but flows mightily into the surroundings".

Today, a visit to Pompeii, buried by an erupting Vesuvius in AD 79, is a high priority for tourists, but this was not always so. Travellers on the Grand Tour in the 1600s and early 1700s preferred the volcanic phenomena of the Solfatara crater and the Phlegraean Fields to the west of Naples. Even in the late 18th century Goethe described the area around Paestum, southeast of Naples, as "anything but picturesque", populated by "buffaloes that look like hippopotami, with wild, bloodshot eyes". Only when the first archaeological digs unearthed the remains of Paestum and the buried cities around Mount Vesuvius, did a tour of the ancient ruins become popular.

The beautiful colour, light and atmosphere found on the islands of Capri and Ischia, and the Sorrento peninsula began to interest landscape painters in the 19th century. The southern flank of the peninsula – the Amalfi coast – remained isolated, and regarded by many as barren, until the mid-1960s, when it attracted visitors in search of an alternative, remote lifestyle. Ironically, the Amalfi coast has since become a very popular holiday area.

Paestum, south of Naples; in the background are the temples of Neptune and Hera

◁ The fishing harbour of Corricella on the island of Procida

Exploring the Coast

THE MAIN CENTRE from which to explore Campania is Naples itself, well situated in the middle of the bay. Road and rail links are generally good in the region, with both state railways (FS) and privately run lines serving a variety of destinations. The Circumvesuviana railway connects all the sights in the area of Vesuvius, including Pompeii. The three islands in the bay are accessible by hydrofoil (half an hour's journey) and by ferry (one hour) from Mergellina. Connections are also possible from Sorrento, Positano, Amalfi and Salerno.

Castello Aragonese in Ischia

SIGHTS AT A GLANCE

The Solfatara at Pozzuoli

SEE ALSO

• **Where to Stay** pp170–71

• **Where to Eat** pp178–89

• **Shopping in Campania** pp194–5

0 kilometres   20

0 miles   20

View of the Phlegraean Fields at Cumae

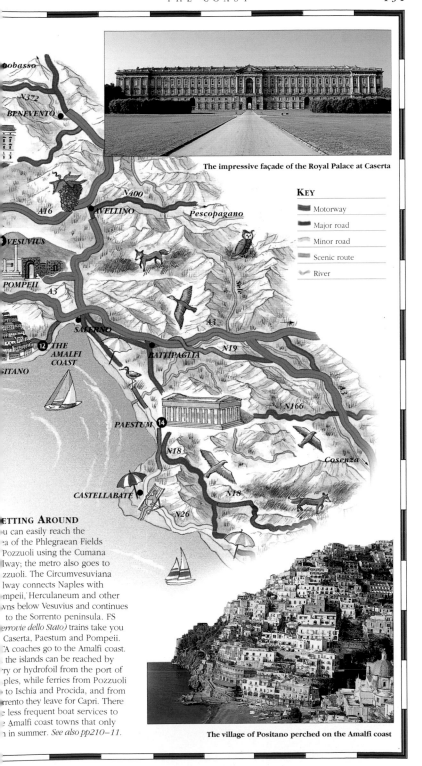

The impressive façade of the Royal Palace at Caserta

KEY

▬	Motorway
▬	Major road
▬	Minor road
▬	Scenic route
〰	River

Molobasso

N372

BENEVENTO

A16

N400

AVELLINO *Pescopagano*

VESUVIUS

POMPEII

A3

SALERNO

⑫ **THE AMALFI COAST**

ITANO

BATTIPAGLIA

N19

A3

N166

PAESTUM ⑭

Cosenza

N18

CASTELLABATE

N18

N26

ETTING AROUND

ou can easily reach the
ea of the Phlegraean Fields
 Pozzuoli using the Cumana
lway; the metro also goes to
zzuoli. The Circumvesuviana
lway connects Naples with
mpeii, Herculaneum and other
wns below Vesuvius and continues
 to the Sorrento peninsula. FS
errovie dello Stato) trains take you
 Caserta, Paestum and Pompeii.
A coaches go to the Amalfi coast.
 the islands can be reached by
ry or hydrofoil from the port of
ples, while ferries from Pozzuoli
 to Ischia and Procida, and from
rrento they leave for Capri. There
 less frequent boat services to
 Amalfi coast towns that only
 in summer. *See also pp210–11.*

The village of Positano perched on the Amalfi coast

Bagnoli ❶

Road map C3. *C1, F9. Cavalleggeri Aosta. Cumana: Bagnoli.*

The area west of Naples, beyond Posillipo, is called "de' Bagnoli" because of the fumaroles and hot springs there. In 1907 the ILVA steelworks was built here *(see pp24–5)*, blighting a beautiful natural setting. The factory has since been closed down. Today part of the site is taken up with the **Città della Scienza** (Science City), first opened in 1996. A series of itineraries features education through games involving science, aimed at both children and adults.

Città della Scienza

Via Coroglio 104. *081 570 17 60. 9am–7pm Tue–Sun (Oct–Mar: until 5pm).*

Pozzuoli ❷

Road Map *C3. 77,000. Azienda Autonoma di Soggiorno e Turismo, Via Campi Flegrei 3. 081 526 14 81/24 19; Via Matteotti 1. 081 526 66 39/ 50 68. Cumana: Pozzuoli. to Ischia & Procida.*

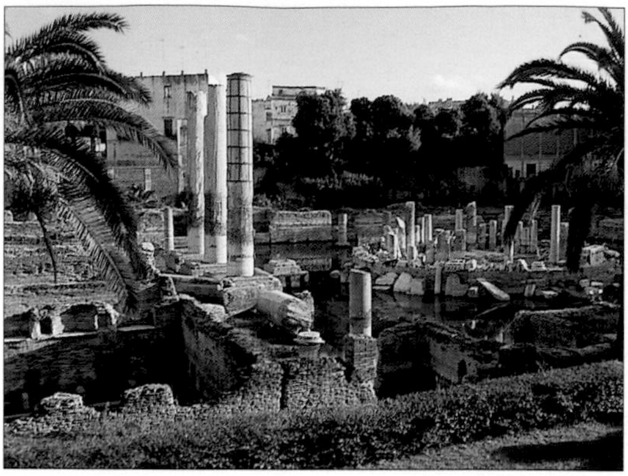

The *macellum* at Pozzuoli, commonly known as the Temple of Serapis

Around the 7th century BC, the Greek colony of Dicearchia was founded on this site overlooking the port. By 194 BC Roman Puteoli was a flourishing trade centre with luxurious villas. The town later became the Rione Terra quarter. Abandoned in 1971 because of the underground volcanic activity that has always affected Pozzuoli, the place is now under restoration.

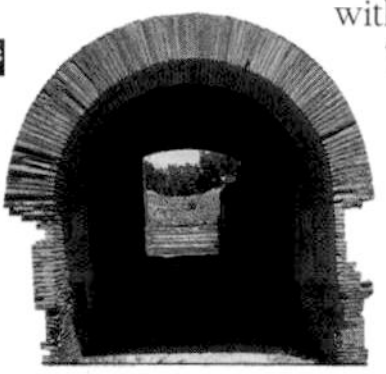

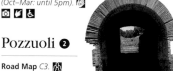

The amphitheatre stage entrance

A Roman temple can still be seen under the San Procolo cathedral. The amphitheatre, one of the most ancient in Italy, shows how important the city once was.

Anfiteatro Grande

Via Terracciano 75. *081 526 23 41. 9am–4pm daily.*

The amphitheatre had a seating capacity of 40,000. The underground area was used for the caged animals and the equipment to lift them up to the arena, as well as a sophisticated drainage system to collect rainwater.

Temple of Serapis

Piazza Serapide. *081 44 01 66. daily.*

The so-called Temple of Serapis (2nd century AD),

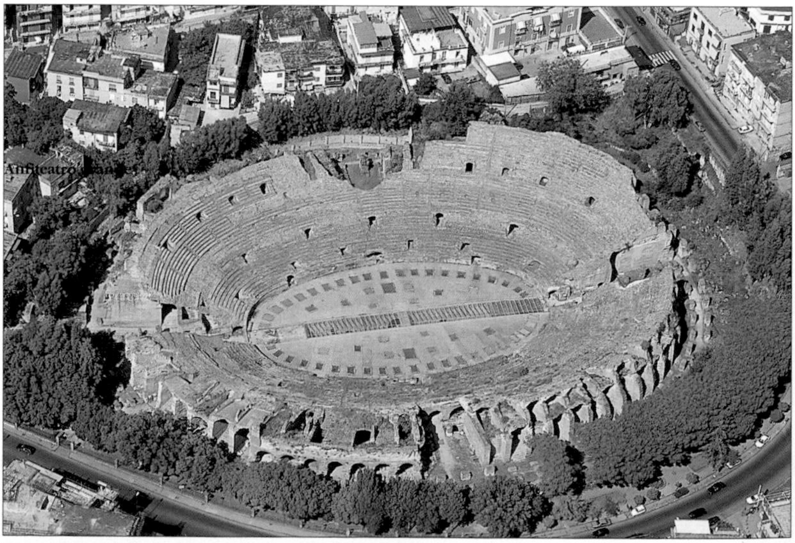

The Anfiteatro Grande at Pozzuoli, with three tiers of seats

The Solfatara in Pozzuoli, known as _Forum Vulcani_ in ancient times

actually the *macellum* or food market, is all that remains of the ancient port district.

🔥 Solfatara

Via Solfatara 161. [081 526 23 41.
⏰ 8:30am–1 hr before sunset daily. 🅿️

This volcanic crater was an obligatory stop for those making the Grand Tour. It is now dormant, but you can see phenomena created by the still molten underground magma and water seepage: fumaroles and sulphur fumes.

🐾 Riserva degli Astroni Oasi WWF

Bypass (tangenziale; 1 km from Agnano exit). [081 588 37 20.
⏰ 10am–2pm. 🅿️ holidays & holiday eves; groups by appt.

This wildlife reserve lies in an extinct crater covered with trees. It was once an Aragonese hunting ground.

Baia and Bacoli ❸

Road Map B3. 🏘️ 27,000.
🚉 Cumana: Baia, Bacoli.

A LONG THE COAST between Pozzuoli and Capo Miseno there are many places that were well-known in antiquity. Baia boasted sumptuous Roman villas with terraces overlooking the sea, famous therapeutic springs (still in use in the Middle Ages) and an Aragonese castle, now an archaeological museum.

Bacoli lies along the coast and runs into the modern town of Miseno, which developed over the site of the Roman town of Bauli. At the time of the Emperor Augustus the port of Miseno was connected to Lake Miseno in the interior. The port was

The Bath of Mercury at Baia

planned so as to avoid silting from volcanic movement, and replaced Porto Giulio *(see p135)*, the headquarters of the Roman navy. The Arco Felice, which in the 1st century AD was the gateway to Cumae *(see pp134–5)*, stands on the peninsula protecting the Bay of Pozzuoli.

Beaches and clubs make this area a summer favourite.

🏛️ Casino Vanvitelliano del Fusaro

Via Fusaro 162, Baia. [081 868 70 80. 🚉 Cumana: Baia.
⏰ 8am–8pm.

In 1794 Vanvitelli built a Casino or hunting lodge on an island in Lake Fusaro for Ferdinand IV. This is the only non-volcanic lake in the area.

⛪ Parco Archeologico di Baia

Via Fusaro 35, Baia. [081 868 75 92. 🚉 Cumana: Baia. ⏰ 9am–1 hr before sunset. 🅿️

The large domes at this archaeological site were once thought to be temples, but are now known to be the remains of a spa that included baths named after Venus and Mercury and the so-called Temple of Diana.

This monumental complex was built from the late 2nd century–early 1st century BC, on two levels, with terraced land descending to the sea.

The site is now used to exhibit excavation finds from the Phlegraean Fields area.

🏛️ Museo Archeologico dei Campi Flegrei

Via Castello, Baia. [081 523 37 97. 🚉 Cumana: Baia. ⏰ 9am–1 hr before sunset. 🚫 Mon. 🅿️

The Castello di Baia was once an Aragonese fortress.

View of the city of Baia; in the foreground, the Roman ruins

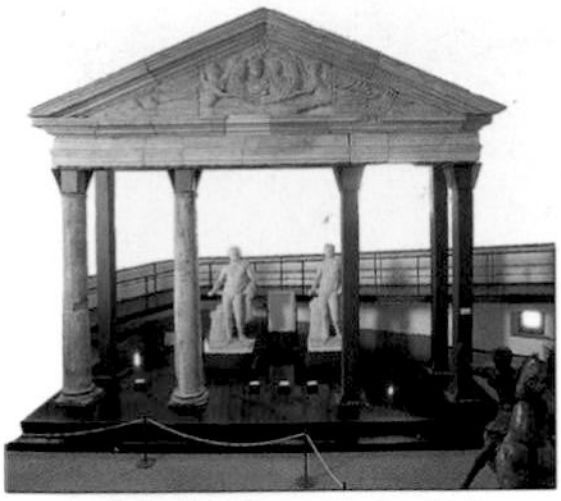

Hall in the Museo Archeologico

It was totally rebuilt in the 1600s and then used as an orphanage from 1927 to 1975. It is now an Archaeological Museum, with finds from the Phlegraean Fields *(Campi Flegrei)*. Also on display are the Roman plaster casts of Greek statues found in Baia. From the northwest tower you can see the reconstructed Sacello degli Augustali, used for worship of the emperor, found near the Forum at Miseno. The zone is now partly under water.

Piscina Mirabilis

Via A Greco, Bacoli. 9am–1 hr before sunset. for inquiries: custodian Ida Basile.

This enormous reservoir, divided into five longitudinal sections supported by pillars, collected water brought by Roman aqueduct from the River Serino, then supplied to the fleet stationed at Miseno.

Cento Camerelle

Via Cento Camerelle 165, Bacoli. for inquiries: custodian Scotto di Vetta. 081 523 36 90.

The tunnels dug out of the tufa contained a series of cisterns placed at different levels. They originally supplied a villa dating back to the Republican era.

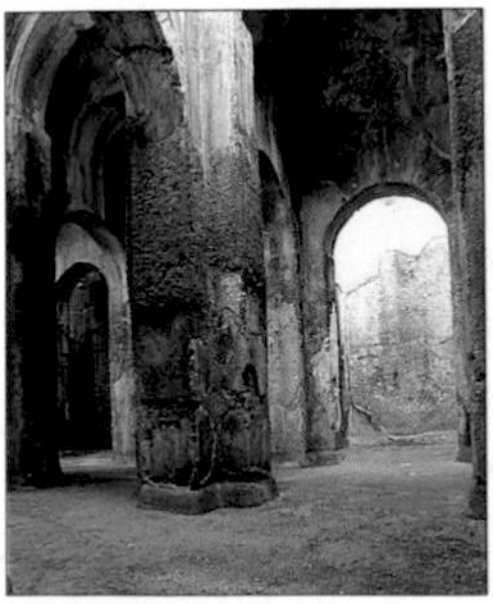

The *Piscina Mirabilis* at Bacoli

Cumae 4

Road map B3. *Cumana: Fusaro. from Fusaro (10 mins to Cumae).*

FOUNDED IN the 8th century BC, probably by Greeks stationed on Ischia, Cumae is one of the oldest colonies of Magna Graecia. A powerful port for centuries, Cumae resisted the Etruscans but succumbed to the Romans in the 3rd century BC and became a Roman colony. A village grew up over the ruins of the upper city in the 5th–6th centuries but was utterly destroyed by the Saracens in 915. The ancient settlement has not yet been completely excavated.

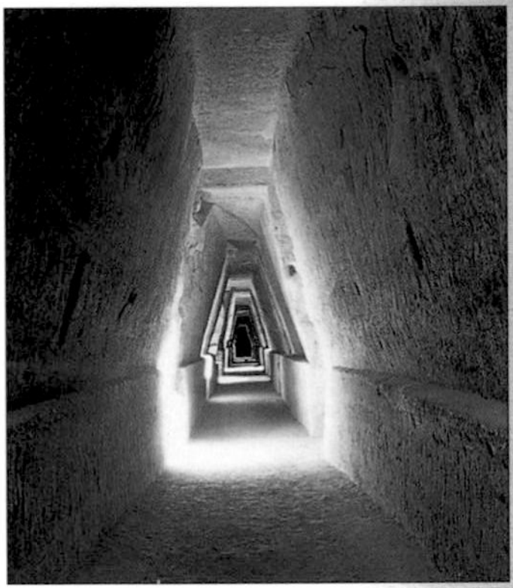

The tufa corridor in the Sibyl's Grotto

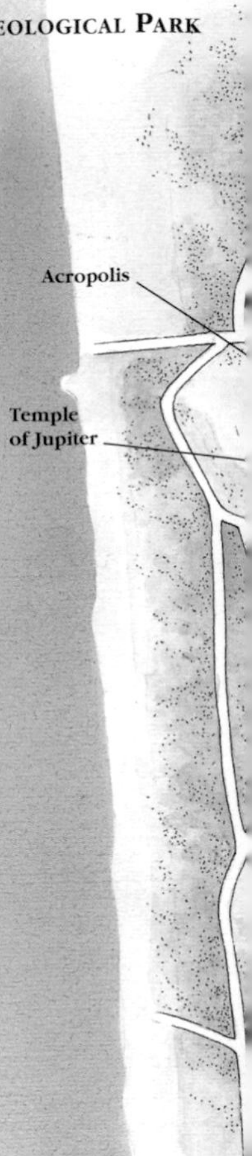

The best-known areas are the acropolis on the rise to the northwest and the necropolis in the plain. The acropolis walls, partly rebuilt, and two huge temples are well preserved. The Temple of Apollo lies on the lower terrace, the Temple of Jupiter on the upper one; both were rebuilt in the age of Augustus and the pre-Christian era. At the foot of the acropolis is the entrance to the so-called Sibyl's Grotto.

The lower city, inhabited at a later period, is still being excavated and studied. There is a forum, various baths and an amphitheatre. There are also remains of different epochs: the Samnite age forum conceals the more ancient *agora*, or Greek city centre. In recent years a sanctuary dedicated to Isis, destroyed with the rise of Christianity, has been discovered in the port area.

Archaeological Park

Via Acropoli. 081 854 30 60. 9am–1 hr before sunset.

Temple of Apollo

Most of the finds from the Temple of Apollo date from the Roman era, when a terrace overlooking the city was added on. In the early Christian period the temple was turned into a basilica and burial pits were hewn out of the ancient foundations.

The Sibyl's Grotto

According to myth this was where to find the Cumaean Sibyl, the oracle consulted by Aeneas. The tufa passageway, trapezoid in section, is illuminated by narrow

View of the Archaeological Park, the site of the excavations revealing ancient Cumae

⋔ Temple of Jupiter
This ancient sanctuary became an early Christian church and remains of the altar and baptistry are still visible today.

⋔ Roman Crypt
The part visible is the last stretch of a long tunnel that begins at Via Sacra and goes through the hill of Cumae.

THE PHLEGRAEAN LAKES

The wide arc of land around the bay of Pozzuoli has been known for centuries as the Campi Flegrei, or Burning Fields, because of the constant volcanic activity. Mud still bubbles from the clay bed of the Solfatara and in places the ground is still hot. Over time some of the Phlegraean craters have become lakes. **Lake Averno**, in ancient times thought to be the entrance to hell, owes its name (*a-ornon* in Greek: "without birds") to the once-suffocating vapours. At the end of the 1st century BC, its almost sacred character declined after the construction of Porto Giulio, a system of channels that connected the sea and the lakes. Ships first reached the outer port in **Lake Lucrino** and then the inner basin of Lake Averno, connected to Cumae by the tunnel through Monte Grillo. The port was abandoned when it silted up and trade was transferred to Miseno. Lake Lucrino again became a pleasure area. Its extent was greatly reduced by the 1538 eruption that created **Monte Nuovo**.

Lake Averno

fissures and ends in a vaulted chamber. Despite its undoubted fascination, there is no proof of the tunnel ever having had a religious function. It seems more likely that the tunnel was part of a network of underground routes used for military purposes. The complex system includes the Roman crypt and the Grotto of Cocceius, which connected Cumae to Lake Averno.

Portici and the Vesuvian Villas ⑤

Road Map C3. 🏛 68,000. 🚌 *Ente Ville Vesuviane Napoli, Piazza del Plebiscito.* 📞 *081 40 53 93.* 🚉 *Circumvesuviana: Portici.* 🚌 *city buses.*

THE COAST east of the city, up to the foot of Mount Vesuvius, has always been dotted with rural estates, owned by the nobility but used for agriculture as much as rural retreats. The luxurious villas now known as the Ville Vesuviane were built in the early 1700s, when the value of land in the area rose because of the interest in the archaeological excavations around the volcano. Prince d'Elbeouf, who discovered Herculaneum in 1709, built a villa here. A few decades later, after the building of the Royal Palace at Portici, these aristocratic villas grew in number, transforming the road between Resina and Torre del Greco into what became known as the **Miglio d'Oro**, or Golden Mile. The presence of the Bourbon palace and the location of these villas, with fine views of, and often access to, the countryside and sea, made this area a favourite resort among the aristocracy. A port was built here in 1773.

Over 100 of the villas are of considerable architectural interest; unfortunately, only a few can be visited. Many are either inhabited or in a state of decay. Some are well worth a stop, if only to see the decorations on the façade or the magnificent gardens that have survived massive urbanization.

🏛 Reggia di Portici
Via Università 100, Portici. 📞 *081 775 12 51.* 🕐 *by appt.*
The Royal Palace *(reggia)* was built between 1738 and 1742 in the centre of a splendid park at the foothills of Vesuvius and overlooking the sea.

The Royal Palace in Portici

Two villas had occupied the site and a road still crosses the large inner courtyard and continues towards Herculaneum. Originally, finds from the site at Herculaneum and the other archaeological sites in the area were kept in Maria Amalia's Porcelain Parlour in the palace, but these have since been transferred to the museum at Capodimonte *(see p99).*

The palace did not have a mooring, so the sovereigns bought the Villa d'Elboeuf for this purpose. Designed by Ferdinando Sanfelice, the villa incorporates some splendid stucco-work and a magnificent circular staircase. The villa was separated from the sea by the Naples-Portici railway *(see p23)* in 1839.

In 1873, the Royal Palace and its park became the home of the Faculty of Agriculture of the University of Naples.

🏛 Villa Campolieto
Corso Resina 283, Ercolano. 📞 *081 732 21 34.* 🕐 *10am–1pm Tue–Sun.*
Built in 1755–75 first by Gioffredo and then by Vanvitelli, this is the only Vesuvian villa that has been completely restored. A monumental staircase links the ground floor and upper floor. Vanvitelli's elegant portico hosts the Festival delle Ville Vesuviane *(see p41)* each summer, and the villa sometimes hosts other events such as the *Terraemotus* modern art exhibition.

🏛 Villa Favorita
Corso Resina 291, Ercolano.
🚫 *to the public.*
This villa, set in an extensive park, was designed by Ferdinando Fuga in 1768 as a royal residence. Ferdinand IV decorated it with paintings, silk from San Leucio *(see p159)* and a mosaic removed from the Villa Jovis in Capri *(see p163).* His son Leopold supervised the layout of the park and stables. The villa was restored in 1854.

🏛 Villa Prota
Via Nazionale 1009, Torre del Greco.
🚫 *to the public.*
This is one of the most spectacular of the Vesuvian villas. Through the large portal, built with balconies and a gateway, you can see the driveway and park. The main wing was built to one side so as not to obstruct the views from the villa.

Vanvitelli's curved portico in Villa Campolieto

Torre Annunziata ❻

Road map D3. 👥 *51,000.* 🛈 *Pro Loco Ufficio Informazioni Turistiche: Via Sepolcri 16.* 📞 *081 862 31 63.* 🚉 🚇 *Circumvesuviana: Portici.*

THE TOWN WAS built over the ruins of ancient Oplontis, which was destroyed in the eruption of Vesuvius in AD 79. Its name derives from a watchtower *(torre)* built to warn the populace of any imminent Saracen raids, and a chapel consecrated to the Annunziata (the Virgin Mary), around which the town grew up.

In the 18th century Charles III founded an arms factory here, designed by a pupil of Vanvitelli and finished by Ferdinando Fuga. In the late 1700s and early 1800s Torre Annunziata became a centre for pasta production. Towards the sea are the spas, Terme Vesuviane Nunziante, named after the general who discovered the ruins of a Roman baths complex here in 1831. He was responsible for the present-day structure, which is still in operation.

🏛 Oplontis Excavations

Via Sepolcri 1. 📞 *081 862 17 55.* 🕐 *9am–1 hr before sunset daily.* 🈳

The excavation area includes the villas of Craxus and Poppaea (the latter was Nero's second wife). Brought to light in 1964, the complex reflects the elegant taste of its owners. As well as large gardens and porticoes, the private baths of the house can also be seen, complete with *calidarium* (the hot room) and *tepidarium* (the warm room). Also interesting are the 1st century BC–1st century AD wall paintings. These frescoes depict still lifes or scenes combining architecture and figures, in some cases with illusionistic effects around the doorways or windows. Many of the rooms in the Villa of Craxus were used as storerooms or shops, and many amphoras were found there.

The harbour at Torre Annunziata

Torre del Greco ❼

Road map C3. 👥 *104,000.* 🛈 *Via G Marconi 14.* 📞 *081 881 46 76.* 🚉 🚇 *Circumvesuviana: Portici.*

THE NAME DERIVES from a watch-tower built by Frederick II and from the vineyards which produce wine from a grape variety called Greco. Torre del Greco is mainly known for its fine coral manufacture. The old town, rebuilt several times after the various eruptions of Vesuvius, lines the coast, while the newer districts, with villas surrounded by gardens, lie on the slopes of the volcano itself. Don't miss Palazzo Vallelonga in Via Vittorio Emanuele and the Camaldoli alla Torre monastery, both 18th-century buildings. The poet Giacomo Leopardi lived in the Villa delle Ginestre (on a road crossing Via Nazionale) and wrote his last poems there, including *La Ginestra* (The Broom).

The imperial villa of Poppaea Sabina at Torre Annunziata

THE RED GOLD AT TORRE DEL GRECO

By the 15th century the main trade in Torre del Greco was coral fishing. Over the centuries the town became a collection point for coral, as other coastal towns followed suit. The first factories were established by foreigners during the course of the 1800s and the Bourbon rulers then set up their own. Local designs were at first inspired by classical models, and subsequently influenced by the Art Nouveau style. As well as coral, there are mother-of-pearl, turtle shell and ivory pieces. The *coralline* boats that went out to collect the coral have been modernized and re-equipped, but today most of the raw material comes from Japan. Admirers of red gold can visit the numerous workshops *(see pp194–5)* in town or the museum at No. 6 Piazza Palomba.

Carved piece of coral

Mount Vesuvius ❽

Carbonized eggs from Pompeii

IN ANCIENT TIMES Vesuvius was simply "the mountain", covered with vegetation and vines. The first person to understand its volcanic nature was the Greek geographer, Strabo (AD 19), who suggested that its rocks had been burned by fire. In AD 79 an almighty eruption smothered the cities on its foothills and greatly altered the surrounding landscape. Ash and debris showered Pompeii, and Herculaneum was buried by a landslide of thick mud. Pliny the Younger recorded the cloud of black smoke that rose "like an umbrella pine" from the mountain. His uncle, Pliny the Elder, was suffocated by the gaseous vapours that engulfed the area. Today, the volcano inspires both fear and fascination and it is constantly monitored for activity.

Layers of ash alternate with lava flow, settle on the sides of the volcano and gradually build up the cone.

Vineyards
The land around volcanoes, rich in alkali and phosphorus, is extremely fertile. On the slopes of Vesuvius, the grapes grown make Lacrima Christi, *once considered one of Italy's best wines.*

Layers of lava

HISTORY OF THE VOLCANO

These sections show the changes in the structure of Vesuvius following the most significant eruptions, from prehistoric times to the formation of the present-day cone.

First eruptions began 35,000 years ago

Further ash and lava flows built up a second cone

8th century BC: Monte Somma is a single cone

After AD 79: Monte Somma is an open caldera

Today's cone, Vesuvius, formed in the old caldera

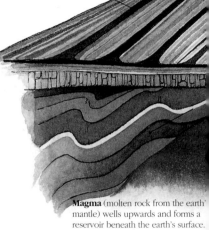

Magma (molten rock from the earth's mantle) wells upwards and forms a reservoir beneath the earth's surface.

Vesuvius Observatory
The observatory on the slopes of Vesuvius was built by Ferdinand II in 1841–5. The Neo-Classical building has a well-stocked library and an interesting collection of minerals. There is a splendid panoramic view from the square. Today it is only used as a base for recording data; the research section has been transferred to Naples.

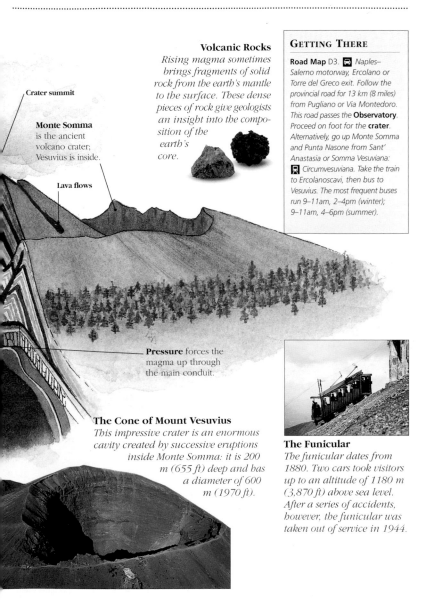

Crater summit

Monte Somma
is the ancient
volcano crater;
Vesuvius is inside.

Lava flows

Volcanic Rocks
*Rising magma sometimes
brings fragments of solid
rock from the earth's mantle
to the surface. These dense
pieces of rock give geologists
an insight into the compo-
sition of the
earth's
core.*

GETTING THERE

Road Map D3. 🚌 *Naples–
Salerno motorway, Ercolano or
Torre del Greco exit. Follow the
provincial road for 13 km (8 miles)
from Pugliano or Via Montedoro.
This road passes the* **Observatory**.
Proceed on foot for the **crater**.
*Alternatively, go up Monte Somma
and Punta Nasone from Sant'
Anastasia or Somma Vesuviana:*
🚆 *Circumvesuviana. Take the train
to Ercolanoscavi, then bus to
Vesuvius. The most frequent buses
run 9–11am, 2–4pm (winter);
9–11am, 4–6pm (summer).*

Pressure forces the
magma up through
the main conduit.

The Cone of Mount Vesuvius
*This impressive crater is an enormous
cavity created by successive eruptions
inside Monte Somma: it is 200
m (655 ft) deep and has
a diameter of 600
m (1970 ft).*

The Funicular
*The funicular dates from
1880. Two cars took visitors
up to an altitude of 1180 m
(3,870 ft) above sea level.
After a series of accidents,
however, the funicular was
taken out of service in 1944.*

TIMELINE (1600–Present day)

1694 Another
eruption, with
lava flow from
the crater

1794 Torre del
Greco destroyed

1906 Another
eruption: the crater
widens by 300 m
(985 ft)

1933 A series of
shocks shows the
volcano is active
once again. Lava
appears on 3 June

1600	1700	1800	1900

1631 On 16 December
the lava claims 600
victims. Naples is saved
and thanks San Gennaro
by building the Guglia in
Piazza Sforza (*see p62*)

1767 The lava
reaches San
Giorgio a
Cremano and
approaches
Naples

1880 The
funicular
opens to
public

1944 After a
final violent
explosion, the
trail of smoke
disappears

Herculaneum 9

Silver disc of Apollo

ANCIENT HERAKLEION fell under Greek influence around the 5th century BC and then under Samnite rule. In 89 BC the town became part of the Roman Empire, a residential *municipium* and resort. The town's quiet existence was brought to an abrupt halt in AD 79, when the eruption of Vesuvius that buried Pompeii covered Herculaneum with a deep layer of lava and mud.

Excavations began in the 18th century, and uncovered Roman houses built around a rectangular plan. Perhaps the best known is the Villa dei Papiri, the inspiration for the J Paul Getty museum in Malibu, Los Angeles. Sculptures found in the villa are now in the Museo Archeologico Nazionale *(see pp86–9)*.

The city baths, built in 10 BC, are divided into two sections. The one for men is larger and decorated, and includes a gymnasium; the women's section is smaller and better preserved.

Decumanus Maximus

★ **Trellis House**
A characteristic example of an inexpensive Roman multi-family dwelling, the Trellis House has wood and reed laths in the crude tufa and lime masonry.

House with the Mosaic Atrium
This house has a famous mosaic floor with geometric patterns, as well as living rooms, and a portico and terrace facing the sea.

0 metres 50
0 yards 50

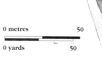

★ **House of the Stags**
The name derives from the beautiful sculpture groups of stags found here. The house is one of the more elaborate: the inner porticoed garden connects the northern section (entrance, indoor triclinium and smaller rooms) to the southern side, which has bedrooms and an arbour with a sea view.

★ House of the Neptune and Amphitrite Mosaic

This mosaic is in the summer dining room. The building and a shop, with wooden shelves for amphoras, are among the best preserved.

VISITORS' CHECKLIST

Road Map C3. 🚇 Portici-Ercolano. 🚋 Circumvesuviana: Ercolano-Scavi. **Digs**: Piazza Museo. 🄲 081 739 09 63. ⏰ 8:30am–3:30pm. 📷

Entrance

House of the Bicentenary
This patrician residence, excavated 200 years after digging began, had mosaic floors and wall paintings.

Decumanus Inferiore

STAR SIGHTS

★ House of the Neptune and Amphitrite Mosaic

★ House of the Stags

★ Trellis House

The Excavation Area

The site of ancient Herculaneum is well below the level of the modern town. The area is still being excavated and some buildings, like the Villa dei Papiri, northwest of the site, remain underground.

The House of Telephus contains a 1st-century BC relief narrating the myth of Achilles and Telephus.

The House of the Gem is named after a cameo portrait from the era of Claudius that was found here.

Pompeii ⑩

AN EARTHQUAKE in AD 62, which shook Pompeii and damaged some of its buildings, was merely a prelude to the tragic day in AD 79, when Vesuvius erupted, engulfing the city and its inhabitants with a terrible storm of cinders and ash. When the remains of Pompeii were discovered around 1750 it looked as though a spell had been cast to freeze all life. The bodies of people were unearthed along with their houses, temples, works of art and everyday objects. The first archaeologists removed the most important finds, which became part of the royal collection and were then transferred to the Museo Archeologico Nazionale *(see pp86–9)*.

"Samovar" from Pompeii

The House of the Golden Cupids *(see pp146–7)* is named after the delightful images in the bedroom.

House of the Faun *(see p146)*

★ House of the Vettii
This is one of the most famous places in Pompeii (see p146). *It has rich wall decoration dating from the last Pompeiian period after AD 62. The array of themes includes Daedalus and Pasiphaë, shown here.*

The Forum
Originally the market place, the Forum (see p144) became the focus for the most important civic functions, both political and religious.

Temple of Apollo *(see p144)*

Porta Marina entrance

Macellum
The macellum was the covered meat and fish market. Fronted by a portico with two moneychangers' kiosks, it opened onto the Forum near the weights and measures office and the Forum Holitorium vegetable market.

Forum *(see p144)*

Basilica *(see p144)*

Temple of Venus *(see p144)*

STAR SIGHTS

★ House of the Vettii

★ Via dei Sepolcri

Fresco from a Lupanare
Most of the guests at the inn – called hospititium *or* caupona – *were gladiators, as important visitors were put up in private homes. Here and in the lupanares, or brothels, paintings and graffiti depict this world and the services offered by waitresses and prostitutes, as well as boys, to satisfy their clients and lovers.*

VISITORS' CHECKLIST

Road Map C3. 🚇 *Pompei-Scavi.*
🚍 *Circumvesuviana: Pompei-Villa dei Misteri.* **Digs:** *Porta Marina, Piazza Esedra, Porta Anfiteatro, Piazza Immacolata.* ☎ *081 861 07 44.* ⏰ *9am–1 hr before sunset.*
🏛 ℹ *Azienda Autonoma di Soggiorno e Turismo, Via Sacra 1.* ☎ *081 850 72 55; Via Porta Marina Inferiore 1.* ☎ *081 861 09 16.* 🌐 *www.pompeiisites.org*

Modesto's Bakery, where carbonized bread was found, is one of several bakeries in Pompeii with wood-fired ovens and millstones.

The Stabian Baths
(see p145), the oldest in the city, had separate sections for men and women.

Plaster Casts
Since 1863, plaster cast techniques have enabled researchers to re-create body shapes. Many were killed by the toxic fumes while engaged in everyday tasks.

VIA STABIANA

VICOLO DEL LUPANARE

VIA DELL ABBONDANZA

Small Theatre
(see p145)

The Large Theatre
(see p144) was built in the hollow of a hill for good acoustics.

Gladiators' courtyard and barracks *(see p145)*

THE ARCHEOLOGICAL SITE
The illustration shows the western section of Pompeii. For a map of the entire area see p147.

Triangular Forum
(see p145)

| 0 metres | 50 |
| 0 yards | 50 |

★ Via dei Sepolcri
"Twenty steps wide, 500 long, the entire length still furrowed by the ancient carriage wheels, completely furnished with pavements like ours, and lined throughout, at left and right, with funerary monuments."
This is how an awestruck Alexandre Dumas described Via dei Sepolcri, outside the northwest city wall, which was discovered in the first digs.

Exploring Pompeii

THANKS TO ITS STRATEGIC position near the Sarno River, Pompeii was a centre of commerce for inland areas. The first town plan (6th century BC) was irregular but, from the 4th century BC on, building developed on a Greek-inspired grid plan. Slabs of old lava from Vesuvius were used to pave the roads. Large villas and houses of different periods and styles, made of brick, stone and cement and often richly decorated, offer an unparalleled view of ancient domestic architecture *(see pp146–7)*. Furthermore, the streets, workshops and public areas are in an excellent state of preservation. Finds such as furnishings, tools, jewellery and even food and drink reveal how the people of Pompeii lived, from the ruling class down to the slaves.

The Forum viewed from the Temple of Apollo

with the fate of Pompeii, her temple was badly damaged in the earthquake of AD 62, then totally devastated by Vesuvius.

The Basilica, Pompeii's ancient judicial seat opening onto the Forum

THE FORUM

THE FORUM, a rectangular paved area, was the centre of public life, and the oldest part of Pompeii, built on the highest spot. Arranged around it are a number of important administrative and religious institutions. To the south is the Basilica, or law court, while opposite are the temples of Apollo, Jupiter and Vespasian, and the Sanctuary of the Lari. The imposing Eumachia building was perhaps used by the wool merchants' guild or, more probably, for commercial transactions. On the other side of the Basilica is the site of the Temple of Venus. The goddess was the protectress of the city, but in tandem

TRIANGULAR FORUM

SURROUNDED BY columns and built on a steep-sided lava mass, the Triangular Forum was the focal point for leisure activities. In front of the Doric temple is a well and also a curious building that scholars think was revered by Pompeiians as the sanctuary of the mythical founder of the city. The sacred area was perhaps dedicated to the gods Hercules and Athena.

THEATRES

THE LARGE THEATRE (2nd century BC) was rebuilt several times in its history and in modern times has again been used as the venue for summer cultural events. It was built to seat about 5,000 people. The quadrangular portico behind the stage, originally designed as a space

The Forum, with Vesuvius in the background

The gladiators' barracks, part of the Large Theatre complex

for the audience to stroll in during intermissions, was turned into a barracks for the gladiators after AD 62. Skeletons, including one of a baby, have been excavated here.

Next door is the indoor theatre, or Small Theatre, used for music concerts. Behind this is the Temple of Isis, the goddess worshipped locally.

VIA STABIANA

THIS AVENUE, passing through the Porta di Stabia, to the south, was a major thoroughfare used by carriages travelling between Pompeii and the port and coastal districts.

On the west side of the avenue are the Stabian Baths, the most ancient in Pompeii; the original structure dates from the 4th century BC. Behind the baths, in the alley, is the best preserved of the city's many brothels. It is the only one with two storeys, two entrances and an independent stairway – all designed to ensure greater privacy for clients. Erotic wall paintings and a dish of pasta were found in this building. At the junction with Via di Nola are the central baths,

which were under construction at the time of Vesuvius' devastating eruption.

Near Porta Vesuvio you can see the remains of an aqueduct. This channelled water from the Serino River aqueduct, built in the era of Augustus, into three conduits that served both private homes and public fountains. The aqueduct fell into disuse after being damaged by the earthquake of AD 62.

An inn in Via dell'Abbondanza

AMPHITHEATRE AND GREAT GYMNASIUM

THE AMPHITHEATRE (80 BC) and the Augustan era Great Gymnasium, with a

swimming pool in the middle, are in an outlying area between the Nocera and Sarno gateways. The amphitheatre was used for gladiatorial combat and is the oldest one of its kind in existence. The stone tiers were separated into different sections for the various social classes. A large cloth canopy (*velarium*) shaded spectators from the sun.

VIA DELL'ABBONDANZA

A public fountain in Via dell'Abbondanza

THE LIVELIEST street in Pompeii was lined with private homes (*see pp146–7*) and shops selling a wide range of goods. The buildings and contents present a vivid picture of everyday life, down to the cart tracks in the street.

You can visit the shop of Verecundus, who made felt and tanned hides; Stefano's well-preserved laundry, where urine was used as a cleaning agent; or the bakery run by Sotericus, where bread was baked but not sold retail. Among the inns, the most famous belonged to Asellina, whose obliging foreign waitresses are depicted in graffiti on the wall. The inn (*thermopolium*) still has the record of the proceeds of that fateful day in AD 79: 683 sesterces.

The Houses in Pompeii

MANY LARGE HOUSES of great historical value and architectural interest are concentrated in the area between Via di Mercurio (the most elegant *cardo*, reserved for pedestrians, in the northwest of Pompeii) and Via Stabiana, and along Via dell'Abbondanza. Wealthy residents had houses with courtyards, living rooms and gardens *(see pp16–17)*, often with decorated walls. A typical Pompeiian house was constructed around two open courts: the atrium, an Italic feature, and the colonnaded garden, a feature of Greek origin. The layout of suburban farmsteads was different; the Villa of the Mysteries is one of the most famous.

Bronze statue, House of the Faun

HOUSE OF THE VETTII

The lari shrine, House of the Vettii

THE OWNERS of the House of the Vettii were freedmen who had become rich merchants. The house has been carefully restored, and its interior walls are adorned with splendid paintings and friezes featuring mythological themes. In the atrium of the more rustic part of the house is the altar of the lari – the deities who protected the place. This depicts the ancestral spirit of the *pater familias* with two lari and, below, a serpent.

On the north side of the house is a kitchen, with a small room decorated with erotic scenes.

HOUSE OF THE FAUN

THE NAME comes from a bronze statue in the middle of the impluvium (pond) in one of the atria. The original is in the Museo Archeologico Nazionale, as are many of the mosaics, including the famous *Battle of Alexander (see pp86–9)*. Built in the 2nd century BC, this is one of the largest private dwellings here.

HOUSE OF THE TRAGIC POET

THE ENTRANCE has a mosaic of a dog with a "beware of the dog" inscription, but many frescoes are in the Museo Archeologico. The name derives from a mosaic showing a drama rehearsal.

HOUSE OF THE GOLDEN CUPIDS

THIS HOUSE, owned by the family of Poppaea, Nero's second wife, was decorated with the elegant taste characteristic of Nero's era. It is not large and is built on an irregular plan because of the limited space. The name derives from the cupids *(amorini)* in gold leaf that decorate the bedroom. Gardens were an important feature at that time, and this garden was well tended and lavished with sculptures, hanging disks *(oscilla)*, theatre masks, marble tables and a swimming pool.

HOUSE OF THE CITARISTA

NAMED AFTER the bronze statue of *Apollo the Lyre Player* found in the central peristyle and now in the Museo Archeologico *(see pp86–9)*, this was really two houses. It is distinguished by the number of open courts: two atria and three peristyles.

HOUSE OF MENANDER

THE WEALTH of decoration and the grandeur of its atrium, peristyle and the rooms facing east make this one of Pompeii's most interesting houses. The walls of this home were decorated with lovely paintings, including a portrait of the Greek playwright after whom it has been named, and

The peristyle in the House of the Golden Cupids

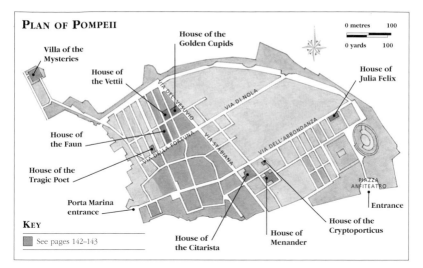

PLAN OF POMPEII

Villa of the Mysteries

House of the Vettii

House of the Golden Cupids

House of Julia Felix

VIA DEL VESUVIO

VIA DI NOLA

House of the Faun

VIA DELLA FORTUNA

VIA STABIANA

VIA DELL'ABBONDANZA

House of the Tragic Poet

Porta Marina entrance

PIAZZA ANFITEATRO

Entrance

House of the Cryptoporticus

KEY

See pages 142–143

House of the Citarista

House of Menander

0 metres 100
0 yards 100

---

images of Ulysses in the Trojan War. A treasure trove of 115 silver objects was also found here in 1930. The bath is quite unusual; it lies on the western side of the peristyle, around a porticoed atrium which still has traces of a fresco portraying divine and mythological figures. The dressing room affords access to the frescoed *calidarium* (warm room).

On the same street is the Samnite period **House of the Labyrinth**. This has two atria and a spacious peristyle with a mosaic on the floor representing *Theseus and the Minotaur in the Labyrinth*.

HOUSE OF THE CRYPTOPORTICUS

THE "hidden portico" that characterizes this house lies under the garden. In AD 79 the owner was probably converting it into a wine cellar, as can be seen by the store of amphoras. The showcases in the corridor contain plaster casts *(see p142)* of the inhabitants who had taken shelter in the *cryptoporticus* during the eruption, but who suffocated from the ashes that made their way in through a vent.

In the *triclinium* (dining room) you can still see frescoes and traces of the rich stuccowork on the vault.

HOUSE OF JULIA FELIX

THE PATRICIAN villas in Pompeii were usually built outside the town centre. The House of Julia Felix occupies an entire block, divided into the owner's quarters and rented dwellings and shops. An inscription with the rental regulations was found here. The house also had baths that were rented and open to the public, who probably flocked here after the Forum Thermae had been damaged by the AD 62 earthquake. The clients waited for their turn in the vast porticoed courtyard, where you can still see the seats. From here they went to the outdoor pool and then to the baths proper, with a *frigidarium* (cold pool) and *tepidarium* (warm pool).

VILLA OF THE MYSTERIES

THIS LARGE VILLA outside the city walls on Via dei Sepolcri was built in the early 2nd century BC. It was converted from an urban dwelling into an elegant country house. The architecture and paintings make it one of the most famous houses in Pompeii. It contains a well-known cycle of frescoes with 29 brightly coloured life-size figures against a red background, who represent a bride's initiation to the Dionysian mysteries or a postulant's initiation to the Orphic mysteries. Some scholars say this subject was depicted because the owner was a priestess of the Dionysian cult, which was widespread in Southern Italy.

Scene from the famous fresco cycle in the Villa of the Mysteries

The Sorrento Peninsula ⓫

Lemons at Sorrento

THE PENINSULA created by the Lattari hills forms a boundary between the bays of Naples and Salerno. The soft tufaceous northern side has been inhabited for centuries, and is dotted with ancient villas dedicated to leisure and culture. The coast becomes rugged and precipitous on the southern side *(see pp150–3)*, after Punta della Campanella *(see pp154–5)*, which was almost isolated until the 19th century. The old Bourbon road passed through Castellammare di Stabia (Roman Stabiae) and served Vico Equense and Sorrento, while the more recent road is higher up and continues to the Amalfi coast via Sant'Agata sui due Golfi.

Vico Equense

CASTELLAMMARE DI STABIA
Road map D4.
🏘 69,000. �· Circumvesuviana: Castellammare. ℹ Azienda Autonoma di Soggiorno e Turismo, Piazza Matteotti. ☎ 081 871 13 34.
Castellammare was totally rebuilt in the 9th century along with the castle used to defend the most important of its many sources of therapeutic waters. The old **thermal baths** are still in use today. The Bourbon rulers built major shipyards here that were later abandoned. Ancient Stabiae, an agglomeration of villas and farmsteads, lies outside the modern town on the Varano plain. Stabiae was destroyed by the Vesuvius

eruption of AD 79, and was only partly excavated in the 18th century. After World War II more ancient houses were found along the coast and in the interior. The oldest is the **Villa di Arianna** on the Varano hill, with a 1st-century BC nucleus and 13 rooms overlooking the bay. Many of these villas were richly decorated and placed in splendid scenic positions.

🏛 Thermal Baths
Piazza Amendola. ☎ 081 871 44 22. 🕒 7am–6:30pm daily.
⋔ Villa di Arianna
Via Passeggiata Archeologica. ☎ 081 871 45 41. 🕒 9am–1 hr before sunset.

🏃 Monte Faito
The prettiest route on foot to the chestnut and beech woods starts from near the Angevin Villa Quisisana. The cable car, which operates from June to September, departs from the Circumvesuviana railway station.

VICO EQUENSE
Road map D4. 🏘 20,000. �· Circumvesuviana: Scraio, Vico Equense. ℹ Via San Ciro 16. ☎ 081 879 93 51, 081 879 88 26, 081 801 57 52.
On a rocky spur with sheer cliffs, this town of Etruscan origin, famous in antiquity for its wine, is now a tourist resort with popular bars and

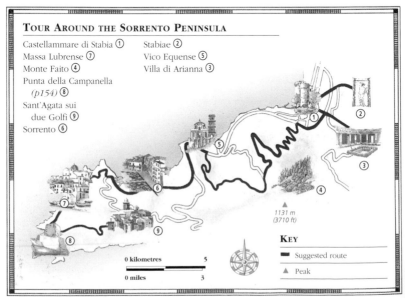

TOUR AROUND THE SORRENTO PENINSULA

Castellammare di Stabia ①   Stabiae ②
Massa Lubrense ⑦   Vico Equense ⑤
Monte Faito ④   Villa di Arianna ③
Punta della Campanella (p154) ⑧
Sant'Agata sui due Golfi ⑨
Sorrento ⑥

1131 m (3710 ft)

KEY
▬ Suggested route
▲ Peak

0 kilometres 5
0 miles 3

View of the Sorrento coast

restaurants. At nearby Scraio freezing sulphurous water continues to flow into the sea.

SORRENTO
Road map C4. 🏛 18,000.
🚆 Circumvesuviana: Sorrento.
⛴ from & to Naples.
🛈 Azienda Autonoma di Soggiorno Sorrento e Sant'Agnello, Via De Maio 21. ☎ 081 807 40 33; Azienda Autonoma di Soggiorno e Turismo, Via de Maio 35. ☎ 081 877 33 97.

You can still distinguish the original Greek town plan in the old centre of Sorrento.

BELLEVUE
Hotel Syrene
SORRENTO

Advertisement for a Sorrento hotel

In the summer months the town is filled with tourists walking along Corso Italia or seated at the cafés in Piazza Tasso. The **Sedile Dominova**, in the square of the same name, is a 15th-century building once used as an assembly hall for the nobility. The **Duomo** is of ancient origin and was rebuilt in the 1400s and then remodelled several times. Inside the cathedral is the archbishop's marble throne, sculpted in 1537, and fine marquetry-decorated choir stalls.

The cloister in the church of San Francesco is a mixture of styles and periods: rounded arches on two sides and interlaced Arabic ones on the other two. The **Museo Correale di Terranova** contains 17th–19th-century objets d'art. Outside the town, towards Capo di Sorrento, you can visit the **Bagno della Regina Giovanna**, with the ruins of Pollius Felix's residence.

Many other ancient villas along the coast were absorbed into more recent ones and have often been converted into hotels. Sorrento has been a popular resort town since the 1700s: Casanova and Goethe were guests of Sir William and Lady Hamilton, and the French generals lodged at the Cocumella, the town's oldest hotel, opened in 1798. Other historic hotels are the Imperial Tramontano *(see p174)* and the Excelsior Vittoria.

🔒 Duomo
Via Santa Maria della Pietà 44.
☎ 081 878 22 48.
🕘 9am–7:30pm.

🏛 Museo Correale di Terranova
Via Correale 50.
☎ 081 878 18 46.
🕘 9am–2pm Apr–Sep; 3–7pm Oct–Mar. 🔲 Tue. 🌐

🏛 Bagno della Regina Giovanna
Punta del Capo descent (Calata).

MASSA LUBRENSE
Road map C4. 🏛 11,869. 🛈 Viale Filangieri 11. ☎ 081 878 91 23.
Massa is a market town and bathing resort on the western end of the peninsula.

SANT'AGATA SUI DUE GOLFI
Road map C4.
Perched on a hill with views north and south, Sant'Agata is a favourite with Neapolitans. It is also famous for the Don Alfonso restaurant *(see p184).*

The harbour at Sorrento

The Amalfi Coast ⑫

Portal of Amalfi Duomo

Suspended between sea, sky and earth, state road 163, which twists and turns along the full length of the Amalfi coast, offers stunning views at every corner. Until the 19th century, this stretch of the "divine coast" was isolated and could only be reached by going up difficult mountain paths on mules. By the early 1900s, this very isolation had become the main appeal and the coast began to attract travellers, artists and writers. Visitors of all kinds were drawn to steep-stepped Positano, clinging to tall cliffs; Amalfi with its glorious past as a marine republic; and Ravello, which Wagner chose as "the magic garden of Klingsor", the setting for his opera *Parsifal*. The limestone islands called Li Galli, southwest of Positano, are traditionally the home of the Sirens made famous by Homer in his accounts of the trials of Odysseus. Exploring by boat *(see pp154–5)* enables you to appreciate this astonishing coast at closer quarters.

A stretch of state road 163

NERANO
Road map D4. 🚌 *Sita.*

The first stop on the Amalfi coast road is the quiet village of Nerano, administratively part of Massa Lubrense. The road to Nerano goes upwards from Sorrento and cuts across the end of the peninsula near the small village of **Termini**. The sea sparkles in the distance, and the panoramic views are stunning. You can even see Capri and the rocky islands of Li Galli *(see p155)*.

Nerano is perched on a ridge; below is the beach and the town of **Marina del Cantone**, popular mostly because of its small seafront restaurants, some supported by stilts. Walkers can descend on foot among the olive trees to the bay of **Ieranto**.

POSITANO
Road map D4.
👥 *3,700.* 🚌 *Sita.* 🚢 *from Capri & Naples.* ℹ️ *Azienda Autonoma di Soggiorno e Turismo, Via Saraceno 1.* 📞 *089 87 50 67 or 089 87 57 60.*

In 1953 John Steinbeck wrote that Positano "bites deep. It is a dream place that isn't quite real when you are there and becomes beckoningly real after you have gone". The town climbs the hill in steps, with the oldest houses in the upper part of Positano, either faded red or pink, decorated with Baroque stuccoes. The traffic-free street going down to the sea, Via Pasitea, penetrates the atmospheric heart of town with its narrow stepped alleys, houses with vaulted roofs, terraces and tiny gardens that defy the

rock. The brightly coloured articles Positano is famous for – such as cloth bags and beachwear – on display inside and outside the many shops, blend well with the pastel-coloured houses, and the local craftsmen are only too happy to make sandals for you while you wait.

Near the beach is the small church of Santa Maria dell'Assunta, whose cupola is covered with yellow, blue and green majolica tiles. The descent ends at Marina Grande, a pebble beach used by fishing boats, lined with bars and restaurants.

If you want to go to inlets inaccessible by land, or to the little islands of **Li Galli**, or take a trip along the coast, boats are always available. If you prefer to go on foot, you can always swim at Ciumicello, Arienzo or take the easy path to Fornillo beach, with its two watch-towers. There are also craggy grottoes in the inlets,

Typical Amalfi scenery, with sheer cliffs overlooking the sea

including La Porta, where there are Palaeolithic and Mesolithic ruins. From Montepertuso, a village above Positano, you can walk along a splendid scenic path to **Nocelle**. For those who love good food, there are plenty of bars and restaurants, including Buca di Bacco (*see p185*), famous for its *arancini* rice croquettes.

The beach at Marina di Praia

PRAIANO
Road map D4.
🏠 *1,900.* 🚌 *Sita.*
This fishing village is perched on the ridge of Monte Sant'Angelo and stretches towards Capo Sottile. The church of San Luca, with 16th-century paintings by Giovan Bernardo Lama, lies in the upper part. In an inlet just outside Praiano is **Marina di Praia**, a small beach surrounded by fishermen's houses. On the road from Positano there are more delightful beaches; just before Praiano is **Vettica Maggiore** and further on, Conca dei Marini. The views are splendid from the terraced square of Vettica Maggiore, by the church of San Gennaro. Before you reach Amalfi, the road widens into an open space where you can go down (by lift) to the **Grotta dello Smeraldo**, where stalagmites and stalactites merge to form great columns in the emerald-green water.

⚓ Grotta dello Smeraldo
🔼 **State road** 163,
4 km (2 miles) from Amalfi. 📷

AMALFI
Road map D4.
🏠 *6,000.* 🚌 *Sita.*
ℹ️ *Azienda Autonoma di Soggiorno e Turismo, Corso Roma 19/21.* 📞 *089 87 11 07 or 089 87 26 19.*
Tucked in between mountains and sea, Amalfi is a perennial favourite with visitors for its scenic beauty and original architecture. It also has a glorious history as a powerful maritime republic – in the 11th century Amalfi was a rival to the ports of Venice and Genoa.

Little remains to show for the colourful trading history of this small town, whose inhabitants once numbered 60,000. Amalfi's cathedral, the **Duomo di Sant'Andrea**, founded in the 9th century, was rebuilt in Romanesque style in the 11th century and then altered several times. The façade and atrium date from the late 1800s, but the carved bronze doors were cast in Constantinople around the year 1000, and the campanile (1276) is decorated with Arabic-like interlaced arches typical of southern Italian Romanesque. Left of the porch, the Chiostro del Paradiso (Paradise cloister)

The rocky Amalfi coastline

was built in around 1266 for Bishop Augustariccio as a cemetery for prominent citizens. The garden is surrounded by an ornate colonnade with interlaced arches supported by paired columns and with fragments of sculpture from different periods. Near Piazza Duomo is the Arsenal; you can still see the ruins of two naves and the vault. Heading inland from Amalfi, you can visit the Valle dei Mulini (Valley of the Mills), famous for its traditional paper production and the **Museo della Carta** or Paper Museum.

🏠 Duomo di Sant'Andrea
Piazza Duomo.
🕐 *9am–1pm, 3–8pm daily.*
🏛 Museo della Carta
Valle dei Mulini.
📞 *089 87 26 15.* 🕐 *9am–1pm Mon, Fri.* ● *Tue–Thu, Sat & Sun.*

Piazza Duomo in Amalfi and the wide steps leading to the cathedral

RAVELLO

Road map D4. 🏠 2,500. 🚌 Sita.
🛈 Azienda Autonoma di Soggiorno
e Turismo, Piazza Duomo 10. [089
85 70 96 or 089 85 79 77;
Ente Provinciale di Turismo, Piazza
Vescovado 1. [089 85 76 57.

Ravello's history is entwined
with that of Amalfi: the
former became part of the
Duchy of Amalfi in the 9th
century. The period of
greatest splendour was the
13th century, when trade with
Sicily and the Orient was at
its height. Somewhat off the
beaten track, Ravello is for
those who love peace and
quiet and stupendous views.

The **Duomo** is dedicated to
San Pantaleone, the town's
patron saint, and the blood of
the saint is kept here. The
church dates from 1086 and
its bronze doors from 1179.
Inside is a splendid raised
pulpit, the work of Niccolò di
Bartolomeo da Foggia in
1272. The twisted columns,
patterned with mosaics, rest
on sculpted lions.

Walking around the town,
Moorish details are evident in
the buildings, in the inner
courtyards and gardens and
the many churches. The
narrow streets and pathways
offer occasional, often
unexpected, glimpses of
marvellous coastal views.
Two highlights are Villa
Rufolo and Villa Cimbrone.

The view from the terrace at Villa Cimbrone

Villa Rufolo, originally built
for the Rufolo family, is a
mixture of 13th- and 14th-
century constructions. It was
remodelled in the 19th
century by a Scottish
enthusiast, who preserved the
Arabic elements. It is famed
for the courtyard with double
arches and even more for the
tropical gardens, which
inspired Wagner's *Parsifal*
(see p35). The Wagner festival
is now held here annually.

On Via San Francesco,
which takes you to Villa
Cimbrone, are the churches
of San Francesco, of Gothic
origin but rebuilt in the 18th
century, and Santa Chiara, the
only one on the coast that has
retained its *gynaeceum*
(women's gallery).

Villa Cimbrone was built
in the late 1800s by the
Englishman Lord Grimthorpe.
An assortment of ancient

architectural elements were
incorporated in the house.
From the villa's clifftop
terrace there is a spellbinding
view of the coast to Punta
Licosa and the Paestum plain.
Villa Cimbrone is now a small
hotel (see p175).

Another place well worth
visiting is the church of San
Giovanni del Toro, in the
square of the same name,
with its three tall semicircular
apses and beautifully
decorated domes.

🛈 Duomo
Piazza Duomo. [089 85 83 11.
⏱ 9am–1pm, 3–6pm.

🛈 Villa Rufolo
Piazza Duomo. [089 85 78 66.
⏱ 9am–5pm May–Feb; 9am–8pm
Mar–Apr. 🅿

🛈 Villa Cimbrone
Via Santa Chiara 26.
[089 85 71 38. ⏱ 9am–1 hr
before sunset. 🅿

The picturesque village of Cetara; standing out among rooftops is the dome of San Pietro

MAIORI, MINORI AND CETARA

Road map D4 & E4.
Maiori: 6,000; **Minori:** 3,100; **Cetara:** 2,500. *Sita.* **Maiori:** *Azienda Autonoma di Soggiorno e Turismo, Viale Capone (Palazzo Zitara).* 089-87 74 52; **Cetara:** *Pro Loco, Via San Francesco 15.* 089 26 14 74.

Ancient *Reginna Minor* and *Maior* are now two popular seaside resorts with a long and noble history. **Minori**, where the Amalfi Maritime Republic arsenals were situated, dates back to Roman times. Near the seafront is the basilica of Santa Trofimena, built in the 12th–13th centuries and then rebuilt in the 1800s. The church houses the relics of the ancient patron saint of Amalfi.

Maiori is like an amphitheatre at the end of the Tramonti valley. It was founded in the 9th century but is today a modern town, rebuilt after a flood in 1954. The fine beaches and good bathing facilities have made it one of the most visited towns on the coast. The 18th-century campanile on 12th-century Santa Maria a Mare towers over the Maior stream.

After the lovely beach of Erchie, **Cetara** was the easternmost possession of Amalfi. At the end of the 9th century it was also a stronghold for the Saracens, who anchored their ships at Cala di Fuenti cove. The name perhaps derives from the Latin *cetaria*, or tunafishing net; the fish, salted and sold in ceramic pots, is a typical local product.

A characteristic ceramics shop in Vietri

VIETRI

Road map E4. *10,000. Sita.*
The majolica-decorated dome and bell tower of San Giovanni Battista (1732) have almost come to symbolize this town overlooking the Bay of Salerno. Vietri is famous as a seaside resort and especially for its ceramics. Cooking utensils, plates, vases and tiles have been manufactured here since the 1400s. In the mid-18th century, Vietri became known as the majolica-makers' district, a suburb of the Cava de' Tirreni (see below). The most original items made were the extremely popular

Porcelain plate made in Vietri

tiles painted with religious subjects. You can still see these tiles in streets, private homes and churches.

Today you can find ceramics of all kinds, either traditional or experimental in colour and shape, catering for all tastes. The green donkey used as the logo of local production is a relatively recent invention, inspired by the 1930s creations of Dutch and German ceramicists. The Villa Guarigli park is home to the **Museo della Ceramica** (Ceramics Museum) featuring local products from the 1600s to the present day.

🏛 Museo della Ceramica

Torretta di Villa Guariglia.
089 21 18 35.
9am–1pm, 3–6pm Tue–Sun.

CAVA DE' TIRRENI

Road map E4.
53,000. Sita.
Lying in a valley in the interior, Cava de' Tirreni is the only town in Southern Italy to have streets lined with porticoes. Go and see the 11th-century abbey of Santissima Trinità and the old Scacciaventi quarter, whose winding streets block the wind (*scacciaventi* means "wind-chaser").

View of Vietri, with the dome and campanile of San Giovanni

Along the Sorrento Coast ⓭

A boat trip

THE BEST WAY to take in all the beauty of the bay is by sea – to discover the isolated beaches, villages perched on the hillsides and ancient watchtowers. From Amalfi, Sorrento and Capri you can rent a launch or a slow *gozzo* boat. In the summer the major centres offer organized excursions on larger boats with a guide, but you cannot stop where you like. A favourite excursion is from the Amalfi coast to Capri (or vice versa), an all-day trip with evening meal at one of the coastal restaurants; the return in the moonlight is an unforgettable experience.

Sorrento Peninsula
An enjoyable way of seeing the coast from the sea is to take a fast motorboat and travel the full length of the Sorrento coastline, rounding Campanella point.

Marina del Cantone is an excellent place to stop for lunch: the local speciality is pasta with courgettes. The small Recommone restaurant in the nearby cove is also good.

Sorrento

Punta della Campanella
An ancient temple of Minerva stood on this rocky cliff; before then the site was possibly dedicated to the cult of the Sirens, after whom Sorrento, or Surrentum (see p149), may have been named. The road to the top is narrow and in poor condition.

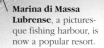

Marina di Massa Lubrense, a picturesque fishing harbour, is now a popular resort.

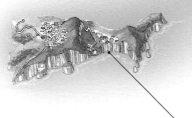

Capri
The island of Capri (see pp162–3) is also associated with the Sirens, as the promontory of Marina Piccola is called Scoglio delle Sirene. Those who want to stroll on the "blue island" can alight here, otherwise take a boat trip around the island, or simply stop for lunch at one of the many restaurants along the coast (see pp186–7).

0 kilometres 4

0 miles 2

VISITORS' CHECKLIST

*At **Positano** you can hire a boat from **Lucibello** on the large beach* 📞 *089 87 50 32; or **Grassi**, on Fornillo beach.* 📞 *089 81 16 20. At **Capri**, from **Sercomar**, Piazza Fontana 64.* 📞 *081 837 87 81; from **Banana Sport**, Via Marina Grande 12.* 📞 *081 837 51 88; and from **Whaels**, Via Colombo 17.* 📞 *081 837 88 94.*

Positano
The square, pastel-coloured houses of Positano (see pp150–51) cling to the steep slopes of Monte Sant'Angelo a tre Pizzi and Monte Comune overlooking the sea. Lush gardens and bougainvillea fill the terraces of these charming houses. This is one of the most popular resorts on the Amalfi coast, famous for its bright, patterned textiles.

Isca
Just offshore is the small island of Isca, where the Neapolitan actor and playwright Eduardo De Filippo (see p37) lived. The house now belongs to his son Luca.

The Li Galli Archipelago
These islands, known as the Sirenuse until the 19th century, were once considered to be the home of the mythical Sirens who lured sailors onto the rocks. The clear water between the three crags, Gallo Lungo, La Rotonda and Castelluccia, makes swimming irresistible.

Paestum ⑭

A NCIENT POSEIDONIA, founded along the Sele River by Greek colonists from Sybaris around 600 BC, became the Roman colony of Paestum in 273 BC. The town began to decline in the 1st century BC due to malaria. Seismic disturbance and deforestation (the local pines made excellent raw material for building ships) had gradually turned the area into marshland. The inhabitants tried to combat the rising water level; they raised their streets and homes, or went to live on higher ground. It was at this time that the Temple of Hera was made into a church by the converted population. Eventually, however, Paestum was abandoned for the nearby town of Capaccio.

Red-figure lekythos

This ancient site was first unearthed in the 18th century during the building of a road, but most of it remained undiscovered until the 1950s.

★ Temple of Ceres
This temple was built around 500 BC and dedicated to Athena. For centuries, until a votive offering was found nearby, it had been attributed to Ceres.

Temple of Neptune
The name of this temple has been a subject of debate. It was probably dedicated to Apollo or Zeus, but it is commonly known as the Temple of Neptune. Built in 450 BC, it is one of the most complete Greek temples in Europe.

THE THREE TEMPLES AT PAESTUM

These plans compare the structure of the 3 main temples at Paestum. The Temple of Hera (6th century BC) has 9 front columns, 18 side columns and 2 aisles divided by a row of columns. The Temple of Ceres (6th century BC) has 6 fluted columns at the front, 13 lateral ones and an undivided *cella*. The largest, Temple of Neptune (5th century BC), has 6 front columns, 14 side ones and its *cella* is divided into 3 aisles by 2 rows of 2-tier columns.

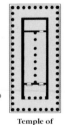
Temple of Ceres

Temple of Hera

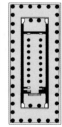
Temple of Neptune

STAR SIGHTS

★ Temple of Ceres

★ Temple of Hera, the "Basilica"

★ Tomb of the Diver (funerary fresco in Paestum Museum)

Paestum Museum

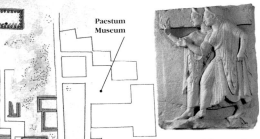

VISITORS' CHECKLIST

Road map F5. Via Magna Grecia.
FS *Napoli–Salerno: Paestum.*
Site ☐ *9am–1 hr before sunset.*
☎ *0828 81 10 16.* **Museum**
☐ *9am–6:30pm daily.* ● *1st &*
3rd Mon of month.
ℹ *Azienda Autonoma di*
Soggiorno e Turismo, Via Magna
Grecia 152. ☎ *0828 72 10 16.*

Metope with Dancing Girls
This metope, on display in the Paestum Museum, comes from one of the two temples in the sanctuary of Hera Argiva at the mouth of the Sele River. Founded by the first colonists, the complex was discovered in 1934–40 after almost two centuries of searching.

The amphitheatre
(1st century BC–1st century AD) has only been partly excavated.

Forum

Baths

★ Tomb of the Diver
The frescoed slabs of the Tomb of the Diver, which date from about 480 BC, were discovered in 1968 about 1 km (half a mile) from Paestum. The image of the diver on the lid symbolizes the passage to the afterlife. These unique examples of Greek funerary painting can be seen in the site's museum.

★ Temple of Hera, the "Basilica"
The absence of religious features led the first archaeologists to believe this was a civic building, when in fact it is the oldest temple in Paestum, built around 530 BC.

0 metres 100
0 yards 100

Antonio Joli, The Temples of Paestum (1758)
Temple ruins had a profound effect on local landscape painters, who often used them in their art. Antonio Joli's painting shows the Basilica, the Temple of Neptune and, beyond, the Temple of Ceres.

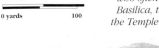

Hoardings and shop signs in present-day Caserta

Caserta ⑮

Road map C2. 👥 *70,000.*
🚉 *Caserta.* 🛈 *Ente Provinciale per il Turismo, Palazzo Reale.* ☎ *0823 32 22 33.*

CASERTA was once known as the village of La Torre, named after a medieval tower of the Acquaviva family. It was only from the middle of the 18th century, when Charles III, Bourbon king of Naples, chose the plain at the foot of the Tifatini mountains as the site for his new centre of administration, that the town began to flourish and expand. It was at this time that it took the name of the nearby medieval village of Caserta Vecchia.

Present-day Caserta is a modern agricultural town that reflects the major rebuilding carried out in the 1950s. A few older buildings remain, such as the church and monastery of Sant'Agostino in Via Mazzini and the former residence of the Acquaviva family in Piazza Vanvitelli. However, the main reason to visit Caserta is the Royal Palace (*see pp160–61*). Conceived by Charles III as the heart of his new administrative centre, the palace was to be a leading European court, modelled on Versailles and linked to the capital and other cities by radial roads and protected by the fortress at Capua.

Façade of the cathedral of San Michele, Caserta Vecchia

This plan to move power away from the capital city was influenced by the apparent vulnerability of the Palazzo Reale on the Naples seafront (*see pp50–51*), a fact that came to light in 1742 when the English fleet had threatened to attack. Once this danger had passed, however, attention was turned to the style of the palace. The king summoned Luigi Vanvitelli, technical adviser at the Vatican, to draw up designs. The palace and the new city were begun in 1752.

When Charles III became king of Spain and returned to Madrid in 1759, construction on the Royal Palace languished. Supervision of the costly and interminable works was handed over to his son Ferdinand IV and in particular, his minister Tanucci. The new king concentrated on the magnificent park and bothered little about the unfinished palace.

Some further work was carried out, but as the two semicircular buildings at the entrance to the grounds illustrate, these were poor substitutes for the splendid buildings proposed in Vanvitelli's original designs.

ENVIRONS
🏛 Caserta Vecchia
Road map C2.

The fascination of Caserta Vecchia, 10 km (6 miles) along a winding road northeast of Caserta, does not lie in the individual monuments but the town itself, which has a remarkably well-preserved medieval character. This small hilltop town was probably founded by the Lombards in the 8th century and then came under Norman rule. When Charles III designed his new palace, activity in this lively community moved into the new town in the plains.

Caserta Vecchia revolves around the main square where the cathedral of San Michele stands. Nearby is the Gothic church of Annunziata with a marble portal opening onto a 17th-century portico. On the eastern side of the village are the ruins of a 13th-century castle, dominated by a 30-metre (98-ft) turret.

🔒 Cathedral of San Michele
🕐 *9am–1pm, 3–7:30pm daily.*
The cathedral in Caserta Vecchia was completed in 1153. The faded yellow and grey tufa façade is simple, with three marble portals. Columns on the triangular tympanum above the middle portal are supported by lions.

Caserta Vecchia, dominated by the cathedral of San Michele

The 14th-century dome has the interlaced Arabic arches often seen on Romanesque buildings in Southern Italy.

The interior of the church is lined with irregular columns and stunning majolica tiles. A starlit sky is represented in the dome, with grey stone for the night and white marble stars.

To the right of the cathedral stands the dark stone bell tower, added a century later, with an archway over the road.

🏛 Village of San Leucio
Road map C2.
This area, 3 km (2 miles) northwest of Caserta was purchased by Charles III in 1750. Five years later Ferdinand IV built a royal lodge here, Casino di Belvedere. In 1789, he founded a progressive community with enlightened laws and based on the production of silk. An existing building was redesigned as a silk factory to be used by the local artisans. All you can see today of the ambitious project are the workmen's dwellings and the Belvedere lodge on the slopes of the hill. The royal lodge was also the residence of the silk factory management.

The Belvedere lodge, San Leucio

🏛 Sant'Angelo in Formis
Road map C2. ◯ daily (ask the caretaker in house opposite). 🎟
The small, Romanesque church of Sant'Angelo in Formis lies 10 km (6 miles) northwest of Caserta. Built on the ruins of an ancient temple to Diana, Roman goddess of the forest, it was reconstructed in 1073. Many features of the temple were incorporated into the church such as the delicate Corinthian columns on the portico, and the church floor.

Inside, a cycle of 11th-century frescoes, painted in Byzantine style by artists from the School of Montecassino, depict stories from the Bible.

THE IDEAL VILLAGE OF SAN LEUCIO

Pretty street in the village of San Leucio

San Leucio was founded in 1789 by Ferdinand IV as a village for workers of the local silk factory. The aim of this social experiment was to create a community dedicated to the pursuit of happiness instead of personal profit. The community had its own laws, attributed to the king but in fact written by Antonio Planelli. These were based on reason and morality, included compulsory education, equal inheritance rights for men and women (who, however, had to marry within the community), the abolition of the dowry and medical assistance for the aged and disabled. The 1799 revolution brought about the end of the most ambitious project of the founders, the creation of an entire model city, Ferdinandopoli, although the designs survive. San Leucio is famous for its silk manufacture and the articles produced here are still very much in demand.

🏛 Roman Amphitheatre
Piazza Adriano, Santa Maria Capua Vetere. 📞 0823 79 88 64. ◯ 9am–1 hr before sunset. 🎟
The amphitheatre at Santa Maria Capua Vetere, 6 km (4 miles) west of Caserta, dates from the 1st century BC. Restored by Hadrian and Antonius Pius, it is still well preserved today, especially its underground structure. Second in size only to the Colosseum in Rome, it had four "storeys": the first three were travertine arches with busts and statues of the gods, while the last was blind and decorated with pilasters. Statues of Eros, Venus and Psyche found here are on display in the Museo Archeologico Nazionale (see pp86–9).

🏛 Ponti della Valle
This viaduct, 2 km (1 mile) from Maddaloni, is over 500 m (1640 ft) long and is supported by three arches. It was built in 1753–8 by Vanvitelli to bring water to the Royal Palace at Caserta.

Ruins of the amphitheatre at Santa Maria Capua Vetere

Royal Palace of Caserta

Statue on a fountain

IN HIS MEMOIRS, the architect Vanvitelli says it was the king who designed the Royal Palace. This may have been adulation, or perhaps Charles III knew what he wanted – to emulate his favourite models, the Buen Retiro in Madrid and Versailles in France. Vanvitelli drew inspiration from the former for this quadrangular, 1,200-room structure, which was finally completed in 1852. The lower ground floor now houses a museum, with photos and exhibits relating to the palace and Caserta culture.

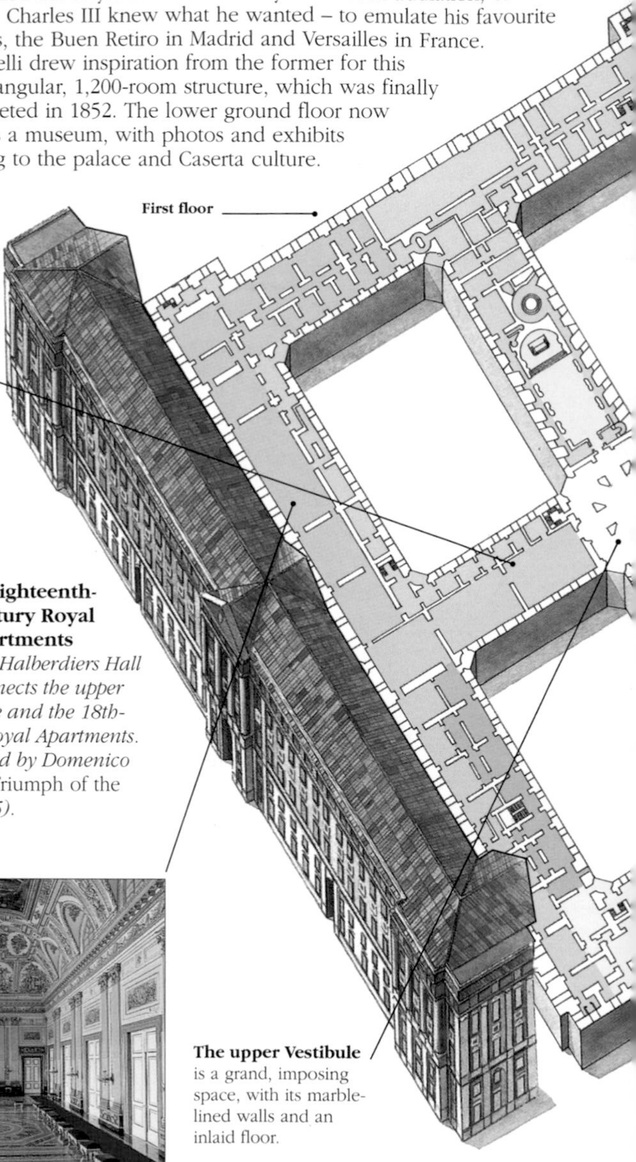

First floor

★ **Eighteenth-century Royal Apartments**
The Halberdiers Hall connects the upper vestibule and the 18th-century Royal Apartments.
The ceiling is adorned by Domenico Mondo's fresco The Triumph of the Bourbon Arms *(1785).*

The upper Vestibule
is a grand, imposing space, with its marble-lined walls and an inlaid floor.

★ **Throne Room**
This is one of the large 19th-century salons – in contrast with the smaller 18th-century rooms – in the palace. It was decorated by Gaetano Genovese in 1844–5 and was once filled with elegant French furniture.

STAR FEATURES

★ **Eighteenth-century Royal Apartments**

★ **Throne Room**

★ **Court Theatre**

Great Staircase
The staircase is positioned to one side so as not to interrupt the splendid view of the park from the main doorway.

VISITORS' CHECKLIST

Road map C2. Piazza Carlo III.
☎ 0823 27 74 33. **Apartments**
⏰ 9am–7:30pm daily. **Park** ⏰
9am–6pm. **Museo dell'Opera**
⏰ 9am–1 hr before sunset.
🎥 for groups. ♿

KEY (UPPER FLOOR)

◻ 18th-century Royal Apartments
◻ 19th-century Royal Apartments
◼ *Terraemotus* exhibition
◻ Cappella Palatina
◻ Biblioteca Palatina
◻ Art Gallery
◻ Non-exhibition space

Art Gallery
Among the portraits in the Art Gallery is that of Maria Carolina, Ferdinand IV's wife, who occupied four elaborate rooms in the 18th-century apartments.

★ **Court Theatre**
The theatre is on the ground floor. The rear of the stage could be opened to the air, creating a natural backdrop.

THE PARK

Luigi Vanvitelli designed this famous park, one of the last examples of the fashion for a regimented garden in the Italian or French style. The long central axis is designed on descending levels, creating a remarkable effect with pools and fountains ornamented with splendid sculptures. The play of flowing water culminates in the **Grande Cascata** waterfall, almost 80 m (260 ft) high, also known as the Fountain of Diana. Next to this is the English Garden, perhaps the first of its kind in Italy. The idea was suggested to Queen Maria Carolina by her friend Lord Hamilton and landscaping work began in 1768.

Flowing water with fountains and waterfalls, the park's central feature

Capri 🔞

Excursion taxi

THE FIRST illustrious residents in Capri were the Roman emperors Augustus and Tiberius. For the last decade of his life, Tiberius ruled Rome from Capri, and the ruins of his luxurious villa can still be seen today. Despite this noble history, the island saw few visitors until the 19th century, when a poet named August Köpisch found the Grotta Azzurra, which was known to locals but not to travellers on the Grand Tour. Tourism began to flourish, and Capri became the haunt of foreign politicians, artists and intellectuals, Alexandre Dumas and Oscar Wilde among them. The singer Gracie Fields and the writer Norman Douglas, author of *Siren Land*, made the island their home.

Marina Grande
Capri's main harbour is a colourful village with seafood restaurants and some Roman and Byzantine remains. A funicular takes you to central Capri in a few minutes.

Rocky Beaches
Sunloungers are set up among the rocks on this island with few sandy beaches.

The Grotta Azzurra, or Blue Grotto, owes its name to the blue colour of the water, the result of light refraction.

| 0 metres | 1000 |
| 0 yards | 1000 |

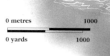

Anacapri
On the slopes of Monte Solaro (see p167) is the second town on the island, Anacapri. Here you can visit the church of San Michele, the Villa San Michele (home of the Swedish physician Axel Munthe), the excavations at the imperial villa of Damecuta and, of course, appreciate the magnificent view from the top of the hill.

Villa Jovis
The retreat built by Emperor Tiberius stands on the mountain named after him. Excavations have unearthed baths, apartments and "Tiberius's drop", from which his victims were supposedly thrown into the sea.

Writer Curzio Malaparte gave this villa, shaped like a hammer with a sickle on the roof, to the Chinese government in 1957.

I Faraglioni, Capri's most striking offshore rocks, soar up to 109 m (360 ft) out of the sea.

Tragara

The Certosa di San Giacomo, founded in 1371, is now occupied by a school and the Diefenbach Museum which has paintings and historical objects.

Marina Piccola

VISITORS' CHECKLIST

Road map C4.
Capri 8,000; Anacapri 5,400.
from Naples & Sorrento.
Azienda Autonoma di Soggiorno e Turismo: *Capri*, Via Marina Grande/Piazza Umberto I.
081 837 06 34 or 081 837 06 86; *Anacapri*, Via Orlandi 19a. 081837 15 24.
Grotta Azzurra: from Marina Grande. from Anacapri, 9am–1 hr before sunset. if the sea is particularly rough.
Certosa di San Giacomo: Viale della Certosa, Capri. 081 837 62 18. 9am–2pm daily.
Villa Jovis: Via A Maiuri, Capri. 9am–1 hr before sunset daily.
Villa San Michele: Via Capodimonte 34, Anacapri. 081 837 14 01. Nov–Feb: 10:30am–3:30pm daily; Mar: 9:30am–4:30pm daily; Apr, Oct: 9:30am–5pm daily; May–Sep: 9am–6pm daily.
Monte Solaro: Anacapri. Chair lift from Via Caposcuro. 081 837 14 28. Jun–Oct: 9:30am–5:30pm daily; Oct–Jun: 11:30am–3pm daily. in adverse weather conditions. www.capri.it

The "Piazzetta" in Capri
In the heart of town the famous "Piazzetta", officially Piazza Umberto I, is an outdoor living room, crowded day and night, packed with café tables buzzing with gossip and animated discussion. Excursions around the island also start from here. Overlooking the scene is the Baroque dome of Santo Stefano.

Via Krupp
Commissioned by the German industrialist Krupp, this famous road makes its vertiginous descent towards the sea in a series of hairpin bends.

Ischia ⑰

Bougainvillea

THE HOT SPRINGS on the volcanic island of Ischia were renowned in antiquity and still draw visitors today. Ancient Pithecusa was founded here in the 8th century BC by the same Greek traders who later founded Cumae on the mainland *(see pp134–5)*. Repeated attacks in the early 1300s forced people to take refuge on the small offshore island which the Aragonese later turned into a castle. A favourite with Bourbon royalty, Ischia also enchanted landscape painters and visitors such as the Irish philosopher Berkeley and the French poet Lamartine. The island is green and rugged, and each coast has a different character, offering beaches or steep hills, busy night-life or quiet seclusion.

Fungo di Lacco Ameno
This "mushroom" rock is a prominent landmark outside Lacco Ameno, where the Greek colonists first landed.

Lacco Ameno is home to the Muse Archeologico di Villa Arbusto wher items from th Greek settle ment are hele

Forio

The beach at Citara is generally considered the most beautiful in Ischia.

Santa Maria del Soccorso
This small sanctuary in the town of Forio combines elements of Gothic, Renaissance and Baroque, and is known for its collection of votive offerings from sailors. The English composer Sir William Walton lived just north of here, at La Mortella.

0 kilometres   2

0 mile   1

Sant'Angelo
Originally a fishing village and now a thermal spa resort, Sant'Angelo lies west of the long Maronti beach. Here "taxi boats" can be hired to take you to coves otherwise inaccessible by land. Nearby are the Nitrodi hot springs.

Monte Epomeo
(see p167) is an extinct volcano. According to mythology, the eruptions and quakes were caused by the wails and sighs of the giant Typhoeus, imprisoned under the island.

Casamicciola Terme
Despite the damage caused by the 1883 earthquake, the spa town of Casamicciola has retained its atmosphere and some Art Nouveau architecture. The Norwegian writer Ibsen wrote Peer Gynt *here.*

VISITORS' CHECKLIST

Road map A4. 🚌 *Ischia 17,000; Barano 7,800; Casamicciola Terme 6,600; Forio 11,600; Lacco Ameno 4,000; Serrara Fontana 3,000.* 🚢 🚢 *from Naples & from Pozzuoli to Ischia Porto.* 🚢 *from Naples Mergellina for Casamicciola Terme.* 🛈 *Azienda Autonoma di Soggiorno e Turismo, Via Colonna 102, Ischia Porto.* ☎ *081 507 42 31; Azienda Autonoma di Soggiorno e Turismo delle Isole, Via Iasolino, Ischia Porto.* ☎ *081 507 42 11.* 🏰 **Castello Aragonese** ◷ *9am–1 hr before sunset daily.* ⬤ *1–26 Dec; 8 Jan–end of Feb.* 🏛 **Museo Archeologico di Villa Arbusto**, *Lacco Ameno.* ⬤ *for restoration.* ☑ www.ischiaonline.it

Ischia Porto is the island's main town where ferries dock.

Ischia Ponte
This village is connected to the small offshore island of Castello Aragonese by a causeway built in 1438.

Maronti beach

Castello Aragonese
Different architectural styles can be seen inside the fortified walls of the island: the Angevin cathedral of the Assunta, a monastery and the church of San Pietro a Pantaniello. There is a lovely view from the Carta-romana belvedere.

Procida ⑱

Road map B3. 🛈 *11,000.* 🚢 🚢
from Naples & from Pozzuoli.
🛈 *Azienda Autonoma di Soggiorno
e Turismo, Via Roma, Stazione
Marittima 1.* 📞 *081 810 19 68.*

MUCH SMALLER than Capri and Ischia and also much less affected by tourism, the third island in the Bay of Naples is a favourite with those who love the simplicity and traditions of the local culture. This is the enchanting world that author Elsa Morante, recollecting her many visits here, evoked in *Isola di Arturo* (Arthur's Island). Procida's economy is sustained not only by tourism but, to a large extent, by the money its emigrants send back home to their families.

Deeply rooted local traditions are evident in the various festivals; for example, the Good Friday procession *(see p40)* that descends to the modern port from so-called Terra Murata – the rise dominated by the Abbey of San Michele – or the Graziella celebration that takes place in the port in mid-August.

The multi-coloured houses resting against the tufa rock make the island architecture one of the most distinctive in the region. Unique to

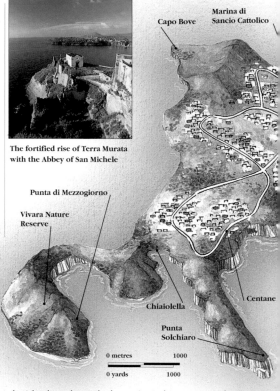

The fortified rise of Terra Murata with the Abbey of San Michele

Capo Bove

Marina di Sancio Cattolico

Punta di Mezzogiorno

Vivara Nature Reserve

Chiaiolella

Punta Solchiaro

Centane

0 metres   1000
0 yards   1000

the island are the vaulted buildings; originally built as winter boat shelters and later enlarged, acquiring among other things façades with arches and half-arches that frame the doors and

windows, terraces, loggias and long external staircases. You can see this type of architecture, albeit in a partially modernized version, on your arrival in Procida in Marina di Sancio Cattolico, the area built up in the 17th

View of Marina di Sancio Cattolico

Punta della
Lingua

Procida

Marina
Corricella

Terra
Murata

Punta di
Pizzaco

Typical Procida architecture

and 18th centuries, and at the small, popular Chiaiolella port on the other side of the island. The Abbey of San Michele, dominating Terra Murata, dates back to 1026, though it has since been rebuilt. Marina Corricella, at the foot of Terra Murata, has been virtually untouched by modern times; the soil is very fertile and the gardens here are filled with lemon trees. You can also visit the luxuriant **Vivara Nature Reserve**, a small island connected to Chiaiolella by a bridge, with examples of Mediterranean flora and an ornithological centre. It was here that intriguing remains of a late Bronze Age Mycenean settlement were found a few years ago.

🔒 **Abbey of San Michele**
Via Terra Murata. 📞 081 896 76 12.
🕐 9am–12:30pm, 3:30–7pm daily.
🌿 **Vivara Nature Reserve**
🕐 ask the Protezione Civile (which manages the park) for permission.
📞 081 896 74 00.

WALKING ON THE ISLANDS

While Procida is almost flat – the highest point, Terra Murata, is 91 m (300 ft) above sea level – Capri and Ischia are steep-sided. On Capri *(see pp162–3)*, the path connecting Monte Solaro (589 m, 1930 ft) to Anacapri is delightful and practicable even for lazy visitors, though there is always the option of the chairlift. Walkers will be well rewarded by the striking view and the 14th-century Santa Maria di Cetrella monastery on Marina Piccola (a detour halfway up). Experienced hikers come back down by the "Passetiello" path which includes a stretch directly above the sea and leads to Capri.

The highest mountain in the bay is the extinct Epomeo volcano (788 m, 2580 ft) on Ischia *(see pp164–5)*. A climb up the cone traditionally starts off at night from Fontana so as to admire the view at dawn. The view takes in the island itself, the Bay of Naples and the Tyrrhenian coast up to Roccamonfina and the Pontine Islands. A rough dirt track leads to the church of San Nicola (1459) and the adjoining monastery, both hewn out of the tufa rock. On your way down you can choose the road to Forio or Casamicciola.

Looking out over Capri from the Monte Solaro chairlift

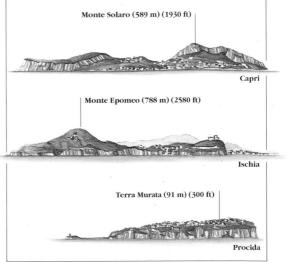

Monte Solaro (589 m) (1930 ft)

Capri

Monte Epomeo (788 m) (2580 ft)

Ischia

Terra Murata (91 m) (300 ft)

Procida

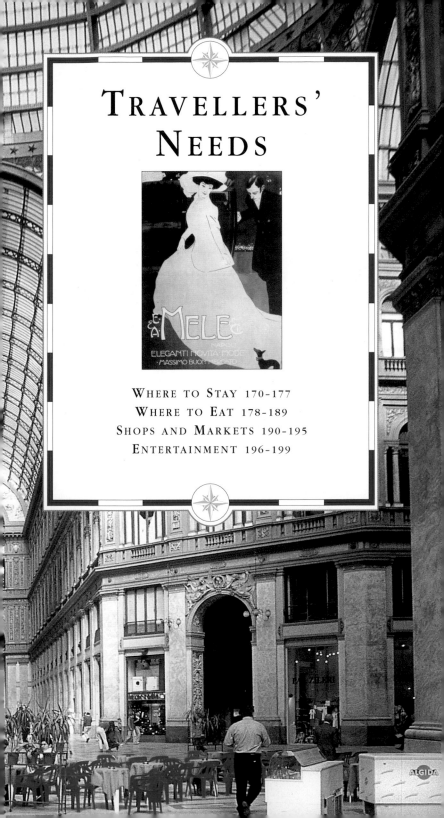

TRAVELLERS' NEEDS

WHERE TO STAY 170–177

WHERE TO EAT 178–189

SHOPS AND MARKETS 190–195

ENTERTAINMENT 196–199

WHERE TO STAY

THE FASCINATION and enchantment of Naples and the surrounding countryside have drawn visitors here for many centuries. Kings and queens, revolutionaries in exile, poets, writers and composers are among the host of celebrities who have wintered at the foot of Mount Vesuvius since the 18th century. Hotels and pensioni in the centre of Naples tend to be fairly expensive, but efforts are being

PRESTIGE
hotels

Logo of the Prestige hotels

made to widen the range of facilities available. Along the Amalfi coastline, around Sorrento and on the islands, traditional holidaying areas, the range of accommodation is much wider. Choices on offer cover all price categories, from simple pensioni to a grand luxury hotel with pools and magnificent views along the coast. This section and the lists of hotels on pages 172–7 will help you make your choice.

Breakfast on the terrace of the Hotel Executive *(see p172)*

cial district is ideal; it may not have the characteristic charm of an older establishment but will be modern and comfortable. The Prestige hotel chain, such as the Grand Hotel Vesuvio, the Excelsior and the Majestic, offer excellent service to an international clientele, and include 42 suites and 22 conference halls. The information bureaux of the Ente Provinciale per il Turismo (**EPT**, the Italian Tourist Board – *see p203*) publishes lists of hotels, pensioni and camp sites. For further information you can also make inquiries at the **Associazione Albergatori Napoletani** (Neapolitan Hotel Owners' Association).

The 5-star Hotel Excelsior *(see p173)* **overlooking the seafront**

WHERE TO LOOK

OUTSIDE NAPLES there is no lack of choice of hotels, from luxury chains to cheaper, family-run pensions. The latter are clean and comfortable, and often have fine panoramic views. In Naples itself, however, the range is rather limited. Hotels can often be expensive and sometimes do not offer good value for money. The most exclusive hotels are usually located on hills or on the seafront with spectacular views.

If you plan to spend a lot of time visiting museums, churches and galleries, it is best to stay in the centre of Naples. You will be within easy reach of the most important sights, and you can go back to your hotel to relax between spells of sightseeing. For those who don't mind the walk, a hotel in the commer-

PRICES AND GRADING

ITALIAN HOTELS are classified by a star-rating system, from one, the lowest, to five stars. Prices including taxes are displayed inside each room. Breakfast is often not

included, and may be an expensive item compared with a coffee and croissant in the nearest local bar. In Naples there is no difference between low and high season, but it is always worth asking about discounts, particularly off season. It is often possible to negotiate special rates for groups or longer stays. On average, single rooms cost two-thirds of the double room rate; rooms without a bathroom may cost up to 30 per cent less. In holiday resorts prices differ in low and high season; during the peak summer months you may be expected to take half-board.

HOTEL FACILITIES

THANKS TO THE World Cup and then the G7 summit, almost all the middle-range and luxury hotels in Naples underwent refurbishment and now provide a high level of comfort, including soundproofing. The cheaper hotels (one or two stars) tend to have clean but simple rooms, often with shared bathroom. Hotels outside Naples usually offer better facilities for less money.

The Hotel Pension Pinto Storey *(see p172)*, **opened in 1878**

The elegant foyer in Parker's Hotel *(see p173)*

BOOKING AND PAYING

Y OU SHOULD BOOK well in advance if you have special requests such as a room with a good view. During July and August, the peak holiday season, hotels along the coast and on the islands get very full, so once again you must book ahead of time. If there are no special events scheduled in Naples, advance booking won't be necessary and you can choose your hotel when you arrive. The local tourist offices will advise you.

If you do book, you will probably be asked to pay a deposit, which can be done by credit card or international money order. When you arrive at your hotel, the reception will ask for your passport; this is to register travellers with the police, a legal formality. By law, the hotel must give you a receipt when you check out.

Telephone calls from the room and drinks from the mini-bar can be very expensive, so it is advisable to check beforehand.

BUDGET ACCOMMODATION

I F YOU ARE on a tight budget you can stay in a hostel. The **AIG** (Associazione Italiana Alberghi per la Gioventù – Youth Hostel Association) has lists of hostels. In Naples, the Ostello Mergellina, near the Mergellina railway station and a stone's throw from the Parco Virgiliano *(see p119)*, is highly recommended. Rooms have washing facilities and breakfast is included. There are also inexpensive family-run pensions with clean, basic rooms, but in general bathrooms are communal.

Interior of the Cappuccini Convento in Amalfi *(see p174)*

(see p173); *(see p119)*; *(see p174)*; *(see p175)*

View from the terrace of the Hotel Poseidon in Positano *(see p175)*

DIRECTORY

Associazione Albergatori Napoletani
Piazza Carità 32.
☎ 081551 49 02.

AIG Ostello Mercellina
Salita della Grotta 23.
☎ 081 761 23 46.

Camping
Camp sites are usually open from April to October, and are often near the sea. Small brown road-signs indicate the nearest site. The one closest to Naples is the **Vulcano Solfatara***. It is easily reached by metro (Ⓜ Pozzuoli), and has bungalows with 2–4 beds as well as a restaurant, swimming pool and a minimarket. Along the coast, at Meta di Sorrento is the* **Blue Village***, while Sorrento offers* **Nube d'Argento***, in the middle of an orange grove, and* **Campo Gaio***, directly overlooking the sea. On Ischia the* **Eurocamping dei Pini** *is about 1 km (half a mile) from the centre. A good alternative for those who want to be at the sea is the* **Mirage***, on Maronti beach. On Procida a good camp site is the* **Punta Serra***.*

Blue Village
Via Alimuri 7 (Sorrento).
☎ 081 878 65 57.

Campo Gaio
Via Capo 41 (Sorrento).
☎ 081 807 35 79.

Eurocamping dei Pini
Via delle Ginestre 28 (Ischia).
☎ 081 98 20 69.

Mirage
Spiaggia dei Maronti (Barano, Ischia).
☎ 081 99 05 51.

Nube d'Argento
Via Capo 21 (Sorrento).
☎ 081 878 13 44.

Punta Serra
Via Flavio Gioia (Procida).
☎ 081 896 95 19.

Vulcano Solfatara
Via Solfatara 161 (Pozzuoli).
☎ 081 526 74 13.

Choosing a Hotel

THE HOTELS in this guide have been carefully selected across a wide price range for the quality of service and location. They are listed by area. For more detailed information on exact locations in Naples, see the Street Finder on pages 212–27; for towns and islands in the rest of the region, see the Road Map on the inside back cover.

	CREDIT CARDS	GARDEN OR TERRACE	PRIVATE PARKING	RESTAURANT	BAR
NAPLES					
TOLEDO AND CASTEL NUOVO: *Jolly* €€€€	V AE DC			●	■
TOLEDO AND CASTEL NUOVO: *Mercure Angioino* €€€€	V AE DC		■		■
SPACCANAPOLI: *Soggiorno Sansevero* €€€€	V AE MC				
SPACCANAPOLI: *Executive* €€€€	V AE DC	●	■		■
SPACCANAPOLI: *Terminus* €€€€	V AE DC	●	■	●	■
DECUMANO MAGGIORE: *Hotel Duomo* €€			■		
CAPODIMONTE AND I VERGINI: *Villa Capodimonte* €€€	V AE DC	●	■	●	■
CASTEL DELL'OVO AND CHIAIA: *Pinto Storey* €€	V				■
CASTEL DELL'OVO AND CHIAIA: *Britannique* €€€	V AE DC	●	■	●	■

TOLEDO AND CASTEL NUOVO: *Jolly* €€€€
Via Medina 70. **Map** 7 B2. 081 41 05 111. FAX 081 551 80 10.
Situated in the heart of the city, in a skyscraper built in the 1950s, this hotel is popular with business people. Well equipped, modern rooms with views.
Rooms: 252 www.jollyhotels.it

TOLEDO AND CASTEL NUOVO: *Mercure Angioino* €€€€
Via A Depretis 123. **Map** 7 B2. 081 552 95 00. FAX 081 552 95 09.
Located between the university area and the port, offering good lodgings. Pleasant, light-filled public rooms; the bedrooms are tastefully furnished and soundproofed.
Rooms: 85 angioino@telnet.it

SPACCANAPOLI: *Soggiorno Sansevero* €€€€
Vicoletto San Domenico Maggiore 9. **Map** 3 B5 (9 C3). 081 551 59 49. FAX 081 21 16 98.
This pension is in an 18th-century building overlooking elegant Piazza San Domenico. Simple, unpretentious rooms for those who want to stay in the historic centre. Family atmosphere.
Rooms: 6

SPACCANAPOLI: *Executive* €€€€
Via del Cerriglio 10. **Map** 7 B1 (9 C5). 081 552 06 11. FAX 081 552 06 11.
Next to Santa Maria la Nova monastery (and occupying part of it), the Executive makes for a comfortable stay with its well-kept rooms, gym with sauna and terrace overflowing with flowers.
Rooms: 19 www.sea-hotels.com

SPACCANAPOLI: *Terminus* €€€€
Piazza Garibaldi 91. **Map** 4 E4. 081 779 31 11. FAX 081 20 66 89.
This hotel facing the railway station is used mostly by businessmen. Well-furnished rooms, each with its own balcony.
Rooms: 167

DECUMANO MAGGIORE: *Hotel Duomo* €€
Via Duomo 228. **Map** 3 C4. 081-26 59 88.
On the first floor of a 19th-century building, this small family-run hotel has pleasantly spacious and quiet rooms.
Rooms: 9

CAPODIMONTE AND I VERGINI: *Villa Capodimonte* €€€
Via Moiariello 66. **Map** 3 C1. 081 45 90 00. FAX 081 29 93 44.
Close to the Palace of Capodimonte, dominating the Sanità district. Its unusual location is ideal for those seeking good hospitality, quiet surroundings and something more unusual.
Rooms: 57

CASTEL DELL'OVO AND CHIAIA: *Pinto Storey* €€
Via G Martucci 72. **Map** 6 D2. 081 68 12 60. FAX 081 66 75 36.
A pension with a homely atmosphere in the elegant part of town. Opened in 1878, Pinto Storey is on the fourth floor and has a small lobby with plants and antique furniture. The rooms are simple, brightly lit and spacious.
Rooms: 25

CASTEL DELL'OVO AND CHIAIA: *Britannique* €€€
Corso Vittorio Emanuele 133. **Map** 6 D1. 081 761 41 45. FAX 081 66 97 60.
A hotel with an old tradition. Comfortable, light rooms with a view of the bay. The small, private garden with exotic plants is reserved for residents.
Rooms: 86 britannique@napleshotels.na.it www.hotelbritannique.it

Price categories for a standard double room per night, with tax, breakfast and service included: € under €52 €€ €52–€102 €€€ €102–€154 €€€€ €154–€206 €€€€€ over €206.	PARKING Private parking on premises or in nearby garage. Hotels usually charge for parking facilities. GARDEN OR TERRACE Public area outdoors reserved for guests. RESTAURANTS The hotel has a restaurant that is also open to non-residents. BAR The hotel has a bar also open to non-residents.	CREDIT CARDS	GARDEN OR TERRACE	PRIVATE PARKING	RESTAURANT	BAR

	CREDIT CARDS	GARDEN OR TERRACE	PRIVATE PARKING	RESTAURANT	BAR
CASTEL DELL'OVO AND CHIAIA: *Canada* €€€ Via Mergellina 43. **Map** 5 B3. **(** *081 68 20 18.* **FAX** *081 26 75 11.* Opposite the small Mergellina port and the hydrofoil embarkation point. The Canada has rooms with good views but rather small public areas. 🛏 TV **Rooms:** *12* @ info@sea-hotels.com 🇼 www.sea-hotels.com	V AE DC		▪		▪
CASTEL DELL'OVO AND CHIAIA: *Miramare* €€€€ Via Nazario Sauro 24. **Map** 7 A4. **(** *081 764 75 89.* **FAX** *081 764 07 75.* Located in a pastel-coloured Art Nouveau villa on the seafront. Rooms with every comfort and a view; a terrace for sunbathing in the summer. 🛏 TV 📧 **Rooms:** *31* @ info@hotelmiramare.com	V AE DC	●	▪		▪
CASTEL DELL'OVO AND CHIAIA: *Parker's* €€€€€ Corso Vittorio Emanuele 135. **Map** 6 D1. **(** *081 761 24 74.* **FAX** *081 66 35 27.* Traces of its history (the hotel dates from the 1870s) can be seen everywhere, starting in the reception rooms with period furniture and fine paintings. Views of the bay and Capri. 🛏 TV 📧 **Rooms:** *83* @ ghparker@tin.it 🇼 www.bcedit.it/parkershotel.htm	V AE DC	●	▪	●	▪
CASTEL DELL'OVO AND CHIAIA: *Santa Lucia* €€€€€ Via Partenope 46. **Map** 7 A4. **(** *081 764 06 66.* **FAX** *081 764 85 80.* The delicately coloured interior with Neo-Classical furnishings creates a romantic atmosphere. One of the historic hotels on the seafront with elegant, light rooms overlooking Castel dell'Ovo and Borgo Marinaro. 🛏 TV 📧 **Rooms:** *100* @ reservations@santalucia.it 🇼 www.santalucia.it	V AE DC		▪		▪
CASTEL DELL'OVO AND CHIAIA: *Excelsior* €€€€€ Via Partenope 48. **Map** 7 A4. **(** *081 764 01 11.* **FAX** *081 764 97 43.* An historic hotel with a view of Castel dell'Ovo and Capri, the Excelsior has accommodated many famous guests. The rooms with Belle Epoque marble, mirrors and curtains are very atmospheric. 🛏 TV 📧 **Rooms:** *120* @ info@excelsior.it 🇼 www.excelsior.it	V AE DC	●	▪	●	▪
CASTEL DELL'OVO AND CHIAIA: *Vesuvio* €€€€€ Via Partenope 45. **Map** 7 A4. **(** *081 764 00 44.* **FAX** *081 764 44 83.* The great tenor Enrico Caruso spent his last night in the suite named after him. This historic hotel, with fine views over the bay, has been popular with celebrities since it opened in the 19th century. 🛏 TV 📧 **Rooms:** *167* @ info@prestigehotels.it 🇼 www.vesuvio.it	V AE DC	●	▪	●	▪
POSILLIPO: *Paradiso* €€€€ Via Catullo 11. **Map** 5 A4. **(** *081 761 41 61.* **FAX** *081 761 34 49.* Quite near the funicular that takes you to Mergellina in a few minutes, this hotel is in an extraordinary position dominating the entire bay. In the summer, romantic breakfasts are served on the terrace with a view of Vesuvius. 🛏 TV 📧 **Rooms:** *75* @ paradiso.na@bestwestern.it	V AE DC	●	▪	●	▪
SORRENTO PENINSULA					
POMPEI: *Hotel Piccolo Sogno* €€ Via Carlo Alberto, Prima Traversa, 2. **Road map** D3. **(** *081 863 12 79.* **FAX** *081 863 12 79.* This recently renovated, family-run hotel is conveniently located within walking distance of the ancient town. 🛏 TV **Rooms:** *7*	V AE		▪	●	
SANT'AGNELLO (SORRENTO): *Cocumella* €€€€€ Via Cocumella 7. **Road map** C4. **(** *081 878 29 33.* **FAX** *081 878 37 12.* Situated in a former 17th-century monastery surrounded by greenery, this hotel has a private beach. Several rooms have terraces overlooking the sea, while the old cloister is now used for functions. ⬤ *Nov–Mar.* 🛏 TV 📧 🏊 **Rooms:** *50* @ hcocum@tin.it	V AE DC	●	▪	●	▪

For key to symbols see back flap

Price categories for a standard double room per night, with tax, breakfast and service included: € under €52 €€ €52–€102 €€€ €102–€154 €€€€ €154–v206 €€€€€ over €206.	**PARKING** Private parking on premises or in nearby garage. Hotels usually charge for parking facilities. **GARDEN OR TERRACE** Public area outdoors reserved for guests. **RESTAURANTS** The hotel has a restaurant that is also open to non-residents. **BAR** The hotel has a bar also open to non-residents.	**CREDIT CARDS**	**GARDEN OR TERRACE**	**PRIVATE PARKING**	**RESTAURANT**	**BAR**

SORRENTO: *Loreley et Londres* €€ Via Califano 2. **Road map** C4. ☎ 081 807 31 87. FAX 081 807 31 87. An hotel with a panoramic view and lift that takes you down to the beach. The retreat of writer Sibilla Aleramo in the early 1900s. ● *Dec–Mar.* 🛏 **Rooms:** 23	V AE	●	■	●	■
SORRENTO: *Bellevue Syrene* €€€€€ Piazza della Vittoria 5. **Road map** C4. ☎ 081 878 10 24. FAX 081 878 39 63. Surrounded by a garden with access to a private beach via a lift, this 19th-century villa has Neo-Classical furnishings and frescoed rooms *(see p149)*. Each room has a balcony and view of the park or sea. 🛏 TV 📶 ♿ **Rooms:** 76 @ info@bellevue.it @ www.bellevue.it	V AE DC	●	■	●	■
SORRENTO: *Excelsior Vittoria* €€€€€ Piazza Tasso 34. **Road map** C4. ☎ 081 807 10 44. FAX 081 877 12 06. This old hotel consists of four buildings in different styles and visitors have included Byron and Goethe. Tastefully furnished rooms, frescoed salons, and a large terrace jutting out over the sea. 🛏 TV 📶 🏊 **Rooms:** 105 @ exvitt@exvitt.it	V AE DC	●	■	●	■
SORRENTO: *Imperial Tramontano* €€€€€ Via Veneto 1. **Road map** C4. ☎ 081 878 25 88. FAX 081 807 23 44. This historic hotel was the birthplace of poet Torquato Tasso *(see p149)*. Surrounded by an ancient park and full of atmosphere, the Tramontano offers comfort and elegance and an easy descent to the sea. 🛏 TV 📶 🏊 **Rooms:** 116 @ imperial@tramontana.it W www.tramontano.it	V AE DC	●	■	●	■

AMALFI COAST

AMALFI: *La Bussola* €€€€ Lungomare dei Cavalieri 1. **Road map** D4. ☎ 089 87 15 33. FAX 089 87 13 69. This family-run hotel is located inside a converted mill. The rooms are clean and simple and the public areas have a view of the sea. Guests can take advantage of the sun terrace on the cliff. 🛏 **Rooms:** 40 @ labussola@amalficoast.it	V AE DC	●	■	●	■
AMALFI: *Luna Torre Saracena* €€€€ Via Comite 33. **Road map** D4. ☎ 089 87 10 02. FAX 089 87 13 33. Ibsen wrote his play *A Doll's House* in one of the cells in this former monastery, which many still find inspirational. Breakfast is served in the impressive Byzantine cloister. 🛏 TV 📶 🏊 **Rooms:** 40 @ luna@amalficoast.it W www.lunahotel.it	V AE DC	●	■	●	■
AMALFI: *Cappuccini Convento* €€€€ Via Annunziatella 46. **Road map** D4. ☎ 089 87 18 77. FAX 089 87 18 86. This old monastery, since transformed into a hotel, stands in the middle of a garden. It has a commanding view of the sea, a chapel and an Arab-Norman cloister. 🛏 TV 📶 **Rooms:** 54 @ cappuccini@amalfinet.it W www.amalfinet.it/cappuccini	V AE DC	●	■	●	■
AMALFI: *Santa Caterina* €€€€€ Strada Statale Amalfitana 9. **Road map** D4. ☎ 089 87 10 12. FAX 089 87 13 51. About a kilometre (half a mile) from Amalfi, this exclusive hotel offers excellent service, graceful salons, an elegant restaurant, rooms with fine views, a garden descending to the sea and a private beach. 🛏 TV 📶 🏊 **Rooms:** 66 @ info@hotelsantacaterina.it W www.santacaterina.it	V AE DC	●	■	●	■
POSITANO: *Casa Soriano* €€ Via Pasitea 108. **Road map** D4. ☎ 089 87 54 94. This 18th-century villa is a real hideaway. It is in an extraordinary location, with spectacular balconies overlooking the sea and its rooms have vaulted ceilings. ● *Oct–Mar.* 🛏 **Rooms:** 8		●			

POSITANO: *Casa Albertina*   €€€
Via della Tavolozza 3. **Road map** D4. 089 87 51 43. FAX 089 81 15 40.
Perched on a ridge (300 steps above the sea), this delightful
family-run hotel is simple and peaceful.
Rooms: 19 @ alcaal@starnet.it

| V |
| AE |
| DC |

POSITANO: *Palazzo Murat*   €€€€€
Via dei Mulini 23. **Road map** D4. 089 87 51 77. FAX 089 81 14 19.
This 18th-century residence with a courtyard lobby was the home
of Joachim Murat, once ruler of Naples. The rooms in the old wing
are furnished with antiques. ● *Jan–Mar.*
Rooms: 30 @ hpm@starnet.it W www.starnet.it/murat

| V |
| AE |
| DC |

POSITANO: *Poseidon*   €€€€
Via Pasitea 148. **Road map** D4. 089 81 11 11. FAX 089 87 58 33.
A romantic, cosy Mediterranean hotel a few minutes from the beach,
with a swimming pool and a health and beauty parlour. It is co-managed
by the Tuscan spa baths Terme di Saturnia. ● *Nov–Easter.*
Rooms: 50 @ poseidon@starnet.it W www.poseidonpositano.it

| V |
| AE |
| DC |

POSITANO: *San Pietro*   €€€€€
Via Laurito 2. **Road map** D4. 089 87 54 55. FAX 089 81 14 49.
Perched over the sea, 2 km (1.5 miles) from Positano, this luxury hotel offers
every comfort. International stars such as Sting, Mick Jagger and Tina Turner
have stayed here. ● *Nov–the week before Easter.*
Rooms: 62 @ info@ilsanpietro.it W www.ilsanpietro.it

| V |
| AE |
| DC |

POSITANO: *Le Sirenuse*   €€€€€
Via C Colombo 30. **Road map** D4. 089 87 50 66. FAX 089 81 17 98.
A noble mansion transformed into an elegant hotel with
precious objects and antique furniture. The rooms have a stunning
view that has enchanted famous guests from John Steinbeck to
Ronald Reagan. ● *Dec–Feb.*
Rooms: 62 @ info@sirenuse.it W www.sirenuse.it

| V |
| AE |
| DC |

RAVELLO: *Caruso Belvedere*   €€€
Piazza San Giovanni del Toro 2. **Road map** D4.
089 85 71 11. FAX 089 85 72 99.
In business for over a century, the Caruso Belvedere has frescoed halls, period
furniture and a terraced garden. Greta Garbo fell in love with this place.
Rooms: 24

| V |
| AE |
| DC |

RAVELLO: *Graal*   €€€€
Via della Repubblica 4. **Road map** D4. 089 85 72 22. FAX 089 85 75 51.
A pleasant family-run hotel in a peaceful location and with a good
swimming pool. All the rooms have balconies and the restaurant
offers excellent home-cooked food.
Rooms: 35 @ info@hotelgraal.it W www.hotelgraal.it

| V |
| AE |
| DC |

RAVELLO: *Villa Cimbrone*   €€€€€
Via Santa Chiara 26. **Road map** D4. 089 85 74 59. FAX 089 85 77 77.
Once the home of an English lord who wanted to reconstruct the original
building in Neo-Gothic style, this hotel, in the middle of the famous Villa
Cimbrone park, is only a ten-minute walk from town. ● *Oct–Mar.*
Rooms: 19 @ info@villacimbrone.it W www.villacimbrone.it

| V |
| AE |

RAVELLO: *Palumbo*   €€€€€
Via San Giovanni del Toro 28. **Road map** D4.
089 85 72 44. FAX 089 85 81 33.
The 12th-century Palazzo Confalone is now a charming hotel. In
the lobby, traces of Moorish architecture frame a panoramic view
of the coast. The rooms, furnished with antiques, look out onto a
citrus grove that descends to the sea.
Rooms: 18 @ reception@hotelpalumbo.it W www.hotelpalumbo.it

| V |
| AE |
| DC |

CAPRI

ANACAPRI: *San Michele*   €€€
Via G Orlandi. **Road map** C4. 081 837 14 42. FAX 081 837 14 20.
A late 19th-century hotel with an appealing, old-fashioned atmosphere.
Quiet and simple, the rooms have a view of the sea or of Monte Solaro.
● *Nov–Mar.*
Rooms: 60 @ smichele@capri.it

| V |
| AE |
| DC |

For key to symbols see back flap

	CREDIT CARDS	GARDEN OR TERRACE	PRIVATE PARKING	RESTAURANT	BAR

Price categories for a standard double room per night, with tax, breakfast and service included:
€ under €52
€€ €52–€102
€€€ €102–€154
€€€€ €154–€206
€€€€€ over €206.

PARKING
Private parking on premises or in nearby garage. Hotels usually charge for parking facilities.
GARDEN OR TERRACE
Public area outdoors reserved for guests.
RESTAURANTS
The hotel has a restaurant that is also open to non-residents.
BAR
The hotel has a bar also open to non-residents.

CAPRI: *La Tosca* € Via Birago 5. **Road map** C5. ☎ 081 837 09 89. Secluded: for those who prefer the appealing silence and simplicity of the "other" Capri. Book well in advance for rooms with a view. ● *Nov–Mar 22.* **Rooms:** *12* @ h.tosca@capri.it	V	●			■
CAPRI: *Belvedere e Tre Re* €€€ Via Marina Grande 138. **Road map** C5. FAX 081 837 03 45. Opened in the mid-1800s. Its name *(tre re)* derives from a visit paid by three Scandinavian kings. Rooms with a view, dining room with large windows overlooking the sea, veranda and piano. 🛏 **Rooms:** *15* W www.belvedere-tre-re.com	V MC	●		●	■
CAPRI: *Gatto Bianco* €€€€ Via Vittorio Emanuele 32. **Road map** C5. ☎ 081 837 02 03. FAX 081 837 80 60. A classic example of Capri hospitality: in the centre of town but quiet, with inviting rooms and quaint furniture, wide sofas and coloured ceramics. Almost all the rooms have a terrace. ● *Nov–Easter.* 🛏 TV **Rooms:** *36*	V AE DC	●		●	■
CAPRI: *La Palma* €€€€ Via Vittorio Emanuele 39. **Road map** C5. ☎ 081 837 01 33. FAX 081 837 69 66. The oldest hotel in Capri, with tastefully furnished rooms. The bar is a fashionable haunt for islanders. ● *Jan, Feb.* 🛏 TV ▤ **Rooms:** *74* @ hlp@caprionline.it W www.lapalma-capri.com	V AE DC	●		●	■
CAPRI: *Villa Krupp* €€€€ Via G Matteotti 12. **Road map** C5. ☎ 081 837 03 62. FAX 081 837 64 89. Once the home of Russian author Maxim Gorky, who entertained Lenin here, the Villa Krupp is quite close to the Piazzetta. Family-run, rooms without frills and with a view of the sea and the Faraglioni rocks. ● *Nov–Feb.* 🛏 **Rooms:** *12*	V	●			
CAPRI: *Quisisana* €€€€€ Via Camerelle 2. **Road map** C5. ☎ 081 837 07 88. FAX 081 837 60 80. In the mid-19th century this was a sanatorium founded by an English physician. Now it is one of the top ten hotels in the world, with large, elegant rooms, a gym, two swimming pools, two restaurants and an ultra-fashionable bar. ● *Nov–one week before Easter.* 🛏 TV ▤ 🏊 **Rooms:** *150* @ info@quisi.com W www.quisi.com	V AE DC	●		●	■
CAPRI: *Villa Brunella* €€€€€ Via Tregara 24a. **Road map** C5. ☎ 081 837 01 22. FAX 081 837 04 30. From the terrace-restaurant a steep stairway leads to the hotel rooms, which are quiet and comfortable. The hotel overlooks a lemon grove, and has a large swimming pool. ● *Nov–one week before Easter.* 🛏 TV ▤ 🏊 **Rooms:** *20* @ villabrunella@capri.it W www.villabrunella.it	V AE DC	●		●	■

ISCHIA

FORIO D'ISCHIA: *Hotel della Baia* €€€ Via San Montano 18/22. **Road map** A4. ☎ 081 98 63 98. FAX 081 98 63 42. A Mediterranean style, pastel-coloured, pleasant hotel a few steps from the San Montano beach and the Negombo thermal park. ● *Oct–Apr.* 🛏 TV ▤ **Rooms:** *20* @ negombo@mklink.it W www.negombo.it	V AE DC	●	■	●	■
FORIO D'ISCHIA: *Il Vitigno* €€ Via Bocca 31. **Road map** A4. ☎ 081 99 83 07. FAX 081 99 83 07. A farm holiday on an ancient farmstead surrounded by vines *(vitigno)*. The rooms are plain and rustic. The excellent food is made from local produce and the wine is from vineyards on the property. 🛏 **Rooms:** *6*		●	■		

FORIO D'ISCHIA: *Mezzatorre* €€€€€
Località San Montano. **Road map** A4. 081 98 61 11. FAX 081 98 60 15.
This magnificent hotel lies at the end of San Montano bay, built around
a Saracen tower, between the sea and a thick grove of pine and
holm-oak trees. ● *Nov–Apr.*
Rooms: 58 @ info@mezzatorre.it

V
AE
DC

ISCHIA PONTE: *Il Monastero* €€
Castello Aragonese. **Road map** B4. 081 99 24 35.
The plain rooms are offset by the unique position: from the Castello
rock there is a magnificent view of ancient Ponte and the sea.
Ideal for those who love secluded spots. ● *mid-Oct–Mar.*
Rooms: 22 @ ilmonasterocastello.it W www.castelloaragonese.it

V
AE
DC

ISCHIA PONTE: *Miramare e Castello* €€€€€
Via Pontano 9. **Road map** B4. 081 99 13 33. FAX 081 98 29 38.
Situated opposite Castello Aragonese, this hotel offers elegant public areas
and rooms as well as perfect service. There is no lack of facilities:
three swimming pools (one with thermal water), a beauty parlour and
a private beach. ● *Oct–Apr.*
Rooms: 40 @ mircastl@metis.it

V
AE
DC

ISCHIA PORTO: *La Villarosa* €€€€
Via G Gigante 5. **Road map** B4. 081 99 13 16. FAX 081 99 24 25.
The original nucleus was a farmhouse. The hotel stands in a shady garden
where there are independent chalets with two-room suites. The rooms,
chalets and public areas are tastefully furnished. Swimming pool and
water cures are available. ● *Nov–Mar.*
Rooms: 37 @ hotel@villarosa.it

V
AE

ISCHIA PORTO: *Il Moresco Grand Hotel e Terme* €€€€€
Via E Gianturco 16. **Road map** B4. 081 98 13 55. FAX 081 99 23 38.
The Moresco, in a pine grove next to the beach, is typical of the high-quality
hotels in Ischia: elegant Moorish-style halls, rooms with terraces, thermal
pools, beauty parlour and tennis courts. ● *Oct–Apr.*
Rooms: 70 @ moresco@leohotel.it W www.ilmoresco.it

V
AE
DC

LACCO AMENO: *Hotel Regina Isabella* €€€€€
Piazza Santa Restituta. **Road map** A4. 081 99 43 22. FAX 081 90 01 90.
Directly overlooking the sea, this luxury hotel was a favourite with
cinema directors and stars in the 1950s. Sophisticated and elegant,
with good facilities: tennis, thermal pools, sauna and private beach.
● *mid-Jan–Mar.*
Rooms: 134 @ info@reginaisabella.it W www.reginaisabella.it

V
AE
DC

SANT'ANGELO: *Casa Conchiglia* €€
Via Chiaia delle Rose 3. **Road map** A4. 081 99 92 70. FAX 081 99 92 70.
Overlooking the sea, this small pension has simple, clean rooms,
all with a balcony and view. ● *Nov–Apr.*
Rooms: 12

SANT'ANGELO: *Park Hotel Miramare* €€€€€
Via Comandante Maddalena 29. **Road map** A4. 081 99 92 19.
Close to the lively village of Sant'Angelo, one of the loveliest spots on
the island, this hotel overlooks the sea and is a short distance from
the famous spa of Aphrodite-Apollon. ● *Nov–Mar.*
Rooms: 55 @ hotel@hotelmiramare.it W www.hotelmiramare.it

V
AE
DC

PROCIDA

MARINA DELLA CHIAIOLELLA: *Crescenzo* €€
Road map B3. 081 896 72 55. FAX 081 810 12 60.
In the atmospheric fishermen's quarter opposite the island of Vivara,
this small hotel has only a few charming, light rooms and is well known
because it has one of the best fish restaurants in Procida.
Rooms: 10

V
AE
DC

MARINA CORRICELLA: *Pensione Gentile* €€
Road map B3. 081 896 77 99. FAX 081 896 90 11.
In the old fishermen's quarter where the steps wind down to the
sea among multi-coloured houses, this small, secluded pension
offers rooms with a terrace and panoramic views.
Rooms: 10

For key to symbols see back flap

RESTAURANTS, CAFÉS AND BARS

Neapolitan pizzeria sign

THE REGION KNOWN to the Romans as *Campania felix* (happy country) revels in food, especially the fruit, vegetables and vines that grow in abundance on every available slope. Neapolitan cuisine is well known throughout the world, thanks to the emigrants who took pizza and pasta with them wherever they went. Neapolitans have never given up their passion for good food, and eating is a social occasion here – all important events are celebrated with huge meals that may last half a day. Key elements in Neapolitan cuisine are pasta, olive oil and tomatoes, but all along the coast and on the islands you'll find the freshest seafood and fish dishes, from simple pasta sauces to generous fish stews. This is also the home of ice cream, and delectable cakes and pastries.

TYPES OF RESTAURANTS AND BARS

NAPLES AND the outlying area offer a wide choice of restaurants, trattorias and bars to suit all budgets. A *ristorante* may be smarter (and more expensive) than a *trattoria*, and a trattoria may be more informal. Every part of Campania has its own specialities and similar recipes may be interpreted in quite different ways in different locations. Family-run trattorias usually offer excellent home-style cooking. Many of the most exclusive restaurants in Naples are located in the seafront area. In Posillipo the famous restaurants are expensive but you will be seated in front of breathtaking views and the mild climate means you can eat outdoors practically all year round.

The city centre is the place to go for less pretentious and cheaper trattorias and pizzerias with typical Neapolitan food. A pizzeria

The Lido Marechiaro *(see p125)* **looking out on to the Bay of Naples**

will offer pasta, meat and fish dishes as well as pizza. In the Spaccanapoli and Decumano Maggiore districts there are trattorias known as *vini e cucina* where you can eat quite cheaply. Besides good wine served by the bottle or from the barrel, these are good places for trying genuine Neapolitan home cooking. They are usually family-run and small, located in the popular areas; the interiors may be quite plain, with plastic tablecloths and paper napkins; and the menu will either be written on a blackboard or recited at your table by the waiter. *Vini e cucina* are popular with locals and students, so you can also experience authentic Neapolitan life. At *tavole calde* (snack bars) first and second courses are economically priced.

The food on sale at the stalls and *friggitorie* (for fried food) is often very good: potato croquettes, fried pizzas *(pizzelle)* and *panzerotti* (ravioli). Bars usually offer filled rolls *(panini)* and sandwiches *(tramezzini)*, as well as cakes and pastries, and assorted drinks. Many bars also operate as *gelaterie*, with a tempting range of ice creams.

HOW MUCH TO PAY

THE AVERAGE PRICE for a full meal at a trattoria is about €14, and it can be as little as €8 in pizzerias and *vini e cucina*. Restaurants cost from €18–€20 upwards. *Vino sfuso*, or house wine, is often served in jugs and is inexpensive. Fresh fish is usually sold by weight, which can make calculating the cost of your meal difficult. You may find it can be quite expensive.

The Da Carmine trattoria *(see p182)*

Eating outdoors, one of the many pleasures of Naples

OPENING HOURS

RESTAURANTS ARE generally open from 12:30 to 3:30pm and from 8pm to midnight, but this may vary somewhat, especially at weekends and in summer, when you can dine until fairly late. Family-run trattorias have more limited business hours and are usually closed on Sundays and in August, especially around Ferragosto (15 Aug), when many shops in the city are closed for holidays. The restaurants in tourist centres on the islands and along the coast usually close in the winter and open around Easter.

A wood-fired pizza oven

MAKING RESERVATIONS AND PAYING

RESTAURANTS AND pizzerias tend to be very crowded on Saturday evening, so it's best to book in advance or arrive early. It is also a good idea to book during the holiday season or on local feast days. Service charges are included in the prices on the menu, but it is customary to leave a tip of around ten per cent. The larger restaurants accept major credit cards.

READING THE MENU

A TYPICAL NEAPOLITAN menu begins with antipasti, which are so varied and interesting they make a meal in themselves: seafood salad, sautéed clams and mussels, or tomatoes, peppers and aubergines cooked in various different ways. The first course *(primo)* will depend on the season: spaghetti with seafood, *parmigiana di melanzane (see p180)* or a simple tomato, mozzarella and basil salad *(insalata caprese)* for lunch at the seaside; pasta and meat sauce or *sartù di riso (see p181)* for a heartier winter lunch. Among the main courses *(secondi)*, you can choose calamari or squid in tomato sauce, assorted fried fish *(fritto misto)* or grilled fish *(grigliata mista)*, or fried

QUI 100 ANNI FA
NACQUE LA PIZZA MARGHERITA
1889   1989
BRANDI
Centenary of the Margherita pizza

baby mozzarella, artichokes and potato or rice croquettes. You must try the vegetable pies; the most famous is made with endive and, in the winter, *friarelli,* a type of broccoli found only in Naples. They are sauteed in a pan with *peperoncino* (hot chilli pepper) and are usually served with sausages.

PIZZERIAS

N APLES IS THE ORIGINAL home of authentic pizza, freshly made and baked in wood-fired ovens. True pizza was originally a peasant dish, made very simply from dough spread with olive oil and tomatoes, and dating from the 18th century. Eaten at any hour of the day in the poorer neighbourhoods of Naples, it was ignored by everyone else until Queen Margherita, the wife of Umberto I, decided to try this famous dish. The pizza Margherita, with mozzarella and basil added to create the colours of the Italian flag – red, white and green – was invented in her honour. It is now found in every pizzeria, not only in Italy but wherever pizza is sold. Neapolitan pizza chefs are famous for their creative flair, and as well as classic toppings like the Margherita and the Marinara (tomato, anchovies), you may find they offer to create their own chef's special.

Inside La Bersagliera restaurant *(see p183)*

What to Eat and Drink in Naples

Colander and oil pourer

Neapolitan cuisine is based on "the three Ps": pizza, pasta and *pomodoro* (tomato). Pizza, perhaps the most ingenious gastronomic invention of all time, was first created here and is now known all over the world. Although pasta is not of Neapolitan origin, the city is its adoptive home. The tomato is a symbol of Southern Italian cooking and is used in an infinite number of ways: fresh with salad, dried, peeled, pulped or concentrated. But there's much more to Neapolitan cuisine: from very simple dishes that require fresh, top-quality ingredients to the rich and elaborate dishes inherited from the aristocratic cuisine of the past, such as timbales, elaborate stuffings and deliciously soft pastries.

Frutti di Mare (Seafood)
Served with spaghetti or risotto, fried or grilled as a main course, fresh seafood is found all along the coast.

Pasta e Fagioli
This is a simple dish of pasta and beans; one of many ideas combining vegetables or pulses with pasta.

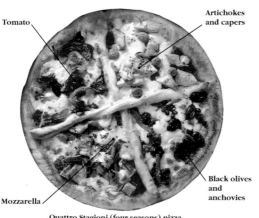

Artichokes and capers

Tomato

Black olives and anchovies

Mozzarella

Quattro Stagioni (four seasons) pizza

Pizza
Pizza is eaten everywhere, and served with a great variety of typical Mediterranean toppings, such as olives, capers, anchovies and herbs. Pizza may even be sold by the metre, as at Vico Equense, near Sorrento.

Spaghetti con le Vongole
This is a typical first course: spaghetti and fresh clams, served plain or with tomato sauce, sprinkled with parsley.

Parmigiana di Melanzane
Layers of aubergines, tomato sauce, mozzarella, grated Parmesan and basil are combined for this dish. Courgettes may be used.

CHEESE AND DAIRY PRODUCE
Mozzarella, made with buffalo milk, is the best of the local cheeses. Fiordilatte and treccia di mozzarella (made from cow's milk) are excellent with tomatoes and basil. There are many types of provolone and scamorza (stuffed, smoked), depending on their origin. Fresh ricotta is used both for savouries and sweet pastries. Grated Parmesan is often added to pasta.

Ricotta

Provolone

Mozzarella   **Parmesan**   *Scamorza*

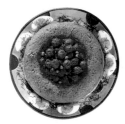

Sartù di Riso
This rice mould, served with garnishes, is one of the more elaborate Neapolitan dishes.

Aubergines, artichokes, peppers
Vegetables are served as antipasti or with main courses.

basil

dried oregano

parsley

Aromatic herbs
Basil and oregano (dried or fresh) are frequently used to flavour dishes based on tomato and mozzarella, while flat-leaved parsley is served with fish dishes.

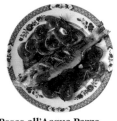

Pesce all'Acqua Pazza
For this dish, fresh fish is cooked in a little water, with tomatoes, garlic and parsley.

Babà
(rum baba)

Sfogliatelle
(millefeuilles)

Zeppole
(doughnuts)

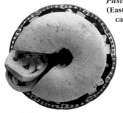

Pastiera
(Easter cake)

Pastries
Sfogliatelle are filled with ricotta, sugar and candied fruit and come as sweet shortcrust pastry or shell-shaped puff pastry. Other special occasion cakes are pastiera *(Christmas and Easter)*, struffoli *(pastries with honey and fruit, for Christmas)* and zeppole *for San Giuseppe* (see p40).

Carne al Ragù
A typical Sunday meal is meat rolls served with savoury tomato sauce.

Casatiello
This traditional country-style pie is made for Easter festivities, with salami, cheese and egg stuffing.

Wines and Drinks
The white Lacrima Christi (see p138) wine, made for centuries by monks on the slopes of Vesuvius, goes well with fish dishes. Greco di Tufo is another good white wine. Limoncello is a lemon-flavoured liqueur.

Lacryma Christi

1989

Limoncello

NEAPOLITAN COFFEE

The coffee made with a typical Neapolitan coffee maker is excellent. It is lighter than espresso and tastes good even when re-heated. The coffee maker consists of two metal cylinders, one with a spout, and a central container to hold finely ground roast coffee. The *caffettiera* is a percolator and not a steam pressure espresso machine.

Neapolitan *caffettiera*

Choosing a Restaurant

THE RESTAURANTS in this chart have been selected for their high quality of food and value for money. They are listed by price category and district (Naples) or region (outside Naples). See the Street Finder on pp212–27 for map references in Naples; for those in other areas, see the Road Map on the inside back cover.

	Credit Cards	Open at Midday	Late Opening	Outdoor Tables	Good Wine List
NAPLES					

TOLEDO AND CASTEL NUOVO: *Amici Miei* €€
Via Monte di Dio 78. **Map** 6 F2. 081 764 60 63. **FAX** 081 245 59 95.
A classic menu with mainly meat dishes. Excellent first courses, especially pasta with vegetables and pulses. The atmosphere is cosy. ▤
● Sun eve, Mon; Aug.
Credit Cards: V AE DC; Open at Midday ●; Late Opening ■

TOLEDO AND CASTEL NUOVO: *Ciro a Santa Brigida* €€€
Via Santa Brigida 71. **Map** 7 A2. 081 552 40 72.
This temple of Neapolitan cuisine opened in the 1930s and has won its share of regular patrons. It features traditional fare such as *sartù di riso* and *minestra maritata* (vegetable soup), and its pizzas are exquisite.
● Sun; 12 days at Ferragosto (15 Aug).
Credit Cards: V AE DC; Open at Midday ●; Late Opening ■; Good Wine List ■

SPACCANAPOLI: *Da Michele* €
Via C Sersale 1/3. **Map** 4 D5 (10 F3). 081 553 92 04.
This 19th-century establishment still has its original marble tables. It prepares only classic pizzas such as Margherita and Marinara.
● Sun; 12 days in Aug.
Open at Midday ●; Late Opening ■

SPACCANAPOLI: *Trianon* €
Via P Colletta 46. **Map** 4 D4 (10 F2). 081 553 94 26.
The city's most popular pizzeria, in business since the 1930s, features three sizes of pizzas: "mignon", normal and "maxi".
● Sun lunch.
Open at Midday ●; Late Opening ■

SPACCANAPOLI: *Lombardi a Santa Chiara* €€€
Via B Croce 59. **Map** 3 B5 (9 C4). 081 552 07 80. **FAX** 081 552 07 80.
Situated in the heart of the old city, Lombardi's is known for its traditional cuisine and especially for its excellent pizzas.
● Mon; Aug.
Credit Cards: V AE; Open at Midday ●; Late Opening ■

SPACCANAPOLI: *La Taverna dell'Arte* €€€
Rampe San Giovanni Maggiore 1/a. **Map** 3 B5 (9 C4). 081 552 75 58.
This restaurant in a pleasant setting has a limited number of tables, so book in advance. The menu is based on traditional Neapolitan recipes, including delectable desserts. In the summer, dinner is served outside under a pergola.
● Sun; Aug.
Credit Cards: V; Late Opening ■; Outdoor Tables ●; Good Wine List ■

DECUMANO MAGGIORE: *Da Carmine* €
Via dei Tribunali 330. **Map** 3 B5 (9 C3). 081 29 43 83.
Don Carmine runs the kitchen, while the rest of the family sees to the table service; the result is wholesome, tasty food and a warm atmosphere.
● 12 days in Aug.
Open at Midday ●; Late Opening ■

DECUMANO MAGGIORE: *Al 53* €€
Piazza Dante 53. **Map** 3 A5 (9 B3). 081 549 93 72.
Traditional cooking that varies according to the season. The antipasti alone are worth the trip; from seafood salad to macaroni omelette.
Credit Cards: V AE DC; Open at Midday ●; Late Opening ■; Outdoor Tables ●

DECUMANO MAGGIORE: *Mimì alla Ferrovia* €€€
Via A d'Aragona 21. **Map** 4 E4. 081 553 85 25.
Traditional, tasty food popular with lawyers from the nearby law courts.
● Sun; 12 days in Aug.
Credit Cards: V AE DC; Open at Midday ●; Late Opening ■; Outdoor Tables ●

VOMERO: *Il Cortile* €€
Via Cilea 129. **Map** 4 D2. 081 560 40 48.
Original, mainly vegetarian dishes – such as small pizzas with *friarelli* (broccoli), ravioli with *caciotta* cheese and marjoram, meat loaf with vegetable stuffing – are rounded off with fine home-made desserts.
● Sun, Mon; 15 days in Aug.
Credit Cards: V AE; Open at Midday ●; Late Opening ■; Outdoor Tables ●

	CREDIT CARDS	OPEN AT MIDDAY	LATE OPENING	OUTDOOR TABLES	GOOD WINE LIST

Price categories for a three-course evening meal for two, including a half-bottle of house wine, tax and service:
€ under €18
€€ €18–€28
€€€ €28–€38
€€€€ €38–€50
€€€€€ over €50.

OPEN AT MIDDAY
Often open all day, with a break in the late afternoon to prepare for the evening session.
LATE OPENING
Orders will be accepted until midnight.
OUTDOOR TABLES
Facilities for eating outdoors, on a terrace (often with a good view), or in a garden during the summer.
GOOD WINE LIST
A wide range of specially selected good wines – local, national and international.

	CREDIT CARDS	OPEN AT MIDDAY	LATE OPENING	OUTDOOR TABLES	GOOD WINE LIST
VOMERO: *Steak House* €€ Piazzetta A Falcone 2. **Map** 1 C5. 081 578 23 06. In rustic surroundings, choose from a menu consisting mostly of variations on the theme of grilled meat and fried potatoes. ● Mon; 15 days in Aug.	V AE		■	●	
CASTEL DELL'OVO AND CHIAIA: *Osteria della Mattonella* € Via Nicotera 13. **Map** 6 F1. 081 41 65 41. This small, family-run trattoria with wooden tables and walls covered with tiles *(mattonelle)* conjures up traditional, tasty food. ● Sun pm; 15 days in Aug.		●	■		
CASTEL DELL'OVO AND CHIAIA: *La Cantina di Triunfo* €€ Riviera di Chiaia 64. **Map** 5 C2. 081 66 01 01. A century ago this was a wine shop. Nowadays, while La Cantina's speciality continues to be its wines and liqueurs (try the *rosolí*) – it also offers a small, daily-changing menu of high-quality cooking. ● Sun; Aug.	V DC AE				■
CASTEL DELL'OVO AND CHIAIA: *Vadinchenia* €€ Via Pontano 21. **Map** 5 B4. 081 66 02 65. Delicate dishes, often based on fish, abound on the innovative, seasonal menu at this restaurant. The regional specialities are prepared with real passion, and the desserts are delicious. ● Sun; Aug.	V AE DC				■
CASTEL DELL'OVO AND CHIAIA: *La Bersagliera* €€€ Borgo Marinaro. **Map** 7 A5. 081 764 60 16. **FAX** 081 764 95 96. The location of this excellent fish restaurant is really special: right on the seafront with views of Castel dell'Ovo and Mount Vesuvius. ● Tue; 10 days Jan.	V AE DC	●	■	●	
CASTEL DELL'OVO AND CHIAIA: *Don Salvatore* €€€ Via Mergellina 5. **Map** 5 B4. 081 68 18 17. **FAX** 081 66 12 41. Back to basics with carefully prepared traditional Neapolitan cuisine and a well-stocked wine cellar. The wide selection of antipasti is accompanied by tasty bread, as well as pizza and wonderfully fresh fish. ● Wed. ♿	V AE DC	●		●	■
CASTEL DELL'OVO AND CHIAIA: *Ciro a Mergellina* €€€€ Via Mergellina 18. **Map** 5 B4. 081 68 17 80. Noisy and crowded, an all-time favourite with Neapolitans, Ciro a Mergellina is known for its antipasti (for example squid in sauce and mixed fried fish), really fresh fish as a main course and excellent pizzas. ● Mon; Fri in summer.	V AE DC	●	■	●	
CASTEL DELL'OVO AND CHIAIA: *Da Dora* €€€€ Via F Palasciano 28. **Map** 5 C2. 081 68 05 19. This family-run trattoria features delicious fish recipes. Try the *linguine alla Dora* with fresh clams, lobster and prawns. 🗏 ● Sun; 15 days in Aug. ♿	V AE DC	●			
CASTEL DELL'OVO AND CHIAIA: *La Cantinella* €€€€ Via Nazario Sauro 23. **Map** 7 A4. 081 764 86 84. **FAX** 081 764 87 69. An elegant restaurant on the seafront offering creative dishes, fish in particular. The house special is *tagliatelle alla Santa Lucia*. ● Sun; 7 days in Aug. W www.lacantinella.it	V AE DC	●	■		■
CASTEL DELL'OVO AND CHIAIA: *Caruso dell'Hotel Vesuvio* €€€€€ Via Partenope 45. **Map** 7 A4. 081 764 05 20. **FAX** 081 764 44 83. On the top floor of this historic hotel, this elegant restaurant offers a splendid view of the bay and cooking based on the freshest local ingredients. ♿	V AE DC	●	■	●	■

For key to symbols see back flap

Price categories for a three-course evening meal for one, including a half-bottle of house wine, tax and service:
€ under €18
€€ €18–€28
€€€ €28–€38
€€€€ €38–€50
€€€€€ over €50.

OPEN AT MIDDAY
Often open all day, with a break in the late afternoon to prepare for the evening session.

LATE OPENING
Orders will be accepted until midnight.

OUTDOOR TABLES
Facilities for eating outdoors, on a terrace (often with a good view), or in a garden during the summer.

GOOD WINE LIST
A wide range of specially selected good wines – local, national and international.

	Credit Cards	Open at Midday	Late Opening	Outdoor Tables	Good Wine List
POSILLIPO: *Al Poeta* €€€ Piazza S Di Giacomo 133. 081 575 69 36. FAX 081 575 69 36. This well-known fish restaurant is always crowded, especially throughout the summer. Try the excellent pizza. ● *Mon; 15 days in Aug.*	V AE DC	●	■	●	
POSILLIPO: *Giuseppone a Mare* €€€€ Via F Russo 13. 081 575 60 02. A classic Neapolitan restaurant, Giuseppone a Mare is famous both for its meticulous service and its excellent seafood. ● *Sun pm, Mon; 15 days in Aug.*	V AE DC	●	■		
POSILLIPO: *'A Fenestella* €€€€ Calata del Ponticello a Marechiaro 23. 081 769 00 20. FAX 081 575 06 86. The window *(fenesta)* in this restaurant is celebrated in an Italian song by Salvatore di Giacomo. The house speciality is linguine with gurnard and cherry tomatoes. ● *Wed lunch; Sun in summer; 7 days at Ferragosto (15 Aug).* www.afenestella.it	V AE	●	■	●	
POSILLIPO: *La Sacrestia* €€€€€ Via Orazio 116. 081 761 10 51. FAX 081 66 41 86. A view of the bay, elegant surroundings, imaginative food, excellent wine list and impeccable service make La Sacrestia the best restaurant in town. ● *Mon lunch; Sun in summer; 15 days in Aug.*	V AE DC	●	■	●	■
PHLEGRAEAN FIELDS					
BACOLI: *La Misenetta* €€€€ Via Lungolago 2. Road map B3. 081 523 41 69. An original, mainly fish, menu, combining tradition and creativity. ● *Mon; Jul–Sep; 23 Dec–4 Jan.*	V AE	●	■		
BACOLI: *Féfé* €€€ Via Miseno 137. Road map B3. 081 523 30 11. Sit outside to enjoy the great views and choose a dish made from local seafood to ensure a wonderful evening in this simple, traditional restaurant. ● *Mon–Fri lunch & Sun pm in winter.*	V	●	■	●	
SORRENTO PENINSULA					
MASSA LUBRENSE: *Antico Franceschiello (da Peppino)* €€€ Via Partenope 27. Road map C4. 081 533 97 80. A historic restaurant with a breathtaking view and a long tradition. This was where *delizia al limone*, a local lemon dessert, was invented. ● *Wed (not in summer).*	V AE DC	●			
MASSA LUBRENSE: *I 4 Passi* €€€ Via Marina del Cantone, Nerano. Road map C4. 081 808 12 71. Tasty dishes cooked in the open kitchen. The *pappardelle* with courgette flowers, broad bean ravioli and fruit mousse are really special. ● *Wed (not in summer); 8 Dec–8 Jan.*	V AE	●	■	●	
MASSA LUBRENSE: *La Taverna del Capitano* €€€€ Via Marina del Cantone, Nerano. Road map C4. 081 808 10 28. La Taverna del Capitano is a restaurant with rooms. Its delicious, genuine cooking is a happy marriage of tradition and invention. ● *Mon (not in summer); 7–31 Jan & Feb.*	V AE DC	●		●	
SANT'AGATA SUI DUE GOLFI: *Don Alfonso 1890* €€€€€ Piazza Sant'Agata 11. Road map C4. 081 878 00 26. One of Italy's most famous restaurants. An elegant setting, and unforgettable dishes prepared with produce from Alfonso and Livia Iaccarino's own farm. ● *Mon, Tue (Mon only Jun–Sep); 8 Jan–25 Feb.*	V AE DC	●			■

SORRENTO: *Antica Trattoria*   €

Via Padre Reginaldo Giuliani 33. **Road map** C4. 081 807 10 82.

The menu is strong on meat, rare for the peninsula, and also has unusual dishes such as *pappardelle* with porcini mushrooms and strawberries.

Mon; Jan. W www.lanticatrattoria.it

| | V AE DC | ● | ■ | ● | |

SORRENTO: *Emilia*   €€

Via Marina Grande 62. **Road map** C4. 081 807 27 20.

One of the typical, family-run trattorias on the Sorrento peninsula, featuring a fine range of fish specialities prepared on the spot.

eve (not in summer); Tue; Jan.

| | | ● | | ● | |

SORRENTO: *'O Parrucchiano*   €€€€

Corso Italia 71. **Road map** C4. 081 878 13 21. W 081 532 40 35.

Classic Sorrento cuisine is the offering from the kitchen of this restaurant, whose doors first opened for business over 100 years ago.

Wed (not in summer). Nov–Mar.

| | V | ● | | ● | |

SORRENTO: *Caruso*   €€€€

Via Sant'Antonino 12. **Road map** C4. 081 807 31 56. FAX 081 807 28 29.

A sophisticated setting, and imaginative cooking. The ravioli with prawn or seafood stuffing are delicious, and the desserts excellent.

Mon (not in summer). @ inforistorantemuseocaruso.com

| | V AE DC | ● | | | ■ |

AMALFI COAST

AMALFI: *La Caravella*   €€€€

Via M Camera 12. **Road map** D4. 089 87 10 29.

Good, interesting, fish-based cooking. A recommended first course is the Amalfi pesto with anchovies, olives, capers and lemon zest.

Tue (not in Aug); Nov.

| | V AE DC | ● | | | |

AMALFI: *Da Gemma*   €€€

Santa Fra Gerardo Sasso 9. **Road map** D4. 089 87 13 45.

The wall is covered with newspaper clippings of this historic restaurant, which has been preparing mouthwatering seafood for over a century.

Wed (not in summer), Aug: midday, Jan–Feb.

| | V AE DC | ● | | ● | |

POSITANO: *Il Grottino Azzurro*   €

Via G Marconi 158. **Road map** D4. 089 87 54 66.

The cuisine is distinctly rustic at Grottino Azzurro: typical dishes include cannelloni, gnocchi, farmyard chicken and home-made desserts.

Wed, Dec, Jan.

| | | ● | ■ | ● | |

POSITANO: *Scirocco*   €

Loc. Montepertuso, Via Pestelle 126. **Road map** D4. 089 87 57 86.

Scirocco's hallmarks are its panoramic location and simple, good food such as fresh fish, grilled vegetables and pizzas cooked in wood-fired ovens.

Mon; 20 days Jan.

| | V AE | ● | | ● | |

POSITANO: *Dona Rosa*   €€€

Loc. Montepertuso, Via Montepertuso 97–9. **Road map** D4. 089 81 18 06.

The kitchen is in full view, so you can watch the bread being made along with the adventurous new dishes that change every day.

Mon & Tue lunch, Jan–Mar (book in advance). @ donarosaristorante@libero.it

| | V AE DC | | | ● | |

POSITANO: *Da Adolfo*   €€

Spiaggia di Laurito. **Road map** D4. 089 87 50 22.

Enjoy spaghetti with clams, squid and potatoes, grilled *fiordilatte* cheese and almond cake while sitting at one of the shaded tables beneath the straw roof of this restaurant – there is no need to change out of your swimming things.

Oct–May: evening.

| | | ● | | ● | |

POSITANO: *La Buca di Bacco*   €€€

Via Rampa Teglia 8. **Road map** D4. 089 87 56 99.

Sooner or later everyone comes to this fashionable and timeless establishment for a drink at its bar or dinner at its restaurant on the beach.

Oct–Apr.

| | V AE DC | ● | | ● | |

POSITANO: *La Cambusa*   €€€€

Piazza Amerigo Vespucci 4. **Road map** D4. 089 81 20 51.

A fine location and super-fresh seafood. In winter the beach terrace is enclosed and the setting becomes even more romantic.

Tue (not in summer).

| | V AE DC | ● | ■ | ● | |

Price categories for a three-course evening meal for one, including a half-bottle of house wine, tax and service: € under €18 €€ €18–€28 €€€ €28–€38 €€€€ €38–€50 €€€€€ over €50.	**OPEN AT MIDDAY** Often open all day, with a break in the late afternoon to prepare for the evening session. **LATE OPENING** Orders will be accepted until midnight. **OUTDOOR TABLES** Facilities for eating outdoors, on a terrace (often with a good view), or in a garden during the summer. **GOOD WINE LIST** A wide range of specially selected good wines – local, national and international.			

	CREDIT CARDS	OPEN AT MIDDAY	LATE OPENING	OUTDOOR TABLES	GOOD WINE LIST
RAVELLO: *Cumpà Cosimo*　€€ Via Roma 42–4. **Road map** D4. 089 85 71 56. Originally a famous wine shop, Cumpà now offers good home-made food. The pasta dishes are recommended, especially the fusilli and gnocchi. ▤ ● Mon (not in summer).	V AE DC	●	■		
RAVELLO: *Palazzo della Marra*　€€ Via della Marra 7/9. **Road map** D4. 089 85 83 02. The arches and vaults of the building in which this restaurant is set were left intact during recent restoration, lending a certain elegance. The menu is a careful and successful blend of tradition and creativity. ● Tue; 10 Jan–10 Feb. ♿	V AE DC	●		●	
CAPRI					
ANACAPRI: *Da Gelsomina*　€€€ Via Migliara 72. **Road map** C4. 081 837 14 99. The rustic surroundings may have disappeared, but the flavoursome food at Da Gelsomina has remained true to the countryside. Try the pasta with *cicerchie* and the *pollo al mattone*. ● Tue & lunch in winter, 1 Jan–10 Feb. ♿	V AE	●		●	
ANACAPRI: *Add'o Riccio*　€€€ Via Grotta Azzurra 11. **Road map** C4. 081 837 13 80. Only a stairway separates Add'o Riccio from the famous Blue Grotto sea cave, a setting with undeniable fascination. It is a firm favourite with seafood lovers, offering dishes such as spaghetti with seafood, or linguine with lobster. ● eve (except summer weekends); Nov–Feb.	V AE DC	●		●	
CAPRI: *La Savardina*　€ Via Lo Capo 8. **Road map** C5. 081 837 63 00. An enjoyable walk takes you to this country trattoria. The simple but delicious home-cooked dishes such as ravioli come to your table in a garden filled with citrus fruit trees and herbs. ● Tue (not in summer); Jan–Feb.	V	●	■	●	
CAPRI: *Le Grottelle*　€€ Via Arco Naturale 13. **Road map** C5. 081 837 57 19. Le Grottelle offers you wholesome country cooking in a family-run trattoria with a magnificent view of the Arco Naturale and beyond. ● Thu & evenings in winter.	V AE	●		●	
CAPRI: *La Pergola*　€€€ Traversa Lo Palazzo 2. **Road map** C5. 081 837 74 14. A pleasant family atmosphere, large garden and delicious food reward the owners of La Pergola with regulars who keep coming back for more. The home-made lemon tart is excellent. ▤ ● Wed; Jan.	V AE DC	●	■	●	
CAPRI: *Settanni*　€€ Via Longano 5. **Road map** C5. 081 837 01 05. A few steps from the square in the main town, this trattoria is well known for its *spaghetti alla chiummenzana*, with cherry tomatoes, oregano, basil and other aromatic herbs found on the island. ● Thu (not in summer); Jan–15 Mar. ♿	V AE	●			
CAPRI: *La Canzone del Mare*　€€€ Via Marina Piccola 93. **Road map** C5. 081 837 01 04. Frequented in the 1960s by film stars, singers and other rich and beautiful characters from the world of show business, La Canzone del Mare is a famous restaurant attached to the most exclusive bathing establishment in Capri. Naturally, the house specials are fish and seafood dishes. ● eve; Nov–Mar. ♿	V AE DC	●		●	

CAPRI: *Faraglioni* €€€€
Via Camerelle 75. **Road map** C5. 081 837 03 20.
In the business of providing traditional fare for locals and visitors to Capri
since the late 19th century, this restaurant, with its tables lined along the Via
Camerelle, is ideal for those who don't mind, or perhaps even relish,
being on view to the throngs who pass by.
Nov–Mar.
V AE DC

CAPRI: *Da Gemma* €€€
Via Madre Serafina 6. **Road map** C5. 081 837 04 61.
More than 50 years of experience have brought Da Gemma considerable
praise, as can be seen by photographs on the wall with dedications by some
of the restaurant's famous guests. The pizza is indeed wonderful.
Mon (winter), 20 days in Jan.
V AE DC

CAPRI: *Luigi ai Faraglioni* €€€
Strada dei Faraglioni. **Road map** C5. 081 837 05 91.
Here you can enjoy an extraordinary, panoramic view of the Faraglioni
and the Monacone rock in the shade of a thatched-roof area while
experiencing classic Capri cuisine.
eve; Oct–Easter.
V AE DC

CAPRI: *Da Paolino* €€€€
Via Palazzo a Mare 11. **Road map** C5. 081 837 61 02.
Eating outside at Da Paolino in the summer evenings, surrounded by
lemon trees, is a really special experience. A chance to tuck into the
marvellous antipasto buffet alone is worth the trip.
Tue (not in summer); Nov–Easter.
V AE DC

ISCHIA

CASAMICCIOLA TERME: *Il Focolare* €€
Via Cretaio 68. **Road map** A4. 081 98 06 04.
Come here for traditional Ischia cuisine cooked by Riccardo and Loretta
D'Ambra, who also run a local winery of the same name.
Wed (not in summer), Mon–Fri lunchtime.
V

FORIO: *Da Peppina di Renato* €€
Via Bocca 42. **Road map** A4. 081 99 83 12.
Good country cooking with local produce. The menu features soups,
rabbit *all'ischitana* and first-rate, home-made desserts.
Wed (not in summer); Dec–Jan.
V

ISCHIA PORTO: *Damiano* €€€
Variante Esterna SS 270. **Road map** A4. 081 98 30 32.
Excellent fish and a magnificent view of the port are the highlights
of this restaurant, unarguably one of the best on the island.
Order the mixed fried fish appetizer to whet your taste buds.
Oct–Mar.
V

ISCHIA PORTO: *Gennaro* €€€
Via Porto 66. **Road map** A4. 081 99 29 17.
This restaurant has the best classic seafood that islands in the Bay of Naples
have to offer, with a great selection of fresh fish, starting with the fine antipasti
and marvellous soup, and continuing through each course.
Nov–Mar; Jul & Aug: midday.
V AE DC

PROCIDA

MARINA CORRICELLA: *Gorgonia* €€
Marina Corricella 50. **Road map** B3. 081 810 10 60.
The *gorgonia* referred to in this establishment's name is a seaweed. The
restaurant's menu is – unsurprisingly – based almost exclusively on fish.
Try the pasta and beans with mussels.
Nov–Apr (not at weekends in Mar, Apr & Oct).
V AE

MARINA DI SANCIO CATTOLICO: *Sent' Cò* €
Via Roma 167. **Road map** B3. 081 810 11 20.
This restaurant's strange-looking name is a dialect form of Sancio Cattolico,
which is the name of the port area where the restaurant is located. Naturally,
the menu offers fish galore. The house speciality is a rather unusual dish –
spaghetti with sea urchins.
at midday (not in summer).
V AE

Light Meals and Snacks in Naples

NAPLES IS FULL of bars, pastry shops, *rosticcerie*, and all kinds of places with stand-up counters where you can stop for a drink and a snack. It is an Italian habit to stop at a local bar to breakfast on a cappuccino and warm croissant, to pause for an apéritif before lunch. or have a coffee in the afternoon. A quick and cheap meal can be bought at the numerous fast food establishments that sell sandwiches, small pizzas and filled rolls, as well as prepared meals like pasta with different sauces, to eat on the spot or take away.

BARS AND CAFÉS

IN NAPLES, unlike most other European cities, the bars generally only have stand-up counters for customers to have a quick coffee. In bars and cafés where seating space is provided, there is usually an additional charge for service at the table. In the summer, however, all available outdoor space is packed with tables. Some of the cafés stay open until the early hours, and are equally popular with the young and the old. Many bars in Naples are also pastry shops (*pasticceria*), ice cream parlours (*gelateria*), quick self-service restaurants (*tavola calda*), or all these combined.

One historic Neapolitan café frequented by celebrities in the past is **Caffé Gambrinus**, one of the most elegant bars in the centre (*see p52*). Here, a short distance from the Palazzo Reale, you can sit outside and admire the lovely Piazza del Plebiscito, which is closed to traffic. Other elegant cafés are **La Caffettiera** in Piazza dei Martiri, or the **Caffetteria Bernini** on Piazza Fanzago. Both of these are in the Vomero district and get very busy in the evenings, especially at weekends.

If you are walking along the seafront (*lungomare*), stop for an apéritif at the **Bar dell'Ovo**. The small and elegant **Bar Prencipe** in Piazza Municipio, which retains its original Art Deco interior, is a good place to pause for breakfast in the city centre. The **Gran Caffè Verdi** on Via Verdi and **Bar Roma** on Via Toledo, with their spacious refreshment rooms, are both popular with office workers during their breaks.

To taste an excellent coffee, try the **Caffè Mexico** in Piazza Dante with superb blends, or the **Café do Brasil** in the Vomero area opposite the Teatro Diana. In the old city centre the **Bar Nilo** is distinguished for its courteous and friendly service.

During the summer months, popular spots for night owls are the **Caffè delle Arti**, opposite the Academy of Art, and the cafés in Piazza Bellini: the **Caffè 1799**, the **Caffè Arabo** and the **Intra Moenia** that also sells books and promotes cultural events.

PASTRY SHOPS AND ICE CREAM PARLOURS

NEAPOLITAN PASTRY shops, known throughout the world and descended from a centuries-old tradition, offer a number of specialities. Among these are the shortcrust or puff pastries called *sfogliatelle*, the *pastiera* eaten at Easter, *babà*, *zeppola di San Giuseppe* and Christmas season pastries such as *rococò* and *struffoli* (pastry rings with honey and candied fruit).

A favourite spot for the locals, particularly on Sundays, is **Scaturchio** in Piazza San Domenico Maggiore, one of the best cafés in the historic centre. Also in Piazza San Domenico Maggiore, **L.U.I.S.E.** sells excellent pastries and sweets, as do **Augustus** in Via Toledo, **Daniele** and **Bellavia** in the Vomero and **Moccia** in the Chiaia district. The **Gran Bar Riviera**, which opened in Chiaia in 1870, also offers many treats; the *tartufo* was invented here, a delectable *semifreddo* ice cream with chestnut cream filling. The best *sfogliatella* can be found

at **Pintauro** on Via Toledo or **La Sfogliatella** in the Galleria Umberto I. Good ice cream parlours are **La Scimmia** in Piazza Carità, the **Bilancione** and **Caraturo** in Posillipo, **Soave** in Vomero and **Häagen-Dazs** in Chiaia.

The *chalets* on the seafront in the Mergellina area are legendary among Neapolitans. The most famous of these is **Chalet Ciro**, specializing in homemade ice cream (*artigianale*). People also come here for coffee or an apéritif. **Chiquito's**, on the Via Mergellina, was once a water vendor and is now famous for his fruit cups and exotic fruit shakes.

TAKE-AWAY FOOD

FOUNDED IN 1887 by Gaetano Cecere, the first Neapolitan fast food establishment is aptly named **Vaco 'e pressa** (I'm in a hurry). True to its founder's tradition, it still has marble furnishings and a quaint atmosphere. Rather than **McDonald's**, the locals usually prefer to drop in at a *tavola calda*, where they can eat a quick plate of pasta, or to buy a sandwich prepared in a delicatessen (*salumeria*), eat a local mozzarella or have hot snacks from a *rosticceria*. Excellent take-aways are **Tavola Calda L.U.I.S.E.** in Via Toledo and **Imperatore** in the Vomero area, where you can also buy tasty roast chicken. **La Piazza**, next to Santa Maria La Nova church, offers a quick snack, and **Hot Stuff** in Via Schipa sells sandwiches or *bruschette* (toasted bread with garlic and oil).

If you like sweet or savoury crêpes, **La Crêperie** in the Vomero area is the place for you. Then there are the many *pizzetterie* such as **Villa Pizza**, **Ciao Pizza**, **Le Focacce Moccia**, **Pizzette e Cornetti** and the *rosticcerie* such as **Elettroforno** in Posillipo which sells pizza by the slice as well as "crocché" (potato croquettes), *arancini di riso* (rice croquettes) and *saltimbocca* (veal). Many of these *pizzerie*, such as the **Cibo** chain, also sell roasted meats.

DIRECTORY

TOLEDO AND CASTEL NUOVO

Bars and Cafés

Bar Prencipe
Piazza Municipio 20.
Map 7 B2.

Caffé Gambrinus
Piazza Trieste e
Trento 38.
Map 7 A3.

Bar Roma
Via Toledo 325.
Map 7 A2 (9 A5).

Gran Caffè Verdi
Via Verdi 23.
Map 7 A2.

Pastry Shops and Ice Cream Parlours

Augustus
Via Toledo 147.
Map 7 A2 (9 A5).

Pintauro
Via Toledo 275.
Map 7 A2 (9 A5).

La Scimmia
Piazza Carità 4.
Map 7 A1.

La Sfogliatella
Galleria Umberto I, 66.
Map 7 A2.

Take-Away Food

Cibo
Via Cervantes 70.
Map 7 A2.

Tavola Calda L.U.I.S.E.
Via Toledo 266.
Map 7 A1 (9 A5).

McDonald's
Via Sanfelice 16/20.
Map 7 B1 (9 C5).

SPACCANAPOLI

Bars and Cafés

Bar Nilo
Via San Biagio dei
Librai 129/130.
Map 3 C5.

Pastry Shops and Ice Cream Parlours

L.U.I.S.E.
Piazza San Domenico
Maggiore 5.
Map 3 B5 (9 C3).

Scaturchio
Piazza San Domenico
Maggiore 19.
Map 3 B5 (9 C3).

Take-Away Food

Ciao Pizza
Via Benedetto
Croce 42.
Map 3 B5 (9 C4).

Cibo
Piazza del Gesù 27.
Map 3 B5 (9 B4).

Le Focacce Moccia
Piazzetta Nilo 16 bis.
Map 3 B5 (10 E3).

La Piazza
Piazza Santa Maria La
Nova.
Map 7 B1 (9 C5).

Villa Pizza
Via Capitelli 28.
Map 3 A5.

DECUMANO MAGGIORE

Bars and Cafés

Caffè Arabo
Piazza Bellini 66.
Map 3 B5.

Caffè 1799
Piazza Bellini 71.
Map 3 B5.

Caffè delle Arti
Via Micco
Spadaro 4/5.
Map 7 B2.

Caffè Mexico
Piazza Dante 86.
Map 3 A5 (9 B3).

Intra Moenia
Piazza Bellini 70.
Map 3 B5.

Scaturchio
Via Portamedina 22.
Map 3 A5 (9 A4).

Take-Away Food

McDonald's
Piazza Dante 92.
Map 3 A5.

Vaco 'e Pressa
Piazza Dante 87.
Map 3 A5 (9 B3).

VOMERO

Bars and Cafés

Café do Brasil
Via Giordano 31.
Map 5 B2.

La Caffettiera
Piazza Vanvitelli 10.
Map 2 D5.

Caffetteria Bernini
Piazza Fanzago.
Map 2 D4.

Caffé Mexico
Via Scarlatti 69.
Map 2 D5.

Pastry Shops and Ice Cream Parlours

Bellavia
Via Luca Giordano 158.
Map 1 C5.

Daniele
Via Scarlatti 104/106.
Map 2 D5.

Soave
Via Scarlatti 130.
Map 2 D5.

Take-Away Food

Cibo
Via Cimarosa 144.
Map 1 C5.

La Crêperie
Via Donadio 1/3.
Map 2 D4.

Imperatore
Via Scarlatti 180.
Map 2 D5.

McDonald's
Via Scarlatti 209.
Map 2 D5.

Pizzette e Cornetti
Via Kerbaker 4.
Map 2 D5.

CASTEL DELL'OVO AND CHIAIA

Bars and Cafés

Bar dell'Ovo
Via Partenope 6.
Map 7 A4.

La Caffettiera
Piazza dei Martiri 30.
Map 6 F2.

Pastry Shops and Ice Cream Parlours

Caraturo
Via dei Mille 57
Map 6 E2.

Chalet Ciro
Via Caracciolo
(opposite Via Orazio).
Map 5 B4.

Chiquito's
Via Mergellina
(opposite the funicular).
Map 5 B3.

Moccia
Via San Pasquale
21/22.
Map 6 E2.

Gran Bar Riviera
Riviera di Chiaia 183.
Map 5 C2.

Take-Away Food

Hot Stuff
Via Schipa 65.
Map 5 B2.

POSILLIPO

Pastry Shops and Ice Cream Parlours

Augustus
Via Petrarca 81 a/b.
Map 5 A4.

Bilancione
Via Posillipo 238/b.
Map 5 A5.

Take-Away Food

Elettroforno
Piazza San Luigi 12/b.

SHOPS AND MARKETS

SHOPPING IN NAPLES is an excellent way to explore the labyrinth of this fascinating city. Expensive boutiques line the main streets such as Via Toledo and Via Chiaia, where good quality, stylish clothes, shoes and jewellery can be bought. However, don't limit yourself to the fashionable areas, but wander around the alleyways in the old town to discover the small specialist shops and artisan workshops. Here visitors can find authentic and hand-made souvenirs.

These streets often bear the name of the trade practised there, such as Piazza degli Orefici (Goldsmiths' Square).

Perhaps the most enjoyable way to shop is to follow the example of most Neapolitans and buy from the numerous markets and stalls along the roadside. These *bancarelle* sell everything from clothes to kitchenware, and children's toys to jewellery. Common items are cheap seconds from the manufacturer or imitation designer labels.

Nativity figure

Coral jewellery in a shop window

OPENING HOURS

SHOPS ARE OPEN from 10am to 2pm and from 4pm to 8pm. They are closed on Sundays and Monday morning in winter, Saturday afternoon and Sunday in summer. Food shops and markets are shut on Thursday afternoons. Before holiday periods like Christmas, many places are open on Sundays and extend their weekly opening hours. In summer most shops close for two weeks around 15 August (Ferragosto).

HOW TO PAY

MAJOR CREDIT CARDS are accepted in most boutiques and department stores. After you have made your purchase, make sure you are given the receipt *(ricevuta fiscale)*. By law the police can make a spot check outside the shop and if you are without a receipt, you may be fined.

SALES

FROM EARLY JULY to early September and early January to mid-March, sales are held in Naples. You can find excellent bargains with discounts of up to 50 per cent and sometimes as much as 70 per cent. It is a good idea to check goods before you leave the shop as a refund is unlikely.

FASHION AND ACCESSORIES

THE EXCLUSIVE SHOPS are concentrated in Via dei Mille and Via Calabritto, in the elegant Chiaia district. Here the great fashion designers, such as **Emporio Armani**, **Prada**, **Gianni Versace** and **Mario Valentino**, have their stores. A new jewellery shop, **Bulgari**, has also recently opened here. In Riviera di Chiaia, **Marinella** sells her famous ties worn by many VIPs.

The shop window of the elegant Livio de Simone boutique

At **Eddy Monetti** the emphasis is on elegant and classical fashion. Clothes with an innovative touch are offered by **Barbaro** in Galleria Umberto I, while avant-garde men's and women's wear is sold by **Maxi Ho**. **Livio De Simone**, a native of Naples, offers stylish clothes in bright Mediterranean colours, while **Amina Rubinacci** is known for her woollen and soft cashmere jumpers. Naples also has boutiques for **Max Mara** and **Max & Co**.

Clothing at more accessible prices is sold at **Camomilla** and **G.B. Pedrini**. Young people have no lack of choice with clothes from the well-known **Benetton** outlets and the **Bamba** boutique in Via Chiaia, famous for its original designs. Modern fashion for young people is also offered in the **Magazzini Generali** (General Store) with a vast stock catering for all budgets. Fun and original second-hand clothes and accessories and personalized T-shirts are sold at **Mu Mu Frequencies**, a multimedia cultural group.

The **Prénatal** chain caters for mothers-to-be and small children. Handbags, belts and other accessories, mostly made by local craftsmen, are sold in the **Spatarella** and **Tramontano** stores.

In the old centre between San Biagio dei Librai and Via degli Orefici there are many jewellers' and goldsmiths' shops. The age-old tradition of engraving and cameo work is still practised in many shops.

Interior of the Colonnese bookshop in Via San Biagio dei Librai

Caso is unrivalled for its coral jewels, and other jewellery shops such as **Ventrella** and **Knight** stock original designs.

DEPARTMENT STORES AND SHOPPING CENTRES

MOST NEAPOLITANS prefer smaller, specialist shops where the service is more personal. However, some department stores such as **La Rinascente** and **Coin** offer a good variety of products from quality clothes, cosmetics and perfumes to household goods and crockery. For specialists in household and kitchen goods, try the **Croff** chain, which also sells a wide variety of modern furnishings. The large chain stores, **Upim** and **Standa**, are generally cheaper and feature average-quality cosmetics, lingerie, household articles and clothes.

The shopping centres, **Galleria Vanvitelli** and the elegant **Galleria Scarlatti** can be found in the Vomero district and the smart 19th-century Galleria Umberto I, off Piazza Trieste e Trento, is an arcade of elegant shops.

Coin
Via Scarlatti 100.
[081 578 01 11.
Via Santa Caterina a
Chiaia 23.
[081 245 19 38.

Croff
Galleria Vanvitelli 16–23
[081 578 96 98.

Galleria Scarlatti
Via Scarlatti.

Galleria Vanvitelli
Piazza Vanvitelli.

La Rinascente
Via Toledo 343.
[081 41 15 11.

Standa
Via Solimene 143.
[081 556 89 00.
Viale Colli Aminei 371.
[081 743 09 51.

Upim
Via A. Doria 40.
[081 239 63 60.
Via Nisco 2.
[081 41 75 20.
Via Scarlatti 16.
[081 556 28 17.

ART, ANTIQUES AND INTERIOR DESIGN

NAPLES IS RENOWNED for its fascinating antique and second-hand shops. The best-known antique dealers can be found in Via Domenico Morelli: **Brandi**, **D'Amodio**, **Falanga** and **Florida** are all specialists in 18th-century furniture and paintings. Shops with historic objects, such as **L'Antiquario** and **Affaitati**, are in Via Costantinopoli. Old engravings, prints and lithographs, picture frames and other *objets d'art*, are on sale at **Bowinkel**, the oldest shop in Piazza dei Martiri. Rare books, prints and gouaches are sold at the **Casella** and **Regina** antiquarian booksellers, while the **Colonnese** bookshop stocks traditional Neapolitan articles. Among the second-hand dealers, the most interesting is **Quagliozza**, who sells all kinds of objects, including lamps, frames and telephones on the steps of the church of San Nicola a Nilo.

The traditional craft of making and restoring string instruments

The **Archivio Fotografico Parisio**, with about 100,000 photographs of Neapolitan life and characters, provides a unique record of the city's history. Art galleries with interesting work on show include the **Galleria Amelio**, **Lia Rumma**, **Studio Morra** and **Studio Trisorio**.

Neapolitan second-hand dealer with goods on display in the street

Restoration of a puppet head in the Ospedale delle Bambole *(see p63)*

Leading interior design shops include **Agorà** in the Posillipo area and **Novelli** in Piazza Amedeo, featuring the latest styles in home furnishings. Simple, clean-cut design solutions for a younger generation are on view at **IdeArredo**.

HANDICRAFTS

THE MANY WORKSHOPS and second-hand shops in the historic centre offer a varied choice of articles, from the kitsch to the well-designed. In Via San Gregorio Armeno is the workshop of the famous nativity scene artisan, **Giuseppe Ferrigno**, while in Via San Biagio dei Librai is the **Ospedale delle Bambole** (hospital for dolls) where porcelain dolls, shepherds, marionettes and puppets are repaired and restored. At the **Liuteria Calace**, in the historic centre, they make and restore violins, violas, mandolins and lutes. **Nel Regno di Pulcinella** is a workshop dedicated to the making of Neapolitan masks.

At **Lunarossa** you can buy objects made of wood, copper, ceramic and stone. Book restoration, bookbinding and elegant objects made from hand-made Amalfi paper make the **Bottega Artigiana del Libro e della Carta** a fascinating place. If you are interested in ceramics, have a look at **Il Cantuccio della Ceramica** and the workshop of **Lisa Weber**.

FOOD, WINE AND SPIRITS

THE LEADING delicatessens in Naples are **La Botteghina** and **Gastronomia L.U.I.S.E.**, all of which sell a variety of local specialities. **Codrington** is known for its large stock of international brands. **Gay Odin** has the finest chocolate in Naples, including the delicious *Vesuvio* chocolate with rum. The old-fashioned **Scaturchio** sells fine cakes and sweets, as well as ice cream. A good selection of wines is to be found at the **Enoteca del Buon Bere** and the **Enoteca Belledonne**.

The inviting entrance of the famous Scaturchio *pasticceria*

OPEN-AIR MARKETS

Street stalls and markets set up in the early morning and usually pack up after midday. Food stalls selling seasonal fruit and vegetables generally have fresher and less expensive produce than the shops. Clothes and household items will be cheap and, although they may not be designer quality, they are perfectly good. Bargaining is not usually done when buying food, but for clothes and other items try asking for a discount *(sconto)*.

Market at Sant'Antonio Abate

Mercatino di Antignano
Piazza degli Artisti. ◖ *8am–1pm Mon–Sat.*
Clothing, shoes, household articles, fabrics.

Fiera Antiquaria Napoletana
Villa Comunale. ◖ *8am–4pm penultimate Sat & Sun of month.*
Antiques market: silverware, jewellery and ornaments.

Mercato del Casale di Posillipo
Posillipo. ◖ *8am–2pm Thu.*
Clothes, accessories, household articles.

Mercato del Ponte di Casanova
Porta Capuana. ◖ *8am–sunset Mon–Sat.*
New and used clothes.

Mercato dei Fiori
Castel Nuovo. ◖ *daily at dawn.*
Flowers.

Mercatino della Pignasecca
Near Piazza Carità. ◖ *8am–2pm Mon–Sat.*
Food.

Mercato di Sant'Antonio
Via Sant'Antonio Abate.
◖ *9am–8pm daily.*
Food market.

Mercato di Porta Nolana
Via Carmignano. ◖ *8am–6pm Mon–Sat (8am–2pm Sun).*
Fresh fish and seafood.

Mercatino della Torretta
Viale Gramsci. ◖ *8am–1pm Mon–Sat.*
Food market and clothing.

DIRECTORY

FASHION AND ACCESSORIES

Amina Rubinacci
Via dei Mille 16.
081 41 30 48.

Bamba
Via Chiaia 209.
081 41 11 14.

Barbaro
Galleria Umberto 44.
081 42 29 71.
One of many branches.

Bulgari
Via Filangieri 41.
081 40 08 56.

Camomilla
Via Toledo 407.
081 551 14 45.
One of many branches.

Caso
Piazza San Domenico
Maggiore 16.
081 552 01 08.

Eddy Monetti
Via dei Mille 45a/b/c.
081 40 47 07.

Emporio Armani
Piazza dei Martiri 61–62.
081 42 23 21.

G.B. Pedrini
Via Toledo 330.
081 40 49 49.

Gianni Versace
Via Calabritto 7.
081 764 42 10.

Knight
Piazza dei Martiri 52.
081 764 38 37.

Livio De Simone
Via D Morelli 15.
081 764 38 27.

Magazzini Generali
Via dei Mille 26/28.
081 41 38 72.

Marinella
Piazza Vittoria 287.
081 245.11 82.

Mario Valentino
Via Calabritto 9/10.
081 764 42 62.

Max & Co.
Corso Umberto I 28.
081 552 62 23.
One of many branches.

Max Mara
Corso Umberto I 134/136.
081 553 85 01.

Maxi Ho
Via Luca Giordano 23.
081 578 04 39.

Mu Mu Frequencies
Piazza Monteoliveto 10.
081 552 41 03.

Prada
Via Calabritto 9.
081 764 13 23.

Prénatal
Via Roma 145.
081 551 07 14.
One of many branches.

Spatarella
Via Filangieri 23.
081 40 17 03.

Tramontano
Via De Pace Antonetta 48.
081 28 56 07.

Ventrella
Via C Poerio 11.
081 764 31 73.

ART, ANTIQUES AND INTERIOR DESIGN

Affaitati
Via Costantinopoli 18.
081 44 44 27.

Agorà
Via Orazio 136/b.
081 714 43 33.

L'Antiquario
Via Costantinopoli 34.
081 564 06 07.

Archivio Fotografico Parisio
Largo Carolina 10.
081 764 51 22.

Bowinkel
Piazza dei Martiri 24.
081 764 43 44.

Brandi
Via D Morelli 57.
081 764 33 75.

Casella
Via C Poerio 92/e.
081 764 26 27.

Colonnese
Via S Pietro a Maiella 32.
081 29 39 00.

D'Amodio
Via D Morelli 6 bis.
081 764 38 72.

Falanga
Via D Morelli 6.
081 764 44 02.

Florida
Via D Morelli 13.
081 764 34 40.

Galleria Amelio
Piazza dei Martiri 58.
081 42 20 23.

IdeArredo
Via R Bracco 41/49.
081 551 09 92.

Lia Rumma
Via V Gaetani 12.
081 764 36 19.

Novelli
Piazza Amedeo 21/22.
081 41 53 50.

Quagliozza
Via San Biagio dei Librai
11 (Church of San Nicola
a Nilo).
081 551 71 00.

Regina
Via Costantinopoli
51/103.
081 45 99 83.

Studio Morra
Via Calabritto 20.
081 763 37 37.

Studio Trisorio
Riviera di Chiaia 215.
081 41 43 06.

HANDICRAFTS

Bottega Artigiana del Libro e della Carta
Calata Trinità Maggiore 4.
081 551 12 80.

Il Cantuccio della Ceramica
Via B Croce 38 (inside).
081 552 58 57.

Giuseppe Ferrigno
Via S Gregorio Armeno 8.
081 552 31 48.

Lisa Weber
Via G Paladino 4.

Liuteria Calace
Piazza San Domenico
Maggiore 9.
081 551 59 83.

Lunarossa
Via B Croce 22.
081 551 70 05.

Nel Regno di Pulcinella
Salita Arenella 56.
081 578 64 50.

Ospedale delle Bambole
Via S Biagio dei Librai 81.
081 20 30 67.

FOOD, WINE AND SPIRITS

La Botteghina
Via Orazio 106.
081 66 05 16.

Codrington
Via Chiaia 94.
081 41 82 57.

Enoteca Belledonne
Vico Belledonne a
Chiaia 18.
081 40 31 62.

Enoteca del Buon Bere
Via M Turchi 15.
081 764 22 55.

Gastronomia L.U.I.S.E.
Piazza dei Martiri 68.
081 41 77 35.

Gay Odin
Via Toledo 214.
081 41 46 40.

Scaturchio
Piazza San Domenico
Maggiore.
081 551 69 44.

Shops and Markets along the Coast

EVERY TOWN AND VILLAGE in the region, from the islands to the coast, offers typical local handicrafts such as ceramics or glassware, as well as foods and wines associated with the history and culture of each place. Wandering through the narrow streets in these lovely seaside spots, you will discover all kinds of customs.

FASHION AND ACCESSORIES

BESIDES SHOPS with designer wear, there are still several old local fashion houses. You can find the top names in Italian and foreign fashion at places such as **Adario & Fiorentino**, who have a shop at Sant'Agata sui due Golfi, or **Dominique** in Ischia and **Elle et Lui** at Lacco Ameno. The shopping street in Capri, Via Camerelle, boasts the elegant **Marcello Rubinacci** boutique, known for top-quality cashmere pullovers. Elegant apparel, mostly made of silk, and typical Capri shoes are among the specialities of **Laura Merola**. Two top jewellers in Capri are **La Campanina** and **Chantecler**, both sited in Via Vittorio Emanuele, who stock precious stones in every colour as well as diamonds and coral necklaces of very fine quality.

Fashion styles in Positano are famous for their originality. Among the town's leading houses is **Maria Lampo**, who are well known for making their articles quickly (*lampo* meaning "in a flash"). Top designer wear as well as handmade patchwork clothing and quilts are sold at **Nadir's**, while **La Bottega di Brunella** and **La Tartana** are distinguished for their fine fabrics and original patterns. If you want the bikini of your dreams, go to **Susy** on Capri, where you can order swim-wear made to measure.

Sorrento, Positano and Capri are famous for their handmade sandals; to have a pair made especially for you, go to **Siniscalchi** in Sorrento, **Costanzo Avitabile** in Positano, the imaginative **Canfora** in Capri or Antonio Viva's shop at Anacapri, aptly called **L'Arte del**

Sandalo Caprese. Again in Anacapri, **Kontiri Boutique** makes various types of shoes to measure. On the mainland, cloth shoes decorated in weird and wonderful ways can be found at **La Gabella** in Amalfi.

ART AND HANDICRAFTS

BY EXPLORING the craftsmen's shops in the towns and villages outside Naples you can really get to know the heart of a place, and discover its cultural and artistic traditions. The boats known as *gozzi* are built by the **Aprea Mare** company in Sorrento, and are world-famous. The ancient tradition of marquetry in the Sorrento peninsula is carried on by craftsmen such as **Salvatore Gargiulo**, **Peppe Rocco** and **Giliberto Attardi**.

Vietri sul Mare is famous for its decorated ceramics; the **Solimene** factory employs at least 40 craftsmen who, despite the large output of the place, make fine handmade products. The **Perrotti** brothers make splendid stained glass, and accept commissions. Other high-quality ceramics are produced by **Taki** in Ischia and **Artigiò** in Procida, while **La Bottega dell'Arte** in Capri – thanks to the well-known ceramicist Sergio Rubini – now has over 200 outlets in the United States alone. Again in Capri, **Carmelina** offers classic naïve painting.

In Amalfi, visit the **Cartiera Amatruda** and **Cavaliere** mills, where fine quality paper is produced. As a souvenir of Capri there are the **Carthusia** perfumes, sold only on the island (you can also visit their laboratories at No. 2 Via Parco Augusto). On the island of Procida, **Maria**

Rosaria Intartaglia makes pretty embroidered lingerie to order. Lastly, the **Emporio Scialò** at Ischia sells raffia dolls and Pulcinella puppets, all made by hand.

FOOD, WINE AND LIQUEURS

MANY FINE DAIRY products such as cheese come from the area around Naples. In Sorrento you can visit the **Apreda** dairy and buy fresh plaits of *fiordilatte*, a type of mozzarella made from cow's milk, in the nearby shop. The **Caseificio Isola di Capri** and **Gabriele** in Vico Equense are also excellent dairies. At Capri, **Sfizi di Pane** offers 15 different types of *tarallini* biscuits as well as various kinds of bread. For the sweet-toothed, Ischia's **Caffè Calise** has orange *sfogliatelle* and at Positano the **La Zagara** pastry shop has delicious fruit tarts called *crostate*. While in Amalfi, try the delightful lemon pastries at **Andrea Pansa**.

Some wine shops also sell local products such as jam, honey and spices: **Piemme** at Sorrento, **Ischia Sapori** on Ischia and **Gusti e Delizie** in Ravello. Good ranges of wine are on sale at **La Valle dei Mulini** in Amalfi, **I Sapori di Positano** in Positano and **Enoteca Casa D'Ambra** at Ischia. **Limoncello di Capri** is the most famous source of limoncello, or lemon-flavoured liqueur, and **I Giardini di Ravello** also stocks a good range.

MARKETS

THERE ARE numerous markets in the outlying areas. The most important in size and tradition is the second-hand market in Resina at Ercolano (Herculaneum), where you will find used clothes and accessories. It is half an hour from the central railway station in Naples: take the Circumvesuviana line and get off at Ercolano.

DIRECTORY

FASHION AND ACCESSORIES

Adario & Fiorentino
Via Nastro Azzurro 1–3
(Sant'Agata sui Due
Golfi).
℡ 081 878 00 65.
One of two shops.

L'Arte del Sandalo Caprese
Via G Orlandi 75
(Anacapri).
℡ 081 837 35 83.

La Bottega di Brunella
Via Pasitea 76
(Positano).
℡ 089 87 52 28.

La Campanina
Via V Emanuele 18
(Capri).
℡ 081 837 06 43.

Canfora
Via Camerelle 3
(Capri).
℡ 081 837 04 87.

Chantecler
Via V Emanuele 51
(Capri).
℡ 081 837 05 44.

Costanzo Avitabile
Piazza A Vespucci 1–5
(Positano).
℡ 081 87 53 66.

Dominique
Corso V Colonna 180
(Ischia).
℡ 081 99 12 21.
One of two shops.

Elle et Lui
Piazza Santa Restituta 8
(Lacco Ameno).
℡ 081 90 02 28.

Kontiri Boutique
Via Capodimonte 54
(Anacapri).
℡ 081 837 36 40.

La Gabella
Via P Comite 37
(Amalfi).
℡ 0330 67 54 03.

Laura Merola
Via Fuorlovado 2
(Capri).
℡ 081 837 04 03.

Marcello Rubinacci
Via Camerelle 9
(Capri).
℡ 081 837 72 95.

Maria Lampo
Via Pasitea 12–16
(Positano).
℡ 089 87 50 21.

Nadir's
Via Pasitea 44
(Positano).
℡ 089 81 16 90.

Siniscalchi
Corso Italia 203
(Sorrento).
℡ 081 878 30 65.
One of two shops.

Susy
Via Le Botteghe 61
(Capri).

La Tartana
Via della Tartana 5
(Positano).
℡ 098 87 56 45.

ART AND HANDICRAFTS

Aprea Mare
Via Santa Lucia 15
(Sorrento).
℡ 081 807 28 18.

Artigiò
Via V Emanuele 10
(Procida).
℡ 081 896 96 69.

Giliberto Attardi
Via Padre R Giuliani 45–49
(Sorrento).
℡ 081 878 12 91.

La Bottega dell'Arte
Via Catena 2–4
(Capri).
℡ 081 837 18 78.

Carmelina
Via Roma (Capri).

Carthusia
Via Camerelle 10
(Capri).
℡ 081 837 05 29.
One of two shops.

Cartiere Amatruda
Via delle Cartiere 100
(Amalfi).
℡ 089 87 13 15.

Cartiera Cavaliere
Via M del Giudice 2.
(Amalfi).

Ceramiche Artistiche Solimene
Via Madonna degli
Angeli 7
(Vietri sul Mare).
℡ 089 21 02 43.

Emporio Scialò
Corso Umberto I, 21
(Forio d'Ischia).
℡ 081 99 75 92.

Maria Rosaria Intartaglia
Via Lubrano di Vavaria 12
(Procida).
℡ 081 896 86 74.

Peppe Rocco
Via San Nicola 12
(Sorrento).
℡ 081 878 48 74.

Perrotti
Via Nazionale Costiera 32
(Vietri sul Mare).
℡ 089 76 15 76.

Salvatore Gargiulo
Via Fuoro 33
(Sorrento).
℡ 081 878 24 20.

Taki
Via Marina 20
(Forio d'Ischia).
℡ 081 98 91 49.

FOOD, WINE AND LIQUEURS

Andrea Pansa
Piazza Duomo 40
(Amalfi).
℡ 089 87 10 65.

Apreda
Via del Mare 20
(Sorrento).
℡ 081 878 13 34.
One of two shops.

Caffè Calise
Via A Sogliuzzo 69
(Ischia Porto).
℡ 081 99 12 70.

Caseificio Isola di Capri
Via Roma 38
(Capri).
℡ 081 837 68 75.

Enoteca Casa D'Ambra
Via Porto 24
(Ischia Porto).
℡ 081 99 10 46.

Gabriele
Corso Umberto I, 5–7
(Vico Equense).
℡ 081 879 87 44.

I Giardini di Ravello
Via Civiltà 19
(Ravello).
℡ 089 87 22 64.

Gusti e Delizie
Via Roma 28–30
(Ravello).
℡ 089 85 77 16.

Ischia Sapori
Via Gianturco 2
(Ischia Porto).
℡ 081 98 44 82.

Limoncello di Capri
Via Roma 79
(Capri).
℡ 081 837 55 61.

Piemme
Corso Italia 161
(Sorrento).
℡ 081 877 35 96.

I Sapori di Positano
Via Mulini 6
(Positano).
℡ 089 81 11 16.

Sfizi di Pane
Via delle Botteghe 15
(Capri).
℡ 081 837 01 06.

La Valle dei Mulini
Via delle Cartiere 55
(Amalfi).
℡ 089 87 32 11.

La Zagara
Via Mulini 8
(Positano).
℡ 089 87 59 64.

ENTERTAINMENT

As you might expect of a major city, Naples offers an exciting range of entertainment, including cultural and sports events as well as other leisure activities. The nightlife is dynamic, the cafés, nightspots and cultural venues are always open late, and just about every taste is catered for. Music and theatre performances take place throughout the year, bolstered by some important international festivals held in summertime, mostly in the holiday resorts.

Tennis at Villa Comunale

For cinema buffs there are two multi-plexes and many cinema clubs. During the week people usually go to the cinema or out to eat; at weekends the piazzas are buzzing with life, as it is customary for Neapolitans to meet up to have a drink before going on to the nearby nightspots, pubs or discos. No one goes dancing before midnight, and those who dance the night away can always have a hot brioche and coffee for breakfast at dawn in one of the all-night bars.

Night-time illuminations in a city that is happy to party until dawn

INFORMATION AND BUYING TICKETS

To find out what's on in Naples, check the listings (and supplements) in the local newspaper *Il Mattino*, or the Naples inserts in the national newspapers. You will also find free entertainment guides in most hotels.

There are two official booking offices: **Concerteria** and **Box Office**. Tickets are usually sold at the door on the day of performance. It might be more difficult, however, to get seats at short notice for premieres; very important events; at theatres like the Diana and Bellini for chamber music concerts; and for the opera season at the Teatro San Carlo.

You can also find out more information via the Internet; the regional website is: www.na.flashnet.it/prov.htm., which provides details on museums, cinemas and parks.

Classical ballet dancers at the Teatro San Carlo

The cultural association called Napoli Porte Aperte provides cultural itineraries in town and also has a website with further information: www.cib.na.cnr.it/Napoli/indice.html.

DANCE, THEATRE AND OPERA

National and international touring productions as well as performances by local companies make Naples one of the leading cities for theatre in Italy *(see p39)*. Each theatre has a published programme (the season runs from October through to

May), though there are exceptions such as the **Augusteo**, which will put on the occasional concert or visiting theatre company production as "extras". Mainstream theatre and musicals are featured at the **Bellini** and leading Italian companies at the **Diana** and the historic **Mercadante**, now restored to its former glory after 30 years of neglect. New small companies play at the **Sancarluccio**, while fringe and experimental theatre are featured at the **Nuovo** and **Galleria Toledo**.

Traditional Neapolitan comedy survives at the **Sannazaro**, a typical 19th-century theatre where Eleonora Duse, Eduardo Scarpetta and the De Filippo brothers performed. The **Totò** was recently opened and is a venue for variety shows. The top venue for opera and ballet, as well as for Neapolitan social occasions, is the **Teatro San Carlo** *(see pp37, 39, 53)*; the opera is world class and top singers perform. A premiere here is always an important international event.

Interior of Teatro San Carlo

CINEMA

THE FOUR multiplexes are the **Plaza**, **Alcione**, **Arcobaceno** and **Modernissimo**. New films are shown at reduced prices on Wednesdays, while on Mondays some of the art-houses feature older films at half-price. In the summer, retrospectives are held in historic sites in and around Naples, including the courtyards of the Castel Nuovo *(see pp54–5)* and Palazzo Reale *(see pp50–51)*.

NIGHTSPOTS

THE TRENDY discos are **La Mela** and **Chez Moi**, which were once decidedly traditional but are now open to avant-garde influences. Two very popular multipurpose nightspots are **Mephisto** and **S'Move** (two storeys, high-volume music and five of the best DJs in Naples). **Queen Victoria**, with a piano bar, offers a mixed bag of live music, South American dances, belly dancing and flamenco. For the latest in dance music there are four good nightclubs: **Velvet Underground** and the **Notting Hill**, which offer interactive, varied programmes with theme evenings; **Riot**, a multimedia club that often hosts exhibitions and concerts; and the recently opened **Vibes Café**, which has a small square at the back for outdoor entertainment.

Lead singer in the Almamegretta group *(see p37)*

LIVE MUSIC

THE CITY that is home to the prestigious San Pietro a Maiella Conservatoire offers plenty of opportunities to listen to masterpieces of classical music. For instance, the symphony season at Teatro San Carlo draws huge numbers of people each year. Furthermore, excellent concerts are organized by the **Associazione Alessandro Scarlatti**, where old and new classical pieces are performed to great critical acclaim.

Pop, rock and jazz evenings are held at the **Antica Birreria Kronenbourg**, **Lido Pola** and the historic **Otto Jazz Club**. Another excellent live music spot is **Rude Pravo**, which opened in 1995 and features new groups. Lastly, **Palapartenope** is the only auditorium that can handle huge audiences.

Carousel at the Edenlandia funfair

AMUSEMENT PARKS

THE MAIN amusement park in Naples is **Edenlandia**. It features the world of fables and Walt Disney favourites, and there are over 200 attractions, with models of settings from the Disney stories and themed merry-go-rounds. The **Q-Zar** park attracts the more competitive, while the lively **Bowling Oltremare** has table tennis and bars as well as bowling.

INTERNET

FOR THOSE ADDICTED TO surfing the Net, there are Internet monitors and terminals for hire at the **City Hall Café** and **Internet Bar**. You can always consult the website devoted to Naples *(see opposite page)*.

Trotting races at Agnano

SPORTS

THE ITALIAN football championship is the sporting event that most fires the passion of Neapolitans. The ritual at the **San Paolo Stadium** *(see p42)* is repeated every time the Naples team plays at home. Tickets always sell out quickly.

The **Ippodromo di Agnano** (race track), where the famous Gran Premio is held every April, lies in a splendid natural location. Tennis is also popular, and courts are in abundance.

But Naples is first and foremost a seaside city. Nautical sports, especially canoeing and sailing, are organized by the seafront clubs. Although strictly reserved for members, they will be happy to accept the foreign guests of a member, so if you are lucky enough to know one, don't miss the chance to enjoy a unique experience. Swimming, diving and especially water polo are extremely popular sports in Naples. All of them are practised at the **Piscina Scandone**, the public swimming pool.

A fast-paced game of water polo, popular in Naples

Reed thickets surrounding a lake at the WWF nature reserve on Vesuvius, a popular destination with walkers

WALKING

THE PLEASURE of hiking through lovely countryside has become popular of late. Maps with suggested routes are distributed free at the **EPT** offices *(see p203)*, and information is also given by associations such as the **Naples WWF**, which runs the Cratere degli Astroni nature reserve on Vesuvius. You can reach this crater by taking the Agnano exit on the *tangenziale* (by-pass road); the paths in its thick woods lead to stretches of water inhabited by herons and other birds. Another classical hiking route is in the park of Vesuvius, where the **Guide Alpine della Campania** organize guided tours. For information on the various routes up Mount Vesuvius, contact the **Ente Parco del Vesuvio**.

OUTSIDE NAPLES

THE FESTIVALS are the real highlights in the calendar of cultural events in the area around Naples. Concerts are very popular as a result, so it is best to book seats well in advance. Among these are the **Estate Musicale Sorrentina**, held in the cloister of the church of San Francesco in Sorrento, and the prestigious **Festival Internazionale di Ravello** *(see p41)*.

There is plenty of nightlife in the Phlegraean Fields area, with its nightspots, bars and discos; the best known is **Michelemmà**, a garden in the heart of Pozzuoli, with a jazz club and pizzeria. In the

The Festival Internazionale at Ravello

same town, the **Havana Club** has three dance floors, an outdoor pool and a pine grove. Towards Licola and in the Sorrento peninsula, the beach bars turn into beach discotheques on summer

evenings. At Sorrento there are the **Kan Kan** disco and the **Filou Club** piano bar. Positano offers good entertainment, such as drinks and conversation at the **Buca di Bacco** and then off to **Music on the Rocks**, a disco and piano bar.

In Capri, after a stroll around the square you could try **Number Two** or **New Penthotal** for a night of energetic dancing, or else to the taverna **Anema e Core** to sing classical Neapolitan songs. Evenings in Procida are spent in the bars in the Marina or Chiaiolella, while Ischia has at least two dance spots which stay open until the small hours – **New Valentino** and **Jane**.

SCUBA AND SKIN DIVING

A GLIMPSE OF marine life and the features of the sea bed in the two bays is an experience you shouldn't miss: make enquiries at the **Capri Diving Club** and **Ischia Diving Center** or **Teresa Lucibello** at Positano's Marina Grande. Or you can explore the magnificent coastal and island sea floor with the small **Sottomarino Tritone** submarine.

Fireworks, a popular tradition in Naples and the Campania region

DIRECTORY

INFORMATION

Box Office
Galleria Umberto I.
081 551 91 88.

Concerteria
Via M Schipa 23.
081 761 12 21.

DANCE, THEATRE AND OPERA

Galleria Toledo
Via Concezione a
Montecalvario 34.
081 42 58 24.

Teatro Augusteo
Via Toledo 262.
081 41 42 43.

Teatro Bellini
Via Conte di Ruvo 14.
081 549 96 88.

Teatro Diana
Via L Giordano 64/72.
081 556 75 27.

Teatro San Carlo
Via San Carlo 93/f.
081 797 21 11.

Teatro Mercadante
Piazza Municipio 64.
081 551 33 96.

Teatro Nuovo
Via Montecalvario 16.
081 425 59 58.

Teatro Sancarluccio
Via San Pasquale a
Chiaia 49.
081 40 50 00.

Teatro Sannazaro
Via Chiaia 149.
081 41 17 23.

Teatro Totò
Via F Cavara 12/a.
081 564 75 25.

CINEMA

Alcione
Via Lomonaco 5.
081 40 63 75.

Arcobaceno
Via Carelli 13.
081 578 26 12.

Multicinema Modernissimo
Via Cisterna dell'Olio 59.
081 551 12 47.

Plaza Sala Bernini
Via Kerbaker 85.
081 556 35 55.

NIGHTSPOTS

Chez Moi
Via Parco Margherita 13.
081 40 75 26.

La Mela
Via dei Mille 40 bis.
081 41 38 81.

Mephisto
Via Medina 12.
081 551 66 42.

Notting Hill
Piazza Dante 88

Queen Victoria
Via V Fornari 15.
081 42 23 34.

Riot
Via S Biagio dei Librai 39.

S'Move
Vico dei Sospiri 10.
0330 99 54 49.

Velvet Underground
Via Cisterna dell'Olio 11.

Vibes Café
Largo San Giovanni
Maggiore 26–7.
081 551 39 84.

LIVE MUSIC

Antica Birreria Kronenbourg
Parco Edenlandia.
081 239 40 90.

Associazione Alessandro Scarlatti
Piazza dei Martiri 58.
081 40 60 11.

Lido Pola
Via Nisida 34.
081 570 19 50.

Otto Jazz Club
Piazzetta Cariati.
081 551 74 53.

Palapartenope
Via Barbagallo.
081 762 82 16.

Rude Pravo
Piazza Fanzago 111.
081 556 01 82.

AMUSEMENT PARKS

Bowling Oltremare
Viale J F Kennedy.
081 62 44 44.

Edenlandia
Viale J F Kennedy.
081 239 40 90.

Q-Zar
Via Lomonaco 1.
081 40 18 15.

INTERNET

City Hall Café
Corso V Emanuele 137a.
081 66 94 00.

Internet Bar
Piazza V Bellini 74.
081 29 50 35.

SPORTS

Ippodromo di Agnano
Via Ippodromo.
081 570 26 10.

Piscina Scandone
Viale Giochi del Mediter-
raneo. 081 570 91 59.

Stadio San Paolo
Fuorigrotta.
081 239 56 23.

WALKING

Ente Parco del Vesuvio
Municipio di San
Sebastiano al Vesuvio.
081 771 82 15.

Guide Alpine della Campania
081 777 57 20.

Naples WWF
081 726 65 11.

OUTSIDE NAPLES

Anema e Core
Via Sella Orta 1 (Capri).
081 837 64 61.

Buca di Bacco
Via Marina (Positano).
089 81 14 82.

Filou Club
Via Santa Maria della Pietà
12 (Sorrento).
081 878 20 83.

Havana Club
Via Fascione 4 (Pozzuoli).
081 526 42 15.

Jane
Via Arenile Pagoda (Ischia).
081 99 32 96.

Kan Kan
Piazza Sant'Antonino (Sorrento). 081 878 11 14.

Michelemmà
Via Rossini 27 (Pozzuoli).
081 326 01 52.

Music On The Rocks
Grotte dell'Incanto (Positano). 089 87 58 74.

New Penthotal
Via V Emanuele 45 (Capri).
081 837 67 93.

New Valentino
Corso V Colonna 97
(Ischia). 081 98 25 69.

Number Two
Via Camerelle 1 (Capri).
081 837 70 78.

DIVING

Capri Diving Club
Località Punta Carena 8.
(Anacapri).
081 837 85 94.

Ischia Diving Center
Via Jasolino 8 (Ischia).
081 98 50 08.

Teresa Lucibello
Spiaggia Marina Grande
(Positano). 089 87 50 32.

Sottomarino Tritone
Via delle Rose 50/A (Piano
di Sorrento).
081 808 66 18.

SURVIVAL
GUIDE

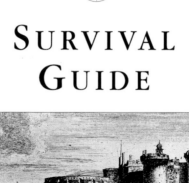

PRACTICAL INFORMATION

Naples is a lively, if somewhat chaotic city which may seem bewildering to visitors. However, over the past few years the city has undergone something of a rebirth. Its rich historic and artistic wealth has been reassessed, with more monuments open at regular hours and reorganization of the major museums to make the most of their world-class collections. Improved facilities and new pedestrian areas have revived public spaces, and cultural and social activities, advertised in the tourist offices, abound.

Visitors will still find the city has its frustrating aspects, with crippling bureaucracy at banks and public offices, and it is wise to be on the lookout for petty crime, keeping money and valuables well out of view. However, only simple guidelines and some forward planning are needed to make the most of this fascinating city and its past.

ITALIA
ENTE NAZIONALE
ITALIANO PER IL TURISMO
The ENIT logo

Looking over Piazza Mercato, one of Naples's liveliest squares

TOURIST INFORMATION

You can begin to organize your own itineraries before you leave for Italy by making enquiries at the **ENIT** office (the Italian national tourist board) in your home country. Once you are in Italy, the network of local tourist offices, known as **EPT** (Ente Provinciale per il Turismo), can provide useful information concerning accommodation, guided tours and excursions in the surrounding area. These information offices can be found at key arrival points such as the airport and the main railway station in Naples, as well as in the city centre.

Outside Naples, the **Azienda Autonoma di Soggiorno, Cura e Turismo**, which is organized by the regional administration, has offices in Naples and the main tourist resorts. They are reliable sources of information and will provide free maps and guide books. Smaller towns will also have an information office, called a *Pro Loco*, often based in the town hall.

INFORMATION FOR STUDENT TRAVELLERS

Students and young people under 26 can obtain air, rail and ferry discount tickets at the local Centro Turistico Studentesco (**CTS**). The membership card costs €22 and includes the ISIC international student identity card and the Italian *Carta Giovani*. This card offers discounts at theatres, bookshops and other businesses in Naples. CTS will also help with cheap car hire and courses for its members. Students from abroad can purchase the ISIC card or the *Carta Giovani* separately for €8 each. The ISIC card offers a 24-hour telephone helpline providing general advice and information.

The **Associazione Italiana Alberghi per la Gioventù** (Youth hostelling association) operates hostels for members of the YHA (Youth Hostel Association). If you are not already a member, the card can be purchased directly from the hostel for €13. There is one youth hostel in Naples, the Ostello Mergellina, which is conveniently located and open all year round. For information on hostels outside Naples, inquire at the youth hostel association office.

ENTERTAINMENT

The monthly magazine called *Qui Napoli*, published by the **Azienda Autonoma di Soggiorno, Cura e Turismo** and available from most hotels and information offices, is a free guide to events in and around Naples. It lists opening hours for monuments and museums and each issue has an updated *Agenda* in both Italian and English with information on exhibitions, theatre, concerts and conferences. More detailed information on lectures, seminars, sports and entertainment can be found in the national magazines or in the relevant supplements of the daily newspapers.

***Qui Napoli*, a free tourist monthly for Naples and Campania**

◁ Busy Piazza Municipio viewed from the air

Modern Neapolitan skyscrapers, a striking contrast with the old city

MUSEUMS AND MONUMENTS

SOME STREETS and squares in the old centre of Naples have information display panels with a map of the area showing the position of museums, monuments and churches. Museums are usually open in the morning and closed on Mondays. Entrance is free for under 18s or those over 60. Churches are usually free, although there may be a charge for areas like cloisters. Visits to underground Naples are organized by **L.A.E.S.** and **Napoli Sotterranea** on Thursdays at 9pm, Saturdays at 10am and noon, and Sundays from 10am to noon. Archaeological sites are generally open every day from the morning to one hour before sunset.

Street clock with the city arms

IMMIGRATION AND CUSTOMS

EUROPEAN UNION (EU) residents and visitors from the United States, Canada, Australia, New Zealand and Japan do not need a visa for stays of up to three months but must have one for a longer stay. Non-European Union citizens must carry a valid passport with them at all times, while for EU citizens an ID card will suffice.

Non-EU citizens can bring in either 400 cigarettes or 100 cigars or 500 grams of tobacco, 1 litre of spirits, 2 litres of wine and 50 grams of perfume. Non-EU citizens can claim back sales tax (IVA) on purchases over €155. For help, call your embassy or consulate.

ITALIAN TIME

ITALY IS ONE HOUR ahead of Greenwich Mean Time in winter and two hours ahead in the summer. The clocks go forward in March and back in September. That means that London is one hour behind Italian time and New York six hours behind; while Tokyo is eight hours ahead of Naples and Sydney is ten hours ahead.

ELECTRIC ADAPTORS

ELECTRIC CURRENT is 220 volts, with two-pin or three-pin round-pronged plugs.

DIRECTORY

TOURIST INFORMATION

Aziende Autonome di Soggiorno, Cura e Turismo
Naples
Palazzo Reale, Piazza Plebiscito.
081 252 57 26.
Piazza del Gesù.
081 551 27 01.
Castel dell'Ovo.
081 764 56 88.

Sorrento
Via De Maio 35.
081 807 40 33.

ENIT

United Kingdom
1 Princes Street, London
WIR 8AY. 020 7408 1254.

United States
630 Fifth Avenue, New York,
NY 10111. 212 245 4822.

EPT

Capodichino Airport.
081 780 30 50
or 081 780 57 61.
Central Railway Station.
081 26 87 79.
Mergellina Station.
081 761 21 02.
Piazza Martiri 58.
081 40 53 11.

L.A.E.S.
081 40 02 56.

Napoli Sotterranea
081 44 98 21.

INFORMATION FOR STUDENT TRAVELLERS

Associazione Italiana Alberghi per la Gioventù
Salita della Grotta 23.
081 761 23 46.

Centro Turistico Studentesco (CTS)
Via Mezzocannone 25.
081 552 79 60.

CONSULATES

South Africa
Corso Umberto I.
081 551 75 19.

United Kingdom
Via Crispi 122.
081 66 35 11.

United States
Piazza della Repubblica 2.
081 583 81 11.

Display panel with local map and tourist information

Security and Public Services

WHILE THE COUNTRYSIDE around Naples does not pose particular problems, petty crime is quite widespread in Naples itself. By taking a few simple precautions you will be able to protect yourself from pickpockets and purse snatchers: don't wear valuable jewellery or watches; handbags are easy targets, so hold onto them tightly and carry your money in your pockets. If possible, keep cameras and video cameras hidden from sight. It's best to be wary in Naples, but don't let apprehension ruin your trip.

Logo of the bank of Naples

LOOKING AFTER YOUR PROPERTY

IT'S BEST NOT to carry large sums of money on you while walking around town – leave it in your hotel safe. Always make photocopies of your vital documents like passports, or at least make a note of the number. Report any loss or theft to the police, while lost or stolen traveller's cheques and credit cards should also be immediately reported to the issuing bank. If you are travelling by car, always park in supervised car parks and do not leave items visible inside the vehicle. In crowded public areas or on public transport, be on your guard against pickpockets, as they are very agile, while purse snatchers on mopeds prefer to take jewels and handbags from strolling pedestrians. The station is best avoided at night, and it is not advisable for single women to go around alone after dark.

A team of policemen

but many Italians usually prefer to drink bottled mineral water. As Neapolitan cuisine includes many seafood dishes, be careful not to eat closed

shellfish and it is advisable to avoid raw seafood.

If you should need urgent medical assistance, call the **Pronto Soccorso** (casualty department) or the **Guardia Medica** at night and at week-ends. All pharmacies will have a list of branches open at night and on public holidays *(farmacia di turno)* posted on their door. The **Farmacia Alma Salus** in Piazza Dante, in the centre of Naples, is open 24 hours a day.

CREDIT CARDS

MAJOR CREDIT CARDS such as VISA, Access/Mastercard, American Express and Diners Card are accepted by the majority of the larger businesses and restaurants. Smaller trattorias may only accept cash, so it is adviseable to carry some cash with you.

Italian pharmacy sign

HEALTH

IN THE SUMMER, if you go to the seaside, watch out for the no bathing signs *(divieto di balneazione)* on the beaches, as this means that the water is polluted. Tap water is drinkable in Naples,

CURRENCY

Twelve countries have replaced their traditional currencies, such as the lira, with the euro. Austria, Belgium, Finland, France, Germany, Greece, Ireland, Italy, Luxembourg, Netherlands, Portugal and Spain chose to join the new currency; the UK, Denmark and Sweden stayed out, with an option to review their situation. The euro was intro-duced on 1 January 1999, but only for banking purposes. Notes and coins came into circulation on 1 January 2002. All euro notes and coins can be used anywhere inside the participating member states.

You can exchange currency at an automatic cash dispenser at certain bank branches in Naples, but it's best to have some euros in cash with you when you arrive. Euro bank notes have seven denominations. The €5 note (grey in colour) is the smallest, followed by the €10 note (pink), €20 note (blue), €50 note (orange), €100 note (green), €200 note (yellow) and €500 note (purple). The euro has eight coin denominations: €1 and €2; 50 cents, 20 cents, 10 cents, 5 cents, 2 cents and 1 cent. The €2 and €1 coins are both silver and gold in colour. The 50-, 20- and 10-cent coins are gold. The 5-, 2- and 1-cent coins are bronze.

Euro notes

BANKING HOURS

Banks are open from Monday to Friday. Opening hours vary but generally run from 8:30am to 1:20pm and 2:45pm to 3:45pm. Queues may be very long, especially in the morning, when it is advisable to arrive early. Identification, such as a passport, is required for any transaction. Cash dispensers (Bancomat) display logos of the cards they accept.

Banco di Napoli
Via Toledo 177–178.
(081 791 11 11.
Banca di Roma
Via Toledo 352/a.
(081 785 41 11.
Cariplo
Via Nuova Marina 20.
(081 550 71 11.

An Italian post box

POSTAL SERVICES

Post offices in Naples are open Monday to Saturday from 8:30am to 1:20pm (noon on the last day of the month). The central Post Office in Piazza Matteotti is open from 8:15am to 7:20pm (8:15am–2pm on Sundays). Branch Post Offices are situated all over the city, in the railway stations and at Capodichino airport. The Italian postal service is by no means a model of efficiency, so for urgent communications, whether you are sending letters or parcels, it is advisable to use the *Postacelere* express service. This is a fast and reliable service for a fee. Throughout Italy, stamps can be bought at the tobacconist *(tabaccaio)* as well as in the post office itself. The postcode for Naples is 80100.

Posta Centrale
Piazza Matteotti.
Operator (081 551 19 47.
Information (081 551 14 56.

Automatic cash dispenser

PUBLIC TELEPHONES

Public telephone boxes in streets and in bars generally accept coins, telephone cards (which can be bought from a *tabaccaio* or a bar) and, sometimes, credit cards. A number of bars use *telefono a scatti* which monitor the number of units used during the phone call and ask you to pay at the end. Offices run by Telecom Italia (the state telephone company) also operate with this system. You can also place reverse charge calls and pay by credit card with these phones.

For international directory enquiries, dial 176. For international operator assistance, dial 170. General information is given on 1400. With Countrydirect service you can call an operator in another country, who will connect you to the number you want: dial 172, followed by the country code (codes are listed in the Telecom directory). With credit card phones you can have your calls charged to your home phone bill; dial 187 to arrange this service. The area code for Naples is 081. Note that hotel phone calls can be very expensive, often up to twice the price of a call from a public phone.

Telecom Italia Office
Via Depretis 4. ○ 9:30am–1pm,
2–5:30pm daily.
(081 551 09 21.

TRAVEL INFORMATION

IN THE WAKE of a campaign to improve transport services in Naples, plans are being made to restructure and develop existing flight, rail and ferry links. The airport, Capodichino, is close to the city and is used for domestic, European and charter flights, with the nearest intercontinental airport in Rome to the north. The fastest means of reaching Naples by land is to travel

An Alitalia airplane

by train, since there are no direct long-distance coach connections with European cities, and cars are far from ideal because of parking and traffic problems in town. Naples also has a large maritime passenger terminal with ferry connections to the islands in the Bay of Naples. Buses, funiculars and two underground lines link all the main sites in the city of Naples itself.

The elegant Campi Flegrei railway station

ARRIVING BY AIR

DAILY FLIGHTS to Naples from London, Paris, Frankfurt and Munich are operated by **Alitalia**, the Italian state airline, as well as non-Italian carriers such as **Air France**, **British Airways** and **Lufthansa**. **Air Littoral**, **Crossair**, **Olympic Airways** and **Sabena** offer direct international services to and from Nice, Lugano, Athens, Marseilles and Brussels.

Capodichino airport is fairly small, even though it is the only one in the region. No direct intercontinental flights are handled, so travellers from countries

outside Europe will probably transfer to a connecting flight to Naples in Rome.

The **C.L.P.** company offers direct coach connections from the airport to the centre of town (Piazza Municipio, on the corner of Via Medina); departures are hourly from 6:30am to 11:30pm (from the airport) and from 7am to midnight (from Piazza Municipio); tickets cost €2 and can be bought on board.

If you go by taxi, make sure you go to the official rank and that the meter is on. The journey lasts about 20 minutes and the fare should be around €20.

Package holidays are often cheaper than independent travel and your onward journey from the airport will be organized for you.

If you have organized a fly-drive deal, you will need to report to the car hire company desk in the airport on arrival. It is usually cheaper to book car hire in advance.

ARRIVING BY TRAIN

THERE ARE THREE MAIN railway stations in Naples – **Napoli Centrale** (Piazza Garibaldi), **Mergellina** (on the seafront) and **Campi Flegrei** (at Fuorigrotta).

The main station in Piazza Garibaldi is also the main interchange for the city's transport systems. Access to the underground (*metropolitana*) and the Circumvesuviana railway (for trains to Pompei-Villa dei Misteri and the coast) is from inside the station. In the square in front you will find the main terminal for the city and suburban buses as well as buses for destinations in Southern Italy.

A programme for the development of high-speed trains called **TAV** (*Treni ad Alta Velocità*) is now under way; it will connect all the major stations. In the meantime, the fastest and most convenient way of travelling by train is the Eurostar (ES), for which you pay a supplement. There is a train every hour on the Naples-Rome line. For

Capodichino airport coach service

The Mergellina railway station

Passenger ferry at the Naples seaport

journeys of less than 200 km (120 miles) you can purchase a discount ticket *(biglietto a fasce chilometriche)* at news-agents in all stations.

Toll booths on the motorway

ARRIVING BY CAR

SHOULD YOU decide to travel into Naples by car, be prepared for highly stressful driving, heavy traffic and parking problems. A car may be convenient for visiting other sites in the region, but in Naples itself it is advisable to use the public transport system or walk.

The **Automobile Club d'Italia** (ACI) provides maps and a towing and repair service to its members as well as to members of affiliated foreign associations. Tolls are charged on the *autostrada* (motorway) and can be paid in cash or with a Viacard magnetic card, available at a

tabaccaio (tobacconist's) or an ACI agency. Emergency telephones are located at intervals along the motorway.

Autostrada A2 exits into the Naples bypass road *(tangenziale)*, which takes you quickly to the centre or the outskirts. For the coastal resorts, follow signs for Autostrada A3, signposted Salerno. The state road 163 runs the length of the beautiful Amalfi coastline.

ARRIVING BY BOAT

THE MAIN MARITIME passenger terminal (Stazione Marittima), used by large and medium-sized ships, is the **Molo Angioino**, opposite Piazza Municipio.

Ferries and hydrofoils for connections to the islands in the bay and the Sorrento peninsula depart from the nearby **Molo Beverello** and **Mergellina** *(see p119)* passenger terminals.

The **Tirrenia** ship line offers direct connections between Naples and Sardinia, Sicily and Tunisia. The **Linee Lauro** company sails twice-weekly to Sardinia, and **Siremar** operates the route from Naples to the Aeolian Islands. **Aliscafi SNAV** runs a high-speed hydrofoil service for the Aeolian islands, Ponza and Ventotene. This route is only operated in the summer, however.

(see p119)

DIRECTORY

AIRLINE INFORMATION

Alitalia
Information 147 86 56 43
Reservations 147 86 56 41 / 2.

British Airways
 199 71 22 66.

Continental
 800 231 0856.

Lufthansa
 06 656 84 004.

**Gesac
(airport services)**
 081 789 61 11.
Information 081 789 62 59.
Parking 081 789 63 25.

C.L.P.
 081 251 41 57.

TRAIN INFORMATION

Ferrovie dello Stato
Centrale Railway Station.
Information 147 88 80 88.

Stazione di Mergellina
 081 68 06 35.

Stazione di Campi Flegrei
 081 239 54 02.

FOR MOTORISTS

Automobile Club d'Italia
Piazzale Tecchio, 49/d.
 081 239 04 10.
Emergencies 116.

PASSENGER SHIP LINES

Tirrenia/Siremar
 081 720 11 11.

Linee Lauro
 081 551 32 36.

Aliscafi SNAV
 081 761 23 48.

Consorzio Autonomo Porto di Napoli
Stazione Marittima,
Molo Angioino.
 081 552 39 68.

A SNAV express hydrofoil to the Aeolian Islands and Ponza

Getting Around Naples

THE CITY TRANSPORT system is being improved and expanded in stages, but it is still fairly unreliable and often rather slow. In fact, it will usually take you less time to travel around the central districts on foot rather than on a bus or tram. With the exception of the underground system *(metropolitana)*, public transport is only really recommended for longer distances. In the main squares in the centre there are display panels with a map of Naples which indicate the main bus, tram and metro stops.

The funicular railway

UNDERGROUND RAILWAY

NAPLES HAS TWO underground lines *(metropolitana)*: one is part of the Ferrovie dello Stato (FS, or state railway), and the other is the hill metro *(collinare)*. The former uses normal train routes and is often subject to delays. It runs from 5:30am to 10:20pm, with departures every 8 minutes. It goes through the main areas in Naples. The hill metro links Vomero with the hospital and the Chiaiano and Secondigliano quarters. It runs from 6:40am to 10:54pm, with departures every 12 minutes.

FUNICULAR RAILWAYS

THERE ARE FOUR funicular routes, run by the Azienda Napoletana Mobilità (ANM) Naples city transport system. Three of these (Funicolare Centrale, Funicolare di Montesanto and Funicolare di Chiaia) connect the centre of the city with the Vomero district, where the museum of San Martino and the museum of Duca di Martina are located, as well as a large shopping area. The Mergellina funicular, run by a separate company, connects the seafront area (Via Mergellina) with Via Manzoni. The funiculars are reliable and fast and run from 7am to 10pm, with departures every 10 minutes.

BUSES AND TRAMS

BUS AND TRAM networks are run by the ANM. You need patience to travel by bus in Naples; even short journeys take time because of the heavy and famously chaotic traffic. Buses and trams are often crowded and have their share of pickpockets, so be alert, and keep valuables carefully tucked away. Recently, four new bus lines (red lines R1, R2, R3, R4) were created to improve the general standard of service; they depart every 5 to 10 minutes between 6am and midnight, while electric buses (E1, E2, E3) now serve the old town and the Quartieri Spagnoli. There are also **ANM** night buses:
Via G Marino 1.
Information [081 763 21 77.

TICKETS AND MONTHLY PASSES

THE "GIRANAPOLI" system of tickets operates in Naples for all local buses, trams, funiculars, the hill metro and the FS metro. A Giranapoli ticket costs about €1 and is valid for 90 minutes. A ticket costing €2 can be used all day. On the metros and funiculars a single ticket is only valid for one journey.

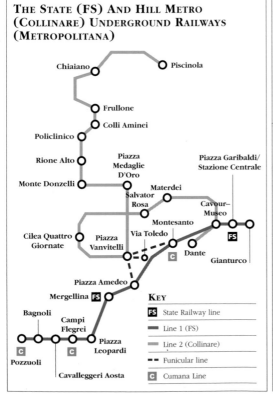

THE STATE (FS) AND HILL METRO (COLLINARE) UNDERGROUND RAILWAYS (METROPOLITANA)

Chiaiano
Piscinola
Frullone
Colli Aminei
Policlinico
Rione Alto
Piazza Medaglie D'Oro
Piazza Garibaldi/ Stazione Centrale
Monte Donzelli
Materdei
Salvator Rosa
Cavour– Museo
Montesanto
Cilea Quattro Giornate
Piazza Vanvitelli
Via Toledo
Dante
Gianturco
Piazza Amedeo
Mergellina
Bagnoli
Campi Flegrei
Piazza Leopardi
Pozzuoli
Cavalleggeri Aosta

KEY

FS	State Railway line
──	Line 1 (FS)
──	Line 2 (Collinare)
▬ ▬	Funicular line
C	Cumana Line

A taxi rank

Giranapoli tickets are sold in the stations, at newsstands and tobacconists. You must validate each ticket before departure by stamping it in a machine. If you are in Naples for several weeks it is worth buying the monthly Giranapoli pass.

TAXIS

IF YOU TAKE A TAXI, make sure it is from an official rank. The meter should read €2 at the start of the ride, which is the local tax. The minimum fare is €3, double for out-of-town trips and rides from the airport to the centre cost an extra €2–3. There is an extra charge of €2 at weekends and public holidays; and 2 from 10pm to 7am; and 50 cents for each item of luggage.

The Neapolitan taxi logo

You can easily find taxis in the official ranks outside the train and metro stations, and in the main squares of Naples. You can also book a taxi over the telephone, but note that a supplement of about 50 cents is charged.

Cotana
☎ 081 570 70 70.
Napoli
☎ 081 556 44 44.
Partenope
☎ 081 560 66 66.

WALKING

THE PEDESTRIAN ZONES are a recent, much-needed development in a city with immense traffic problems. You can now walk along streets in the historic centre and admire the monuments in relative peace and quiet. To shop away from traffic, go to the pedestrian-only Via Chiaia, Via Toledo or Via Scarlatti (in Vomero). Every Sunday part of Via Partenope is closed to traffic, enabling you to admire Vesuvius and Castel dell'Ovo. However, be careful crossing the road elsewhere: drivers often ignore traffic lights and people waiting at zebra crossings, and fast-moving scooters appear from nowhere. Fortunately, Neapolitans have quick reflexes and usually manage to avoid accidents.

Traffic policeman

DIRECTORY

PARKING

Parcheggio di Interscambio
Via Benedetto Brin.
☎ 081 763 28 32.

Grilli
Via G Ferraris 40.
☎ 081 26 43 44.

Mergellina
Via Mergellina 112.
☎ 081 761 34 70.

Santa Chiara
Pallonetto Santa Chiara 30.
☎ 081 551 63 03.

Supergarage
Via Shelley 11.
☎ 081 551 31 04.

Turistico
Via A De Gasperi 14.
☎ 081 552 54 42.

PARKING

IN 1998 designated parking areas were introduced to relieve congestion in Naples. They are marked with blue lines and cost a €1–2 per hour to use. Cheaper parking can be found at Brin and Lungomare. Brin's **Parcheggio di Interscambio** also offers electric cars for rent, enabling you to drive in areas normally closed to traffic and enjoy free parking in the city centre car parks.

SCOOTER AND MOPED HIRE

The brave may find that mopeds and scooters are the best method of negotiating the heavy Naples traffic. At least you can easily find parking space. They can be hired at some car-hire agencies:

Italrent
Via Comunale Tavernola 166–7.
☎ 081 575 63 12.
Capodichino Airport.
☎ 081 599 13 16.

Motorbike hire: **Bernini**
Via Torrione San Martino 29.
☎ 081 556 71 12.

A scooter, the most practical way of getting around Naples

Travelling Outside Naples

SEPSA
coaches logo

EVEN IF YOU ARE BASED IN NAPLES it is not difficult to visit ancient sites such as the Phlegraean Fields, the archaeological sites at Pompeii and Herculaneum, the towns on the Amalfi coast (Amalfi, Positano and Ravello) and the enchanting islands of Capri, Ischia and Procida. Most places are accessible by local train or bus, and excursions are available from bigger hotels and local travel agents.

Interior of the Centrale station

A Circumvesuviana train

LOCAL TRAINS

THE CIRCUMVESUVIANA train service connects Naples with the towns around Mount Vesuvius (including ancient Pompeii) and those on the Sorrento peninsula. The main terminus is in Corso Garibaldi, with the next stop in Piazza Garibaldi (at underground level), where moving walkways connect the metro station to the **Circumvesuviana**. There are four routes: Naples-Sorrento, Naples-Pompei-Poggiomarino, Naples-Ottaviano-Sarno and Naples-Nola-Baiano. In addition there are three types of train: the *accelerato* (ACC), which stops at all stations, the *diretto* (DIR), stopping only at the main

ones, and the *direttissimo* (DD), stopping at even fewer. Services run from 5am to midnight, with trains departing roughly every 20 minutes. You may want to avoid travelling late at night, though, because trains are infrequent and there are fewer people around. From 1 March to 1 November there is a seasonal service run by the Funivia di Monte Faito cableway, starting from Castellammare di Stabia station. To reach the towns on the Phlegraean Fields and the coast you can take the **Ferrovia Cumana**, while the **Ferrovia Circumflegrea** serves the towns in the interior. The main station is in Piazza Montesanto and the service is fast and efficient. The Cumana service has departures every 10 minutes for Bagnoli and every 20 for Pozzuoli and runs from 5:21am to 9:41pm. The main stops on the Circumflegrea

A hydrofoil in the Bay of Naples

line are Montesanto, Soccavo, Quarto, Licola and Torregaveta; departures are every 20 minutes until 9:43pm. Six trains per day stop at Cuma, Lido Fusaro and Torregaveta.

HYDROFOILS AND FERRIES

VARIOUS SHIPPING LINES offer frequent crossings from Naples to the islands in the bay. The Sorrento peninsula and some Amalfi coast towns can also be reached by boat. Ferries and hydrofoils depart from the Molo Beverello in Piazza Municipio, near the Stazione Marittima, and from Mergellina (hydrofoils only). From the port of Pozzuoli the crossing to Procida and Ischia is shorter and cheaper; you can also take your car on board, but check on available space beforehand. The **Caremar** line operates a ferry to Procida, Ischia and Capri which departs from the Molo Beverello and from Pozzuoli. **Linee Lauro** serves the Naples-Ischia route with ferries and hydrofoils departing from the Molo Beverello, while Sorrento and Capri are served by hydrofoil from the port of Mergellina.

SNAV logo

Coach for the Amalfi coast

Mergellina is also the departure point for the **SNAV** line's hydrofoils for Procida, Ischia (Casamicciola) and Capri. **Alilauro** offers a hydrofoil service to Ischia, Sorrento and Capri from the Molo Beverello and to Ischia, Capri and the Amalfi coast (Amalfi, Positano and Salerno) from Mergellina. Hydrofoils run by **Navigazione Libera del Golfo** go to all the islands from Mergellina and to Capri, Amalfi and Positano from the Molo Beverello.

the Phlegraean Fields area (Baia and Bacoli), while the blue SITA coaches go to various towns and resorts on the Sorrento peninsula, the tourist sights on the Amalfi coast (Amalfi, Maiori, Minori, Positano, Ravello, and so on) and Salerno. The **SITA** terminus is at Nos. 3–7 Via Pisanelli (near Piazza Municipio). Departures are every half an hour on weekdays and Saturdays and every two hours on Sundays and public holidays.

Three of the main car hire firms

TRAVELLING BY COACH

YOU CAN ALSO reach towns and resorts in the region by coach. Local companies depart from the terminus in Piazza Garibaldi or from the airport at Capodichino. The bus company **ACTP** serves the towns in the Vesuvius area and Caserta, with departures every 20 minutes on weekdays and every 40 minutes on Sundays and public holidays. The **SEPSA** company covers the towns in

CAR HIRE

IN ITALY CAR HIRE is quite expensive, and driving in Naples is highly stressful. If you are determined to drive, it is best to pre-book through an international agency or organize a fly-drive deal and use the vehicle only for visiting the tourist attractions outside the city. To rent a car you must be over 21 and have held a valid driver's licence for at least a year. Agencies are listed in the Yellow Pages (Pagine Gialle) under Autonoleggio.

DIRECTORY

LOCAL TRAINS

Circumvesuviana
Corso Garibaldi 387.
(081 772 24 44.

Ferrovia Cumana/Circumflegrea
Piazza Montesanto.
(081 551 33 28.

HYDROFOILS AND FERRIES

Alilauro
(0761 10 04.

Caremar
Molo Beverello. (081 551 38 82.
Pozzuoli. (081 526 27 11.

Linee Lauro
(081 551 32 36.

Navigazione Libera del Golfo
(081 552 72 09.

SNAV
(081 761 23 48.

COACH COMPANIES

ACTP
Via Arenaccia 29.
(081 700 11 11.

SEPSA
Via Cisterna dell'Olio 44.
(081 542 91 11.

SITA
Via Pisanelli 3–7.
(081 552 21 76.

CAR HIRE

AVIS
Piazza Garibaldi 1
(Centrale Railway Station).
(081 553 71 71.
Via Partenope 32.
(081 764 56 00.
Capodichino Airport.
(081 780 57 90.

Hertz
Via Nazario Sauro 21.
(081 764 53 23.
Piazza Garibaldi 93
(Centrale Railway Station).
(081 20 62 28.
Capodichino Airport.
(081 599 09 24.

CIRCUMVESUVIANA

Napoli   Torre Annunziata   Castellammare   Sorrento

Torre del Greco   Pompei   Meta

The main stations on the Circumvesuviana line

NAPLES STREET FINDER

THE PAGE GRID superimposed on the *Area by Area* map below shows which parts of Naples are covered by this Street Finder. The map references given for the restaurants, hotels and sights in Naples refer to the maps in this section. Central Naples has been enlarged on map pages 9 and 10 to make it easier to read. Sights in this area will give both map references. A complete index of the street names and major sights in the city follows on pages 214–17. The key on the opposite page shows the scales of the maps and explains the symbols. All the main sights in the city are clearly indicated in pink so they are easy to find.

0 metres   500

0 yards   500

1

2

3

9

10

Decumano Maggiore

Spaccanapoli

Vomero

7

5

6

Castel dell'Ovo and Chiaia

HOW TO USE THE MAPS

The first number corresponds to the Street Finder map.

Gesù Nuovo ❸

Piazza del Gesù Nuovo. **Map** 3 B5 (9 B4).
📞 081 44 05 11. ⏰ 6:30am–12:45pm
(1:30pm Sun), 4:15–7:30pm daily.

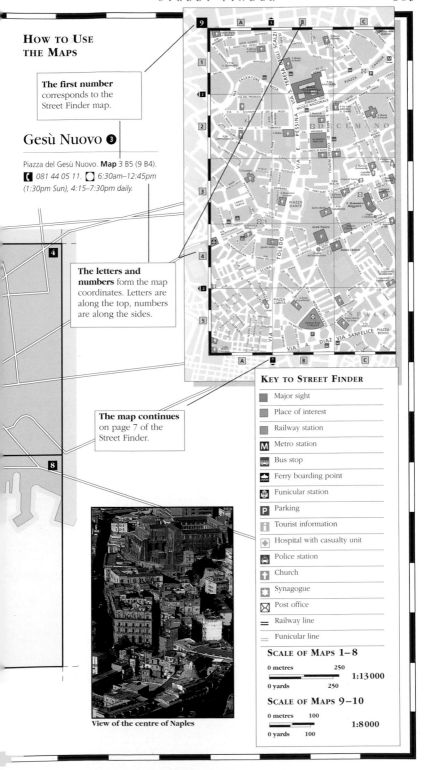

The letters and numbers form the map coordinates. Letters are along the top, numbers are along the sides.

The map continues on page 7 of the Street Finder.

View of the centre of Naples

KEY TO STREET FINDER

⬛	Major sight
⬛	Place of interest
⬛	Railway station
Ⓜ	Metro station
🚌	Bus stop
⛴	Ferry boarding point
🚟	Funicular station
🅿	Parking
ℹ	Tourist information
✚	Hospital with casualty unit
🚓	Police station
✝	Church
✡	Synagogue
⊠	Post office
=	Railway line
=	Funicular line

SCALE OF MAPS 1–8

0 metres	250	
0 yards	250	1:13 000

SCALE OF MAPS 9–10

0 metres	100	
0 yards	100	1:8 000

Street Finder Index

Map references in brackets
refer to enlarged map section

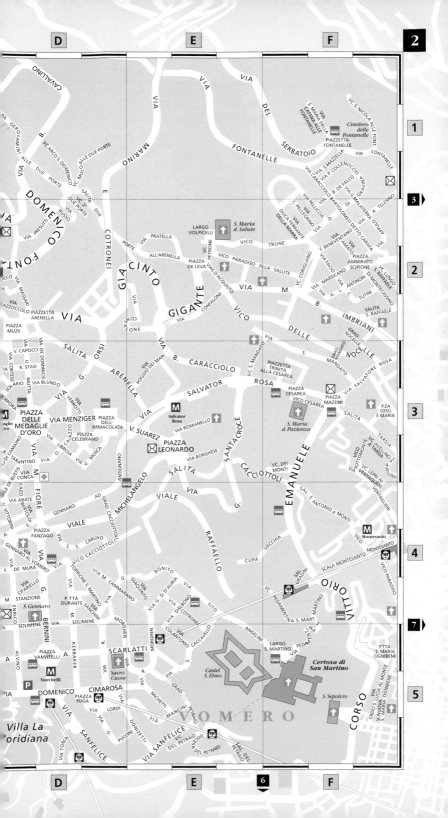

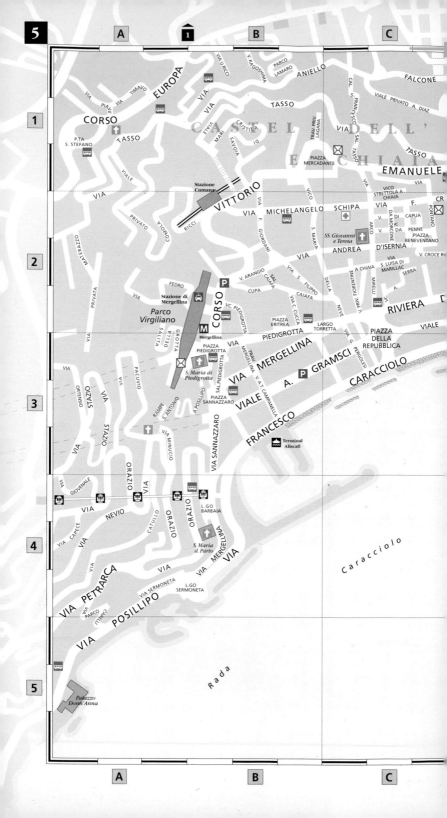

A
3
B
C

SEE PAGES
9 & 10 FOR
ENLARGEMENT
OF THIS AREA

SEE PAGES
9 & 10 FOR
ENLARGEMENT
OF THIS AREA

1

2

2

2

3

4

6

5

A
B
C

PARADISO
SCURA
VIA
V. SENISE
V. DI LIOY
VIA
CARROZZIERI
L.GO
S. GIOVANNI
MAGGIORE
VIA TARI
VIA
VIA E. CAPOCCI
P.
SAL.
VIA
P. PIGNASECCA
VC. SOCCORSO
VC. TRUCCO
VIA PUOTI
LIBORIO
FORMALE
S. CARAFA
V. CARAFA P.ZZO
MONTELIVETO
V. MONTELIVETO
BANCHI NUOVI
CA. SS. COSMA
S. Giovanni
Pappacoda
C.SO
UMBERTO
VIA MAROTTA
1°

VIA G. SIMONELLI
VIA
VC. CAMPANILE
GIRARDI
S.
GELSO
S. Anna
d. Lombardi
PIAZZA
CARITÀ
Palazzo Poste
e Telegrafi
DONNALBINA
VIA MARIA LA NOVA
Santa Maria
La Nova
VIA SEDILE DI PORTO
S. Pietro
Martire
VIA DI COSTANZO

L.GO
MONTE
CALVARIO
PORTACARRESE A.M.
MATTEO
RENINE
S. TERESELLA
VIA BATTISTI
VIA A.
DIAZ
TOLEDO
VAVEDRA
FIORENTINI
VIA DEL
CARRETTO
MADENA
V. SANFELICE
RUA V.BASILE
V. GRAZIELLA
GRIFFI
CATALANA
DEPRETIS
VIA MARCHE
V.G.C. CORTESE
PIAZZA
BOVIO
RUSSO
S. Maria di
Porto Salvo

VIA
PORTA PICCOLA
VICO
SEPOLCRO
VC. S. DE'
DEO
S. GIACOMO
SPERANZELLA
VIA S.
VIA
TOFA
VIA PONTE DI TAPPIA
VIA CERVANTES
V. CERVANTES
Incoronata
V. MEDINA
V. S BARTOLOMEO
V. DI GIOIA
V. SPADARI
S. Maria
MELISURGO
VIA ALCIDE DE GASPERI
LEONE
PIAZZA
CASTEL NUOVO

LUNGO MONTECALVARIO
VICO
LUNGO
VICO DELLA
VC.
D'AFFLITTO
VIA
GIARDINETTO
VIA P. E. IMBRIANI
S. Giacomo
d. Spagnoli
CAL.S. MARCO
La Pietà
di Turchini
P.ZZA
FRANCESE
Teatro
Mercadante
CASTEL NUOVO
VIA
CREPSE
E

VIA S. MATTIA
VC. BERIO
VIA
S.
VIA S.
VERDI
S. Brigida
BRIGIDA
VIA VITTORIO EMANUELE III
PIAZZA
MUNICIPIO
Castel Nuovo
ACTON
NUOVA CALATA PILIERO
NUOVA
CALATA PORTA DI MASSA
MOLO
IMMACOLATELLA
VECCHIA

Galleria
Umberto I
P.TA
SERAO
VIA S. CARLO
S. Ferdinando
VIA
MARCO DEL CASTELLO
Stazione
Marittima

NARDONES
PIAZZA
TRIESTE
E TRENTO
Teatro
San Carlo
VIA F. ACTON

VIA CHIAIA
Caffè
Gambrinus
VIA SERRA
VIA
PIAZZA
PLEBISCITO
Palazzo Reale
Giardini
Pubblici
MOLO
SAN VINCENZO

VIA NIZZ CALICE
S. Francesco di Paola
VIA
EGIZIACA
SOLITARIA
VC. SOLITARIA
VIA CESARIO CONSOLE
VIA
MEGARIDE
LUCIA
OASIN
PETRONIO
S. Lucia
MOLO SIGLIO

PIZZOFALCONE
PALLONETTO
VC. STORTO PALLONETTO
VIA
SANTA
SERAP.ORE
VIA
CUMA
VIA DE
GENERALE
CESARE
TURCHI

VIA ECHIA
SAL. LUCIA
VIA N. SAURO
VIA PALEPOLI
VIA LUCILIO

VIA A.
SUMAS
CHIATAMONE
VIA
PARTENOPE

BORGO
MARINARO

Golfo
di

Castel
dell'Ovo

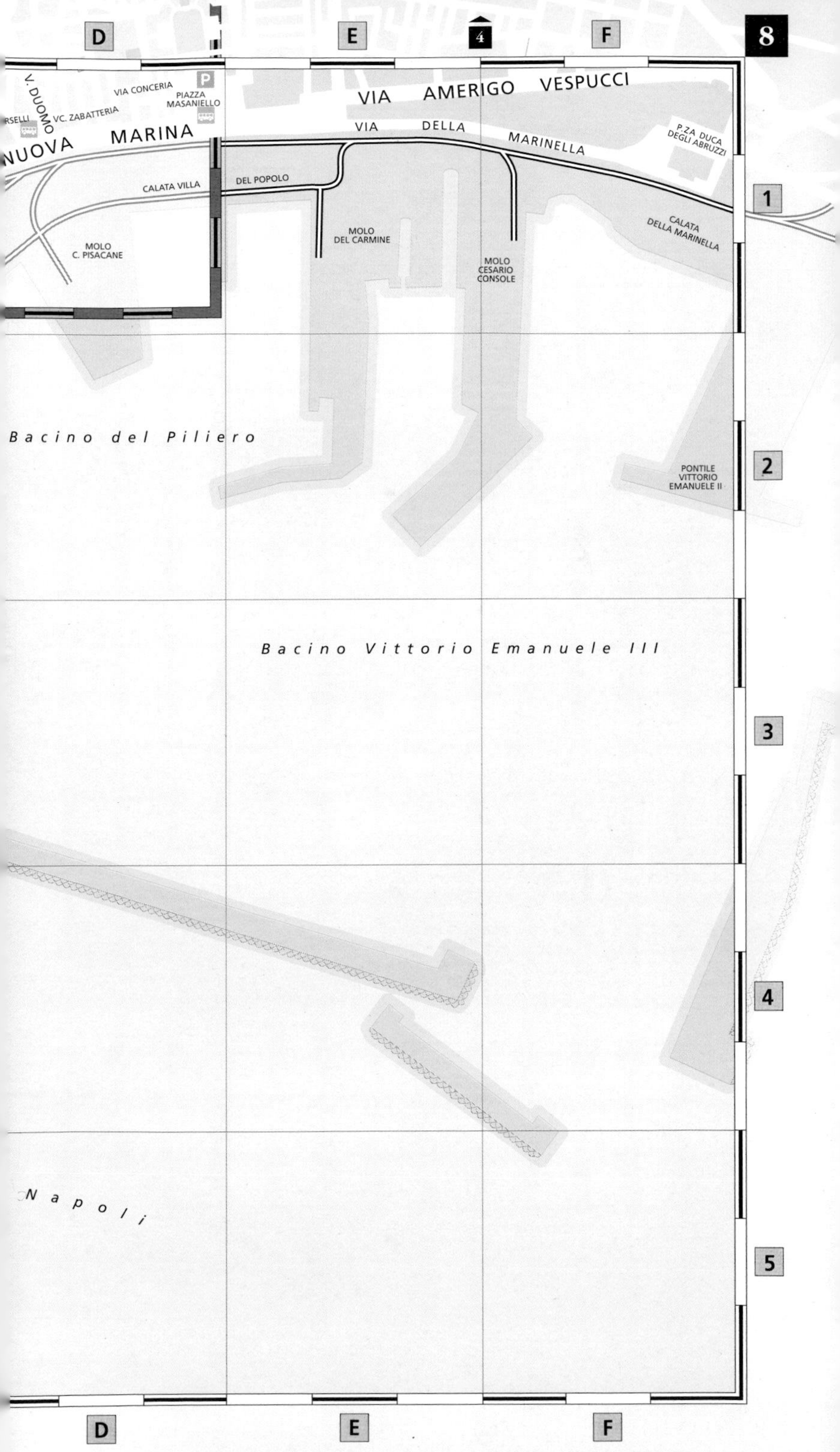

VIA AMERIGO VESPUCCI

VIA DELLA MARINELLA

V. DUOMO

VIA CONCERIA

RSELLI   VC. ZABATTERIA

PIAZZA MASANIELLO

P

NUOVA   MARINA

CALATA VILLA

DEL POPOLO

MOLO C. PISACANE

MOLO DEL CARMINE

MOLO CESARIO CONSOLE

P.ZA DUCA DEGLI ABRUZZI

CALATA DELLA MARINELLA

Bacino del Piliero

PONTILE VITTORIO EMANUELE II

Bacino Vittorio Emanuele III

N a p o l i

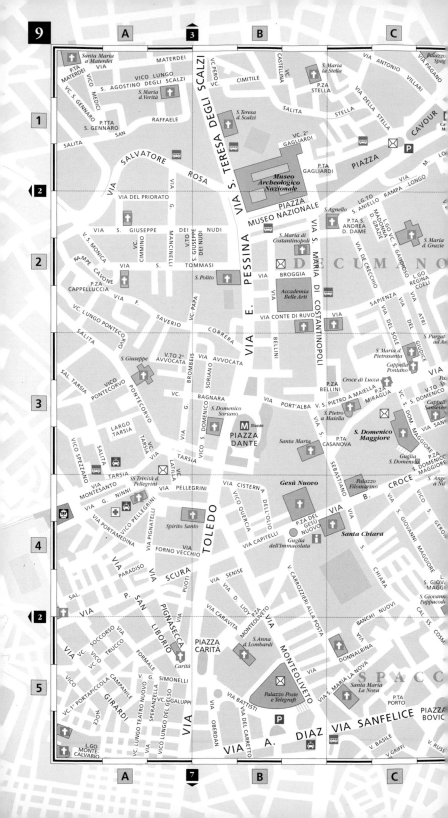

General Index

Acknowledgments

DORLING KINDERSLEY WOULD LIKE to thank the following people whose contributions and assistance have made the preparation of this book possible: Guido Bevilacqua, Luigi Consiglio, Diana Georgiacodis, Costantino Pantano, Adriana Sandrini Maione. Dorling Kindersley would also like to thank all the museums and tourist information offices, too numerous to mention individually, for their assistance and kind permission to photograph at their establishments.

EDITORIAL ASSISTANCE
Gillian Allen, Riccardo Baldini, Cooling Brown, Felicity Crowe, Vivien Crump, Annette Jacobs, Felicity Laughton, Georgina Matthews, Ferdie McDonald, Giorgio Padovani, Ingrid Vienings.

PICTURE CREDITS
Key: t = top; tl = top left; tlc = top left centre; tc = top centre; trc = top right centre; tr = top right; cla = centre left above; ca = centre above; cra = centre right above; cl = centre left; c = centre; cr = centre right; clb = centre left below; crb = centre right below; cb = centre below; bl = bottom left; br = bottom right; b = bottom; bc = bottom centre; bcl = bottom centre left; bcr = bottom centre right.

Every effort has been made to trace the copyright holders. The publisher apologizes for any unintentional omissions and would be pleased, in such cases, to add an acknowledgment in future editions. All the photographs reproduced in this book are from the Overseas S.r.l. Milano picture library except for the following:

ASSOCIAZIONE CULTURALE ARCHIVIO PARISIO, NAPLES: 22br, 24c, 24bl, 25tl, 26bc, 42tr, 55cl, 85cl, 125c, 127c, 130c, 139cr.

CORBIS: Jonathan Blair 27bl.

GIUSEPPE AVALLONE, NAPLES: 1, 19cr, 21cr, 27cr, 29bl, 31tl, 33tl, 34tl, 34tr, 35tr, 37tr, 37cl, 38cl, 38br, 41tl, 41br, 55cr, 60, 63tl, 65tc, 76tr, 77bc, 89bl, 92br, 102, 120, 124, 130bc, 130cl, 131br, 136cl, 140cl, 150tl, 152tr, 153tr, 153bl, 155tr, 155b, 163tl, 165b, 166b, 191cl, 192c, 196c, 196tc, 196cl, 198c.

FORNASS s.a.s., Portici (Napoli) 83cr, 192tl, 196br.

IMAGE BANK, MILAN: 2–3, 10–11, 28–29, 30tr, 30cl, 38tr, 38tl, 39cl, 40cr, 42br, 44–45, 105cl, 107tl, 112, 115c, 117b, 126–127, 131tl, 132bc, 132cl, 133ca, 139bl, 142tr, 145tl, 149br, 150tr, 151tr, 151cl, 154tr, 154br, 156cl, 159cl, 159tr, 160tl, 162tl, 163bl, 163br, 164cl, 164bl, 165tl, 165cr, 200.

MIMMO JODICE, NAPLES: 40tc, 68bc, 80tr, 96bc.

LUCIANO PEDICINI, NAPLES: 19tc, 68c, 69tl, 71c, 81c, 84c, 84bl, 97bl, 147br, 156tr, 157cl, 157tr, 157tc, 160bl, 161cr, 203tr.

MARKA, MILAN: D. Donati 62bc; R. Benzi 204bl; L. Sechi 207t.

SCALA GROUP S.P.A: 72tl.

JACKET
Front – CAPRI ONLINE; D'Aniello main image; CERAMICA PINTO bc; CORBIS: Archivo Iconografico, S.A bl; DK PICTURE LIBRARY: Ian O'Leary br. Back – CORBIS: John and Lisa Merrill b; Richard T. Nowitz t. Spine – CAPRI ONLINE: D'Aniello.

DORLING KINDERSLEY SPECIAL EDITIONS

Dorling Kindersley books can be purchased in bulk quantities at discounted prices for use in promotions or as premiums. We are also able to offer special editions and personalized jackets, corporate imprints, and excerpts from all of our books, tailored specifically to meet your own needs.

To find out more, please contact:
(in the United Kingdom) – SPECIAL SALES, DORLING KINDERSLEY LIMITED, 80 STRAND, LONDON WC2R ORL;

(in the United States) – SPECIAL MARKETS DEPT., DK PUBLISHING, INC., 375 HUDSON STREET, NEW YORK, NY 10014.

Phrase Book

IN EMERGENCY

Help!	Aiuto!	eye-yoo-toh
Stop!	Fermate!	fair-mah-teh
Call a doctor.	Chiama un medico.	kee-ah-mah oon meh-dee-koh
Call an ambulance.	Chiama un' ambulanza.	kee-ah-mah oon am-boo-lan-tsa
Call the police.	Chiama la polizia.	kee-ah-mah lah pol-ee-tsee-ah
Call the fire brigade.	Chiama i pompieri.	kee-ah-mah ee pom-pee-air-ee
Where is the telephone?	Dov'è il telefono?	dov-eh eel teh-leh-foh-noh?
The nearest hospital?	L'ospedale più vicino?	loss-peh-dah-leh pee-oo vee-chee-noh?

COMMUNICATION ESSENTIALS

Yes/No	Sì/No	see/noh
Please	Per favore	pair fah-vor-eh
Thank you	Grazie	grah-tsee-eh
Excuse me	Mi scusi	mee skoo-zee
Hello	Buon giorno	bwon jor-noh
Goodbye	Arrivederci	ah-ree-veh-dair-chee
Good evening	Buona sera	bwon-ah sair-ah
morning	la mattina	lah mah-tee-nah
afternoon	il pomeriggio	eel poh-meh-ree-joh
evening	la sera	lah sair-ah
yesterday	ieri	ee-air-ee
today	oggi	oh-jee
tomorrow	domani	doh-mah-nee
here	qui	kwee
there	la	lah
What?	Quale?	kwah-leh?
When?	Quando?	kwan-doh?
Why?	Perchè?	pair-keh?
Where?	Dove?	doh-veh?

USEFUL PHRASES

How are you?	Come sta?	koh-meh stah?
Very well, thank you.	Molto bene, grazie.	moll-toh beh-neh grah-tsee-eh
Pleased to meet you.	Piacere di conoscerla.	pee-ah-chair-eh dee coh-noh-shair-lah
See you later.	A più tardi.	ah pee-oo tar-dee
That's fine.	Va bene.	va beh-neh
Where is/are ...?	Dov'è/Dove sono ...?	dov-eh/doveh soh-noh?
How long does it take to get to ...?	Quanto tempo ci vuole per andare a ...?	kwan-toh tem-poh chee voo-oh-leh pair an-dar-eh ah ...?
How do I get to ...?	Come faccio per arrivare a ...?	koh-meh fah-choh pair arri-var-eh ah..?
Do you speak English?	Parla inglese?	par-lah een-gleh-zeh?
I don't understand.	Non capisco.	non ka-pee-skoh
Could you speak more slowly, please?	Può parlare più lentamente, per favore?	pwoh par-lah-reh pee-oo len-ta-men-teh pair fah-vor-eh?
I'm sorry.	Mi dispiace.	mee dee-spee-ah-cheh

USEFUL WORDS

big	grande	gran-deh
small	piccolo	pee-koh-loh
hot	caldo	kal-doh
cold	freddo	fred-doh
good	buono	bwoh-noh
bad	cattivo	kat-tee-voh
enough	basta	bas-tah
well	bene	beh-neh
open	aperto	ah-pair-toh
closed	chiuso	kee-oo-zoh
left	a sinistra	ah see-nee-strah
right	a destra	ah dess-trah
straight on	sempre dritto	sem-preh dree-toh
near	vicino	vee-chee-noh
far	lontano	lon-tah-noh
up	su	soo
down	giù	joo
early	presto	press-toh
late	tardi	tar-dee
entrance	entrata	en-trah-tah
exit	uscita	oo-shee-ta
toilet	il gabinetto	eel gah-bee-net-toh
free, unoccupied	libero	lee-bair-oh
free, no charge	gratuito	grah-too-ee-toh

MAKING A TELEPHONE CALL

I'd like to place a long-distance call.	Vorrei fare una interurbana.	vor-ray far-eh oona in-tair-oor-bah-nah
I'd like to make a reverse-charge call.	Vorrei fare una telefonata a carico del destinatario.	vor-ray far-eh oona teh-leh-fon-ah-tah ah kar-ee-koh dell dess-tee-nah-tar-ree-oh
Could I speak to...	Potrei parlare con...	po-tray par-lah-reh con
I'll try again later.	Ritelefono più tardi.	ree-teh-leh-foh-noh pee-oo tar-dee
Can I leave a message?	Posso lasciare un messaggio?	poss-oh lash-ah-reh oon mess-sah-joh?
Hold on.	Un attimo, per favore.	oon ah-tee-moh, pair fah-vor-eh
Could you speak up a little please?	Può parlare più forte?	pwoh par-lah-reh pee-oo for-teh?
local call	telefonata locale	te-leh-fon-ah-tah loh-cah-leh

SHOPPING

How much does this cost?	Quant'è, per favore?	kwan-teh pair fah-vor-eh?
I would like ...	Vorrei ...	vor-ray...
Do you have ...?	Avete ...?	ah-veh-teh.. ?
I'm just looking.	Sto soltanto guardando.	stoh sol-tan-toh gwar-dan-doh
Do you take credit cards?	Accettate carte di credito?	ah-chet-tah-teh kar-teh dee creb-dee-toh?
What time do you open/close?	A che ora apre/ chiude?	ah keh or-ah ah-preh/kee-oo-deh?
this one	questo	kweh-stoh
that one	quello	kwell-oh
expensive	caro	kar-oh
cheap	a buon prezzo	ah bwon pret-soh
size, clothes	la taglia	lah tah-lee-ah
size, shoes	il numero	eel noo-mair-oh
white	bianco	bee-ang-koh
black	nero	neh-roh
red	rosso	ross-oh
yellow	giallo	jal-loh
green	verde	vair-deh
blue	blu	bloo

TYPES OF SHOP

antique dealer	l'antiquario	lan-tee-kwah-ree-oh
bakery	il forno/ il panificio	eel forn-oh/ eel pan-ee-fee-choh
bank	la banca	lah bang-kah
bookshop	la libreria	lah lee-breh-ree-ah
butcher	la macelleria	lah mah-chell-eh-ree-ah
cake shop	la pasticceria	lah pas-tee-chair-ee-ah
chemist	la farmacia	lah far-mah-chee-ah
delicatessen	la salumeria	lah sah-loo-meh-ree-ah
department store	il grande magazzino	eel gran-deh mag-gad-zee-noh
fishmonger	il pescivendolo	eel pesh-ee-ven-doh-loh
florist	il fioraio	eel fee-or-eye-oh
greengrocer	il fruttivendolo	eel froo-tee-ven-doh-loh
grocery	alimentari	ah-lee-men-tah-ree
hairdresser	il parrucchiere	eel par-oo-kee-air-eh
ice cream parlour	la gelateria	lah jel-lah-tair-ree-ah
market	il mercato	eel mair-kah-toh
newsstand	l'edicola	leh-dee-koh-lah
post office	l'ufficio postale	loo-fee-choh pos-tah-leh
shoe shop	il negozio di scarpe	eel neh-goh-tsioh dee skar-peh
supermarket	il supermercato	eel su-pair-mair-kah-toh
tobacconist	il tabaccaio	eel tab-bak-eye-oh
travel agency	l'agenzia di viaggi	lah-jen-tsee-ah dee vee-ad-jee

SIGHTSEEING

art gallery	la pinacoteca	lah peena-koh-teh-kah
bus stop	la fermata dell'autobus	lah fair-mah-tah dell ow-toh-booss
church	la chiesa/ la basilica	lah kee-eh-zah/ lah bah-seel-i-kah
closed for holidays	chiuso per le ferie	kee-oo-zoh pair leh fair-ee-eh
garden	il giardino	eel jar-dee-no
library	la biblioteca	lah beeb-lee-oh-teh-kah
museum	il museo	eel moo-zeh-oh
railway station	la stazione	lah stah-tsee-oh-neh
tourist information	l'ufficio di turismo	loo-fee-choh dee too-ree-smoh

STAYING IN A HOTEL

Do you have any vacant rooms?	**Avete camere libere?**	*ah-veh-teh kah-mair-eh lee-bair-eh?*
double room	**una camera doppia**	*oona kah-mair-ah doh-pee-ah*
with double bed	**con letto matrimoniale**	*kon let-toh mah-tree-moh-nee-ah-leh*
twin room	**una camera con due letti**	*oona kah-mair-ah kon doo-eh let-tee*
single room	**una camera singola**	*oona kah-mair-ah sing-goh-lah*
room with a bath, shower	**una camera con bagno, con doccia**	*oona kah-mair-ah kon ban-yoh, kon dot-chah*
porter	**il facchino**	*eel fah-kee-noh*
key	**la chiave**	*lah kee-ah-veh*
I have a reservation.	**Ho fatto una prenotazione.**	*oh fat-toh oona preh-noh-tah-tsee-oh-neh*

EATING OUT

Have you got a table for ...?	**Avete una tavola per ... ?**	*ah-veh-teh oona tah-voh-lah pair ...?*
I'd like to reserve a table.	**Vorrei riservare una tavola.**	*vor-ray ree-sair-vah-reh oona tah-voh-lah*
breakfast	**colazione**	*koh-lah-tsee-oh-neh*
lunch	**pranzo**	*pran-tsoh*
dinner	**cena**	*cheh-nah*
The bill, please.	**Il conto, per favore.**	*eel kon-toh pair fah-vor-eh*
I am a vegetarian.	**Sono vegetariano/a.**	*soh-noh veh-jeb-tar-ee-ah-noh/nah*
waitress	**cameriera**	*kah-mair-ee-air-ah*
waiter	**cameriere**	*kah-mair-ee-air-eh*
fixed price menu	**il menù a prezzo fisso**	*eel meh-noo ah pret-soh fee-soh*
dish of the day	**piatto del giorno**	*pee-ah-toh dell jor-no*
starter	**antipasto**	*an-tee-pass-toh*
first course	**il primo**	*eel pree-moh*
main course	**il secondo**	*eel seh-kon-doh*
vegetables	**il contorno**	*eel kon-tor-noh*
dessert	**il dolce**	*eel doll-cheh*
cover charge	**il coperto**	*eel koh-pair-toh*
wine list	**la lista dei vini**	*lah ee-stah day vee-nee*
rare	**al sangue**	*al sang-gweh*
medium	**al puntino**	*al poon-tee-noh*
well done	**ben cotto**	*ben kot-toh*
glass	**il bicchiere**	*eel bee-kee-air-eh*
bottle	**la bottiglia**	*lah bot-teel-yah*
knife	**il coltello**	*eel kol-tell-oh*
fork	**la forchetta**	*lah for-ket-tah*
spoon	**il cucchiaio**	*eel koo-kee-eye-oh*

MENU DECODER

l'acqua minerale gassata/naturale	*lah-kwah mee-nair-ah-leh gab-zah-tah/ nah-too-rah-leh*	mineral water fizzy/still
aceto	*ah-cheh-toh*	vinegar
aglio	*al-ee-oh*	garlic
l'agnello	*lah-niell-oh*	lamb
al forno	*al for-noh*	baked/roasted
alla griglia	*ah-lah greel-yah*	grilled
l'aragosta	*lab-rah-goss-tah*	lobster
arrosto	*ar-ross-toh*	roast
basilico	*bah-zee-lee-koh*	basil
la birra	*lah beer-rah*	beer
la bistecca	*lah bee-stek-kah*	steak
il brodo	*eel broh-doh*	broth
il burro	*eel boor-oh*	butter
il caffè	*eel kah-feh*	coffee
i calamari	*ee kah-lah-mah-ree*	squid
i carciofi	*ee kar-choff-ee*	artichokes
la carne	*la kar-neh*	meat
la cipolla	*la chip-oh-lah*	onion
i contorni	*ee kon-tor-nee*	vegetables
le cozze	*leh coh-tzeh*	mussels
i fagioli	*ee fah-job-lee*	beans
il fegato	*eel fay-gah-toh*	liver
il finocchio	*eel fee-nok-ee-oh*	fennel
il formaggio	*eel for-mad-joh*	cheese
le fragole	*leh frah-goh-leh*	strawberries
il fritto misto	*eel free-toh mees-toh*	mixed fried dish
la frutta	*la froot-tah*	fruit
frutti di mare	*froo-tee dee mah-reh*	seafood
i funghi	*ee foon-ghee*	mushrooms
i gamberi	*ee gam-bair-ee*	prawns
il gelato	*eel jeh-lah-toh*	ice cream
l'insalata	*leen-sah-lah-tah*	salad

il latte	*eel laht-teh*	milk
lesso	*less-oh*	boiled
la melanzana	*lah meb-lan-tsah-nah*	aubergine
la minestra	*lah mee-ness-trah*	soup
l'olio	*lob-lee-oh*	oil
il pane	*eel pah-neh*	bread
le patate	*leh pah-tah-teh*	potatoes
le patatine fritte	*leh pah-tah-teen-eh free-teh*	chips
il pepe	*eel peb-peh*	pepper
la pesca	*lah pess-kah*	peach
il pesc⌢	*eel pesh-eh*	fish
il polipo	*eel pob-lee-poh*	octopus
il pollo	*eel poll-oh*	chicken
il pomodoro	*eel poh-moh-dor-oh*	tomato
il prosciutto cotto/crudo	*eel pro-shoo-toh kot-toh/kroo-doh*	ham cooked/cured
il riso	*eel ree-zoh*	rice
il sale	*eel sah-leh*	salt
la salsiccia	*lah sal-see-chah*	sausage
le seppie	*leh sep-pee-eh*	cuttlefish
secco	*sek-koh*	dry
la sogliola	*lah soll-yoh-lah*	sole
i spinaci	*ee speenah-chee*	spinach
succo d'arancia/ di limone	*soo-koh dah-ran-chah/ dee lee-moh-neh*	orange/lemon juice
il tè	*eel teh*	tea
la tisana	*lah tee-zah-nah*	herbal tea
il tonno	*eel ton-noh*	tuna
la torta	*lah tor-tah*	cake/tart
l'uovo	*loo-oh-voh*	egg
vino bianco	*vee-noh bee-ang-koh*	white wine
vino rosso	*vee-noh ross-oh*	red wine
il vitello	*eel vee-tell-oh*	veal
le vongole	*leh von-goh-leh*	clams
lo zucchero	*loh zoo-kair-oh*	sugar
gli zucchini	*lyee dzu-kee-nee*	courgettes
la zuppa	*lah tsoo-pah*	soup

NUMBERS

1	**uno**	*oo-noh*
2	**due**	*doo-eh*
3	**tre**	*treh*
4	**quattro**	*kwat-roh*
5	**cinque**	*ching-kweh*
6	**sei**	*say-ee*
7	**sette**	*set-teh*
8	**otto**	*ot-toh*
9	**nove**	*nob-veh*
10	**dieci**	*dee-eh-chee*
11	**undici**	*oon-dee-chee*
12	**dodici**	*doh-dee-chee*
13	**tredici**	*tray-dee-chee*
14	**quattordici**	*kwat-tor-dee-chee*
15	**quindici**	*kwin-dee-chee*
16	**sedici**	*say-dee-chee*
17	**diciassette**	*dee-chah-set-teh*
18	**diciotto**	*dee-chot-toh*
19	**diciannove**	*dee-chah-nob-veh*
20	**venti**	*ven-tee*
30	**trenta**	*tren-tah*
40	**quaranta**	*kwah-ran-tah*
50	**cinquanta**	*ching-kwan-tah*
60	**sessanta**	*sess-an-tah*
70	**settanta**	*set-tan-tah*
80	**ottanta**	*ot-tan-tah*
90	**novanta**	*nob-van-tah*
100	**cento**	*chen-toh*
1,000	**mille**	*mee-leh*
2,000	**duemila**	*doo-eh mee-lah*
5,000	**cinquemila**	*ching-kweh mee-lah*
1,000,000	**un milione**	*oon meel-yob-neh*

TIME

one minute	**un minuto**	*oon mee-noo-toh*
one hour	**un'ora**	*oon or-ah*
half an hour	**mezz'ora**	*medz-or-ah*
a day	**un giorno**	*oon jor-noh*
a week	**una settimana**	*oona set-tee-mah-nah*
Monday	**lunedì**	*loo-neh-dee*
Tuesday	**martedì**	*mar-teh-dee*
Wednesday	**mercoledì**	*mair-koh-leb-dee*
Thursday	**giovedì**	*joh-veh-dee*
Friday	**venerdì**	*ven-air-dee*
Saturday	**sabato**	*sah-bah-toh*
Sunday	**domenica**	*doh-meh-nee-kah*

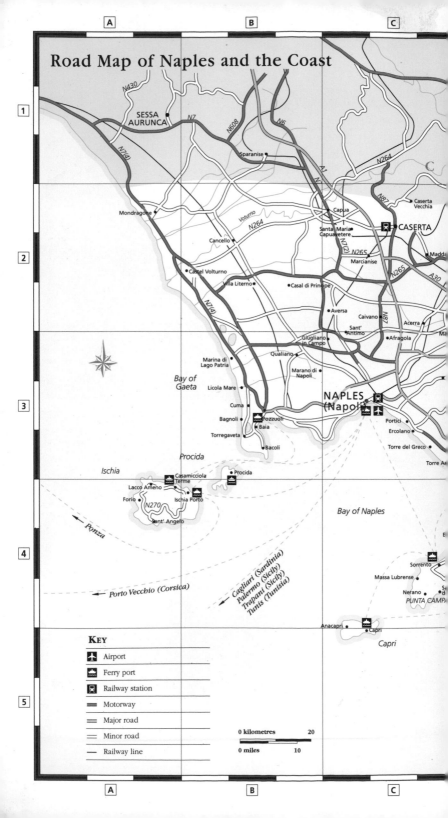